Leading
Teams

Leading Teams

SETTING THE STAGE FOR GREAT PERFORMANCES

J. Richard Hackman

HARVARD BUSINESS SCHOOL PRESS
Boston, Massachusetts

06 05 04 03 02   5 4 3 2 1

Requests for permission to use or reproduce material from this book should be directed to permissions@hbsp.harvard.edu, or mailed to Permissions, Harvard Business School Publishing, 60 Harvard Way, Boston, Massachusetts 02163.

Library of Congress Cataloging-in-Publication Data
Hackman, J. Richard.
   Leading Teams : setting the stage for great performances / J. Richard Hackman.
      p. cm.
Includes bibliographical references and index.
   ISBN 1-57851-333-2
   1. Leadership. 2. Teams in the workplace. 3. Performance. I. Title.
   HD57.7 .H336 2002
   658.4'092—dc21

                                                        2002000757

The paper used in this publication meets the requirements of the American National Standard for Permanence of Paper for Publications and Documents in Libraries and Archives Z39.48-1992.

Contents

Preface

Let's start with a pop quiz. Here are three items from a citizenship test given to all fourth-grade students in Ohio.

1. Which branch of Ohio's state government makes laws?
   a. Judicial
   b. Executive
   c. Legislative

2. Which of the following people is consuming something?
   a. Carmen is walking her dog.
   b. Jaleel is buying a new shirt.
   c. Dale is sorting baseball cards.

3. When people work together to finish a job, such as building a house, the job will probably
   a. get finished faster.
   b. take longer to finish.
   c. not get done.

I'm fairly certain of the answer to the first item (the legislative branch) and the second (buying a shirt), which means that my knowledge of government and economics is at least at the fourth-grade level. But how about that third item? The Harvard student from Ohio who brought me the test said that alternative *a* (get finished faster) is scored as correct. But as she and I reflected on our own experiences in various kinds of work teams, we wondered about that. Too many of the teams we had been in barely worked at all.

There is a puzzle here. On the one hand, alternative *a* really should be the right answer. Work teams have more resources, and a greater diversity of resources, than do individual performers. Teams have great flexibility in how to deploy and use their resources. Teams provide a setting in which members can learn from one another and thereby build an ever-larger pool of knowledge and expertise. And there is always the possibility that a team will generate magic—producing something extraordinary, a collective creation of previously unimagined quality or beauty. These are significant benefits, and they help explain why teams are such a popular device for accomplishing organizational work these days.

On the other hand, team magic, as wondrous as it can be, is rarely seen. More commonly, teamwork really does take longer to finish (alternative *b*) or doesn't even get done at all (alternative *c*). When I announce on the first day of class that there will be group projects in my undergraduate course, there invariably are a few groans from students who have suffered through such projects in other courses. Moreover, research that compares the performance of teams with what is produced by an equivalent number of individuals who work by themselves almost always finds that the individuals outperform the teams.

This book seeks to resolve this puzzle, and do it in a way that can guide the actions of team leaders and members who seek to help their own teams perform well—and maybe even generate a little magic now and then.

THE MAIN MESSAGE

Work teams perform poorly when leaders have focused on the wrong things in designing or supporting them. This book identifies what the right things are—five specific conditions that foster work team effectiveness—

and points to the right times to establish them. Although few in number, these conditions are great in impact. When leaders focus on creating and sustaining them, teams really can perform superbly.

The leader's main task, therefore, is to get a team established on a good trajectory and then to make small adjustments along the way to help members succeed, not to try to continuously manage team behavior in real time. No leader can *make* a team perform well. But all leaders can create conditions that increase the *likelihood* that it will.

There are better and worse times to intervene with teams. Certain acts of leadership are best done when a team is just starting out, others around the midpoint of a work cycle, and still others when a team has finished up a significant piece of work. Leadership initiatives that are done at the wrong times rarely make a constructive difference, and sometimes they backfire.

Anyone who succeeds in getting performance-enhancing conditions in place or helps strengthen them is exercising team leadership. That can be a person who is designated as "team leader," to be sure. But it also can be a team member, an external manager, or even an outside consultant or client. It is not important who creates the conditions, how they go about doing it, or what their personality characteristics are. What is important is that the conditions that foster team effectiveness be put in place and stay there.

The five conditions—having a real team, a compelling direction, an enabling team structure, a supportive organizational context, and expert team coaching—are easy to remember. The challenge comes in developing an understanding of those conditions that is deep and nuanced enough to be useful in guiding action, and in devising strategies for creating them even in demanding or team-unfriendly organizational circumstances. People who are natural team leaders seem to know intuitively how to do these things. In this book, I have attempted to capture what natural leaders know, integrate that with social science research findings about team behavior, and generate a set of lessons that leaders can use to set the organizational stage for great team performances.

ABOUT THE BOOK

If I have achieved my aspiration in writing this book, four different groups of readers will find it informative and useful: (1) practitioners who want to help the teams they lead, or on which they serve, perform as well as possible; (2) scholars who conduct research on team behavior and performance who seek fresh ways of thinking about the factors that most powerfully shape team effectiveness; (3) consultants who may find it useful to inspect and analyze teams through a somewhat unconventional lens; and (4) general readers who are curious about why it is that some teams sail into orbit while others either struggle unpleasantly to an unsatisfactory outcome or crash and burn shortly after launch.

Although the assertions and conclusions in the book are grounded in up-to-date research and theory about work team behavior and performance, I've done my best to avoid the use of academic and management jargon (the term *empowerment,* for example, is used but once in the entire book, and that time reluctantly). Instead, I have tried to use language, concepts, and extended examples that make the material as engaging, concrete, and useful as possible.

The book is optimistic about what team leaders can accomplish. Providing first-rate team leadership unquestionably is a significant personal and organizational challenge. But good team leadership really does make a difference. I reject the views of some contemporary scholars that leadership is mainly a symbolic activity of no real consequence, that leaders are but pawns in larger dramas driven by external forces, and that the best that high-status leaders can hope to do is compose a team well and then keep their distance to avoid unduly influencing members' deliberations. Instead, I have attempted to lay out a way of thinking about team leadership that can increase leaders' leverage in helping a team perform superbly and, in the process, become stronger over time as a performing unit and contribute positively to the personal learning and well-being of individual members.

A Brief Road Map

The book opens with an extended description of how senior leaders at two different airlines structured and supported teams of flight attendants. One airline achieved a great deal of control over flight attendant behavior, but at considerable cost in motivation and creativity. The other airline achieved nearly the opposite outcomes. The experiences of those two airlines are helpful in reflecting on what it means to say a team is "effective," and they highlight the trade-offs that must always be managed in structuring, supporting, and leading organizational work teams. I refer back to the flight attendant teams frequently throughout the book.

Each of the next five chapters explores one of the five conditions that foster team effectiveness: a real team, a compelling direction, an enabling structure, a supportive context, and expert coaching. Then, in the last two chapters, I discuss the opportunities that the present approach provides for some new ways of thinking about team leadership and organizational change processes.

Much of what I say is based on research conducted by myself and my collaborators on a highly diverse set of work teams—musical ensembles, economic analysts, manufacturing teams, airline cockpit crews, and more. It turns out that many of these teams are similar in one significant respect: Their work requires members to generate performances "live" and in real time, often without the chance to go back and try again if things don't go well. Because team design and leadership are so consequential for such teams, they provide a stringent and informative test of the ideas set forth in this book. If the enabling conditions enhance the performance of teams that have little room for error, they surely also should help other teams that have more latitude for trial-and-error learning.

Things Are Not Always What They Seem

Here are four assertions about work teams that, unless I miss my guess, will not seem terribly controversial.

1. Teams whose members work together harmoniously perform better than those that have lots of conflict about how best to perform the work.

2. A primary "cause" of team dynamics is the behavioral style of the team leader, especially the degree to which he or she is authoritative versus democratic.

3. Larger teams perform better than smaller teams because they have more, and more diverse, member resources on which to draw in carrying out the work.

4. The performance of teams whose membership stays intact for a long time gradually deteriorates, because members get careless, insufficiently attentive to environmental changes, and too forgiving of one another's mistakes and oversights.

Although perhaps not controversial, each of these assertions is wrong. The way things *seem* to operate in groups is, surprisingly often, not how they *actually* operate. By drawing on evidence from both social science research and organizational practice, I seek in this book to provide readers with a new set of lenses for analyzing team dynamics—lenses that bring into focus aspects of team functioning that are invisible to casual observers, and that correct commonly held views of teams that are more illusory than real.

A Note on Notes

One of the great features of documents posted on the Internet is their use of hyperlinks—highlighted terms or phrases that, with a single click, take you to another place where you can learn more about something that interests, intrigues, or confuses you. And then, with but one more click, you can return to the text you were reading. The printed page cannot include hyperlinks, but notes serve much the same function. This book has lots and lots of notes, grouped by chapter at the end of the book.

Some of the notes identify the basis for assertions made in the text. Others point you to other books or articles where details about a point being made can be found. Others provide in-depth analyses of certain issues, and therefore may be of interest only to a subset of readers. Still others merely give an unusual example, a tidbit, or an aside that may make you smile or frown. Because the notes are grouped at the end, you can read through the book without distraction. But I hope many readers will insert a bookmark at the start of the notes section and frequently flip back to them to learn more about things that engage their interest.

ACKNOWLEDGMENTS

Much of what I describe and discuss in this book is based on findings from research conducted with a wonderful group of doctoral student and faculty collaborators over the years. Their names are prominent in the notes and the bibliography, and I am enormously in their debt. I am especially grateful to Joe McGrath, Chris Argyris, and Ed Lawler, whose guidance over the years has helped keep me, if not on the straight and narrow, at least from straying too far from productive research paths.

I also thank the individuals and organizations who participated in the several research projects on which the book is based. Special thanks go to Don Burr and his colleagues at People Express Airlines, to David Mathiasen at OMB, to Louise Illes and the late Hank Verwer at Signetics, and to Julian Fifer, Harvey Seifter, and the musicians of the Orpheus Chamber Orchestra. Financial support for the research was provided, in part, by the National Aeronautics and Space Administration, Hay McBer, Pfizer Inc., the Research Division of the Harvard Business School, and both the Hauser Center and the Center for Public Leadership at Harvard's Kennedy School of Government. Facilities and support for writing were provided by the Center for Advanced Study in the Behavioral Sciences at Stanford University and by the Ucross Foundation at the base of the Big Horns in Ucross, Wyoming.

Research and bibliographic assistance were provided by Laura Bacon, Adam Galinsky, Anna Skotko, and Matthew Segneri; graphics consultation was provided by Susan Choi. Special thanks go to Ruth Wageman of Tuck School at Dartmouth College, whose research colleagueship and manuscript critiques have been invaluable in preparing this book.

And then there is Erin Lehman. Erin and I began working together when I first came to Harvard fifteen years ago. She started as a secretary fresh out of college, stayed with me through thick workloads and thin funding, and this year will receive her own doctorate in the behavioral sciences. Her competence, commitment, and loyalty have been more than any professor deserves.

Finally, my deep gratitude to my family—Beth, Catherine, Laura, Lauren, Judith, and Trex—whose presence, support, and patience with me have made writing this book possible.

Richard Hackman
26 November 2001

Leading
Teams

PART I

TEAMS

I

The Challenge

You are director of in-flight services for a major airline, responsible for some 2,000 flight attendants who look after passenger service and cabin safety.

Most of the markets in which your company operates are highly competitive. You dominate a few of them, but rank second or third in others. Recently, your load factors (the percentage of available seats actually occupied) slipped a couple of points in some key markets. The vice president of marketing, to whom you report, commissioned a study to find out why. The results reinforced what was found in previous market research. After price and schedule, the most important factor affecting repeat business is the quality of the service passengers receive.

Although your position is a responsible one, you have no direct influence on price or schedule. There may be little leverage in these factors anyway, since these days the fares and schedules of competing carriers scarcely can be distinguished from one another. What you *do* control is the work performed by flight attendants. Given the current competitive situation, you expect that the vice president would allow you to do whatever you think needs to be done—so long as your actions eventually result in a quality and consistency of on-board service that surpasses that of your competitors.

That is your opportunity. Your problem is that the key encounters between flight attendants and customers occur in a metal tube moving through the atmosphere at 500 miles an hour some 35,000 feet above the ground. Worse, there is no manager on board to make sure the flight attendants perform well. First-line management is provided by a group of flight service managers (FSMs), each of whom has administrative responsibility for a subset of flight attendants. The FSMs also manage, under your direction, the selection, training, and scheduling of in-flight staff. But all the FSMs work on the ground, at headquarters, rather than in the air. They rarely even see the flight attendants, except when someone has a personal problem or there has been an in-flight incident or complaint that requires a headquarters discussion. So there is no realistic way that the FSMs can monitor and manage what really counts—flight attendants' direct encounters with the customers whose patronage is so critical to your airline.

It is time for some fresh thinking about the design, staffing, and management of in-flight services. You have considerable power and influence, and you have a clean slate: Anything and everything is open for consideration. Thus, the question is,

What would you do to increase the likelihood that flight attendant teams at your airline consistently provide superb service to their customers?

Airline managers around the world wrestle every day with precisely this question. Different airlines have answered it in quite different ways. The strategies used by two airlines my colleagues and I have studied illustrate two radically different alternatives for structuring and leading work teams. Managers at both airlines realized that, for better or for worse, flight attendants become self-managing teams the moment they step on board an aircraft. The first airline to be described, an international carrier, attempted to minimize the risks that invariably accompany team self-management; the other airline, a domestic carrier, sought to exploit the many benefits that self-management can bring. Neither strategy worked as well as airline managers hoped. By analyzing what went well and poorly in the experiences of these two carriers, we will begin to see what is needed to set the stage for great performances by work teams more generally.

THE INTERNATIONAL AIRLINE

When we studied this airline several years ago, it employed over 2,500 cabin crew members for work on aircraft such as the Boeing 747, which routinely carried 350 or more passengers on intercontinental flights.[1] Seven supervisors each looked after some 400 flight attendants—a span of control that ensured that the cabin crew teams would indeed be self-managing.

Cabin services at this carrier were part of the marketing organization, and a marketing orientation is evident in the statement of objectives that management printed and distributed to all staff: "Every passenger, from the moment of entering the aircraft to the moment of leaving it, shall receive such a degree of service, attention, care, courtesy and consideration that, by the end of their flight, they are committed to [our airline] for their next trip."

Management carefully designed a cabin product and in-flight delivery routines to achieve that ambitious objective. Analysts researched competitors' products and customers' preferences and then generated detailed specifications for food, beverage, and entertainment services. Workflow experts laid out the exact procedures flight attendant teams were to use in delivering the service product, and fine-tuned these routines using full-scale cabin mockups at the airline's headquarters. Cabin services management conducted rigorous training programs to ensure that every flight attendant understood both the airline's service objectives and the specific procedures to be used to achieve them.

The level of detail was impressive. The overall team task was broken down into specific duties to be provided by specific crew members at specific times. Each position on the team was designated by an alphabetic letter, and flight attendants were trained in the duties required for any lettered position to which they might be assigned. Most positions involved either galley work or serving food or drink to passengers, but special duties also were specified in detail. The flight attendants assigned to the "A," "B," and "D" positions, for example, were responsible for tending to the special needs of any unaccompanied children, mothers with infants, and sick or very elderly passengers. Flight attendant "C" was responsible for tidying the galley areas and for keeping track of equipment the crew brought on board. And so on.

The idea was to create a choreographed team performance that, although carefully worked out in advance, would not seem so to customers. What customers would see was seamless service of such quality and consistency that they would insist on being booked on the same carrier for their next trip. It was a beautifully engineered product and, importantly, one that could be implemented with no manager on board. All that the flight attendants had to do was to execute their duties, to dance the choreographed ballet, with competence and style.

The flight attendants had more than enough knowledge and skill to execute the work. The variety and glamour of work as an international flight attendant attracted many more applicants than there were positions, so the carrier was able to be very choosy about whom it hired. After a demanding initial training course, recruits started work with the title of Flight Attendant I. They became eligible for promotion to Flight Attendant II after a year of satisfactory service and could apply for a senior flight attendant position after three years. Although advancement to Flight Attendant II was routine, promotion to senior flight attendant was a higher hurdle. Not all eligible candidates chose to submit to the rigorous review for promotion to senior status, since the small increment in pay seemed to some insufficient compensation for the relatively large increase in worry and responsibility they would take on.

At the time of the research, crews on board 747s at this carrier consisted of fourteen members, of whom at least three were senior flight attendants. One of the seniors was the flight attendant in charge. He or she conducted the preflight briefing of the crew, handled various administrative chores, and had primary responsibility for coordination with ground staff and with the flight deck crew. Two other seniors served as subleaders for the first class and economy cabins.

Crews were formed essentially randomly. Each day, scheduling staff listed the trips that would begin twenty-eight days in the future, and then went down the list of available flight attendants until the crew roster for each trip was filled. Trips ranged from three days (for example, across the

Atlantic and back) to almost three weeks (an extended set of flights with numerous layovers in cities around the world).

A Trip through Europe and Asia

You are a Flight Attendant II at the international carrier with over two years of service behind you. It is early in the morning on the first day of a five-day trip that will dogleg through Europe and Asia. You arrive at the crew base (a building about a mile from the airport) an hour and a half before your flight's scheduled departure. The deadline for reporting is seventy-five minutes prior to departure, so there is time to spare. First you stop by the check-in desk, where your arrival is noted and you receive your duty assignment card, which brings some good news and a small disappointment. The good news is that your assignment for the next five days will be to provide meal service in the middle of the economy cabin. Your position involves no extra duties, so if passenger loads are light and the weather is good, this could be a routine, nondemanding trip. The disappointment comes as you scan the roster and find that you know no one else on the crew; you like it better when there are at least a couple of people with whom you have worked before. (This is not unusual. I asked an operations researcher at the airline to estimate, if he and I were rostered together on a trip, how long it would be before we could expect to be rostered together again. The answer was 5.4 *years*.)

You next check your mail slot and find it empty except for a routine management notice announcing changes in expense allowances for certain cities. A glance at the union bulletin board reveals nothing of special interest, nor do you see any friends in the crew lounge as you pass by. So you head down to the briefing room. About half the crew is already there, including the in-charge senior flight attendant, who is looking through the papers for the trip. You nod vaguely at those colleagues who glanced up when you walked in, and then settle into a chair to wait for the rest of the crew to arrive.

A few minutes before the seventy-five-minute deadline, the in-charge looks up, finds everyone present, and begins her briefing. She introduces herself and quickly reviews the itinerary for the trip and the passenger loads for the two legs that will be flown today. She then conducts the required preflight safety briefing, asking a few individuals "What would you do if . . . " questions (she has the authority to request replacement of any crew member whose responses are unsatisfactory). "Good," she concludes. "Now, do we have any nurses in the crew?" There are none. "And what foreign languages do we have?" Hands go up, and you learn that the crew includes two members with French, one with German, and one with Italian. "We'll pick up a national for the Asian segments," she notes, referring to the airline's practice of adding a crew member with knowledge of local culture and language for regional portions of an extended trip. "So. Does anyone have any questions or special requests?" Hearing none, the in-charge wraps up the briefing by suggesting that the crew go immediately to the van that will take it to the aircraft. The few extra minutes will let you get settled without rushing, give you time to tidy the cabin if necessary, and allow the crew members assigned to galley duty to check the catering. That pleases you, because nothing gets a crew off to a worse start than finding out in flight that you are short on ice or drinks or meals.

The briefing took about ten minutes. As you heft your suitcase and head for the loading dock, you notice that, as usual, crew members are keeping mostly to themselves, each occupied with his or her own thoughts. It is a collection of individuals. Not until tonight at the hotel will you find out what this crew is going to be like, whether this will be a fun trip or one that seems to drag on forever.

The first few minutes aboard the aircraft pass quickly. You get your suitcase stowed, introduce yourself to the other crew members working your cabin, and take a look around to make sure everything is in order. Then the voice of the in-charge comes over the public address system: "Gate says they're ready to board whenever we are. Anybody need more time?" Hearing no response, she tells the lead gate agent to proceed. In a few minutes, a stream of passengers begins wending its way down the two aisles of the 747, heads swiveling as people try to locate their seat number (or, for some veteran fliers, eyes darting as they try to find their seats without seeming to actually look for them).

Eventually, everyone is boarded and seated. Bags that can be stuffed into the overhead bins have been so stuffed, and the large suitcases and boxes brought aboard by the most optimistic passengers have been tagged and sent down to the baggage hold. The in-charge climbs the circular stairs to the upper deck, steps into the cockpit, and informs the captain that the cabin is ready. You strap yourself into the aft-facing jumpseat by your exit door and, after a few moments, the aircraft is pushed back from the gate. You like this time. It is your first break in activity since you left home this morning, and it will last until the captain signals that it is safe to begin cabin service. You decide not to make eye contact with the exit row passengers you face, and instead use the time to relax. You hardly notice takeoff.

Soon you hear a single chime and the No Smoking sign cycles off and on. Finally favoring with a smile the exit row passengers who have been watching you ever since you strapped in, you go to work. The in-charge makes her announcement describing today's service, galley ovens are turned on, and the drink carts come out and begin their slow journeys down the aisles. The ballet of intercontinental 747 service has begun.

There is little to say about the service itself—it is pretty much what passengers on long-haul flights have come to expect. Today's flight poses no special challenges to the service team, and the choreography works. The plane lands at its first destination, most of the passengers leave, you tidy up your section of the cabin, new passengers board, and the ballet is performed again. Then, after saying good-bye to the passengers at the second destination, you and your teammates retrieve your luggage and proceed through the special immigration and customs lanes for working crew.

There will be no curbside delay today, as two hotel vans are waiting as you emerge from the airport. One is for the cabin crew and the other, from a slightly higher-class hotel, is for the flight deck crew—testimony to the negotiating success of the pilots' union. You suspect that the pilots' bargaining agenda had less to do with in-room amenities than with maintaining status differences between their group and yours, but you stopped being irritated about this long ago. Your main emotion as you climb aboard is gratitude that the van is there, on time, and warm.

En route to the hotel, one crew member announces that a collection of liquor miniatures has mysteriously wound up in his flight bag. Should people be interested in joining him in the hotel's crew lounge, he says, he would be happy to share the fruits of this mysterious occurrence. You silently marvel at how, on virtually every trip, there is someone who finds a way to circumvent the airline's tight liquor control procedures the first night out. And of course you will show up. Even the slam-clickers (those of your colleagues who will, each night, go immediately to their hotel rooms, slam the door, click the lock, and not be seen again until pickup the next day) rarely miss the first-night party.

Within an hour, you and almost all of your teammates—including the in-charge senior flight attendant—are arrayed across the special suite the hotel makes available to overnight crews. Dress is decidedly casual. People-known-in-common are identified and discussed. Strange happenings on previous flights are recounted. Dinner plans are made. An informal pecking order starts to become established. The crew, after having been together for nearly ten hours, finally becomes a group.

The next day, the routine repeats itself; the same ballet is danced. Your crew has the middle day of the trip off, holding in place to relieve the crew on that night's inbound flight. So you see some sights with a few other crew members and do some reading, but mostly you relax. Then it is back to the routines. The last night out, some crew members, mostly the younger ones, perform the "address book ritual." This involves carefully copying into one's book the telephone numbers of new friends and vowing that you will soon get together for dinner back home. But it rarely happens, and most veteran crew members eventually stop pretending that it will.

The first thing you do when you get home is flip through your accumulated mail, where you find among the bills a notice from scheduling that next month you will have three over-and-back trips—good news, because that means fewer days away from home. You take a few minutes to catch up with your significant other, and you grab a bite to eat. But the main thing you want to do is sleep. There were just too many time zone changes over the last five days, something that you suspect you may *never* learn how to handle well.

How It Worked

A superbly engineered service product, carefully tailored to fit market research findings about what customers want. Bright and attractive crew members. Extensive training to ensure that each individual knows exactly what he or she is supposed to do at each point in the service routine. Designated leaders within the team to coordinate the work and deal with unanticipated problems. A schedule that is demanding but not exhausting.

It worked well most of the time for the international airline. There were extremely few service disasters—and those that did occur invariably were rooted in exogenous events such as weather delays, mechanical problems, or catering errors. Moreover, marketing surveys showed that, by and large, passengers were happy with the airline's service. Back in headquarters, managers and supervisors, although burdened with paperwork, were generally calm and confident. They knew that so long as everyone on board was doing what he or she was supposed to do, customers in the dozens of aircraft in flight at any given moment were indeed receiving the service that they were supposed to receive.

The way this carrier structured and supported its self-managing flight attendant teams, then, resulted in predictability, competent in-flight performance, and low risk that a team might go off on its own and do damage to the airline or its passengers. Significant benefits, these. But the airline did incur some costs to obtain them.

One cost, of special concern to the marketing department, was that the company often found itself trailing competitors in service innovations. When a competitor introduced a new twist, months could pass before the international airline matched or leapfrogged the competitor's innovation. Because all procedures were specified in such detail, changes in service required reengineering the workflow, rewriting procedures, and (if the changes were large) waiting for all crew members to cycle through their semiannual, recurrent training before the new service package could be introduced.

Another cost was the disinclination of crews to tailor their services to the special circumstances of a given flight. To specify the "one best way" to accomplish a task necessarily requires that some assumptions be made about the conditions under which the work will be done. For cabin service work, these assumptions involve, among other things, the length of the flight and the number of passengers on board. The procedures that will be most pleasing to passengers on a short, full flight differ from those that will work best on a long, mostly empty flight.

Work system designers at the international carrier did what engineers often do—they optimized procedures for a "typical" flight. Therefore, their routines worked best for flights of about five hours in duration, with about 275 people on board. They did not work as well for eight-hour flights with 100 passengers (cabin crew tended to complete their work very quickly, and on more than one occasion I observed them retire to the galley, close the nonsoundproof curtain, and begin discussing how poorly the airline was managed). Nor did the routines work very well on short flights with every seat occupied (to get through them, the crew had to be constantly in motion, with not a minute to waste chatting with passengers).

Flight attendant teams did not feel that they had the *right* to alter the routines, even when it was clear that they were less than ideal for the special circumstances of a given flight. Instead, the teams typically just went ahead and did what they had been told and trained to do. Toward the end of our research project, a number of cabin services managers became concerned that crew members were, too often, merely "reading their lines," neither attentive enough to passenger needs nor responsive enough to unique in-flight circumstances. Management took several initiatives to correct this problem, including publication of a revised statement of cabin service standards. It began as follows: "Service standards have all too often been thought of in terms of in-flight routines and procedures, particularly those connected with food and drink. When standards have been stated at all, they have centered on cabin crew activity, not on the passenger."

The statement went on to emphasize that the focus of crews' work should be to achieve the ultimate objective for cabin services (that is, service so pleasing that it generates repeat business), even if that meant occasional deviation from standard routines. The message was reinforced in special instructions issued to senior cabin crew: "Instructions and guidelines exist for every aspect of inflight service. Properly followed, they provide the highest standards of professional and technical service. It is, however, entirely within the discretion of the senior cabin crew member to vary normal procedures and allocated duties if doing so achieves a higher level of passenger satisfaction."

Management meant what it said. But the new directives did not generate much change in what actually happened on board company aircraft. The rhythm of the standard routines may have been too strong. Or, perhaps, predictability had over time come to be something as ingrained, and as valued, by crew members as it previously had been by their management.

Management's attempt to alter by exhortation what had become a well-established way of operating points to what is perhaps the major lost opportunity in the "engineering" strategy for managing teamwork—namely, underutilization of members' intelligence, initiative, and ingenuity. The magnitude of this loss became vivid for me when my colleague, Victor Vroom, returned from a trip on the same carrier that we were studying. Vic had a story to tell.

"What wonderful flight attendants that airline has," Vic began. He went on to describe the emergency that had occurred on his flight. There had been indication of an engine fire, and the captain had discharged the fire extinguisher for the suspect engine and then proceeded to land at the nearest airport able to accept a jumbo jet. The fire warning turned out to have been false, but the aircraft could not take off again until the discharged fire bottle was replaced—and it was uncertain when a replacement bottle would arrive. Worse, the city where the aircraft had landed was not served by the airline, which meant that there were no company employees on the ground to help out. So the cabin crew found itself in an unfamiliar city with a planeload of passengers on its hands. "It was amazing," Vic continued. "As soon as we were off the airplane, they immediately got themselves organized, started making calls and negotiating with local innkeepers, and within a couple of hours they had arranged meals and lodging for everyone on board."

I agreed with Vic that the crew had dealt superbly with the emergency. But I had another question. How, I asked, had the service been before the emergency? Vic had to think about that—his recollection of the flight understandably was dominated by the emergency. "I guess it was routine," he finally responded. "Nothing really memorable."

Routine. Nothing really memorable. Those phrases capture the downside of the engineering approach to team management. Even people who arrive for work rich with talent and ready to use it fully to help their teams and their organizations succeed can, eventually, come to experience the work as "just a job." Once that happens, they can find it difficult to generate the extra effort, the additional measure of ingenuity and improvisation, that can spell the difference between team performance that is competent and that which is, indeed, memorable.

Flight attendants at the international airline almost always performed competently. Moreover, our data revealed no pattern of deep-seated angst, hostility, or alienation among them. Yet the sense of excitement and opportunity that had drawn many of them to the airline in the first place had worn off. Being a flight attendant had become just a job, and one that required relatively little thinking, planning, or team decision making. As

Vic's story makes clear, these teams had much more to offer the airline and its customers than the company asked them—nay, *allowed* them—to give.

THE DOMESTIC AIRLINE

The domestic airline was, at the time we studied it, a small, fast-growing carrier that flew Boeing 737 aircraft on flights rarely exceeding two hours in duration.[2] The 737 is a two-engine jet aircraft that, as configured by this airline, could carry up to 118 passengers.

Like the international carrier, the domestic airline sought to provide such superb service that passengers would insist on flying the airline again whenever they had the chance. And teams at both airlines were composed of bright, attractive individuals who were eager to immerse themselves in meaningful work. At the domestic carrier, however, flight attendants performed service-related tasks on the ground and at company headquarters in addition to their in-flight duties. The airline's employment advertisements emphasized the challenging service aspects of the job—often not even mentioning that much of this service would be provided in the air for fear of attracting applicants who mainly sought the glamour of being a flight attendant. Recruiting managers at the domestic airline were so proud of their choosiness that for a time they wore lapel buttons reading "One in 100."

Cabin crew members at the domestic airline were called Customer Service Managers (CSMs). Their work for the airline began with a two-week initial training course, at which they learned everything from three-letter airport codes to techniques for using emergency slides to evacuate a 737 aircraft. Midway through the second week of the training came "team formation day," which class members approached with a combination of anticipation and dread. For it was on that day that class members would arrive as twenty-four individuals and leave as six four-person teams.

The design of the day would have warmed the heart of an organization development consultant. "What makes for a good team?" the instructor would ask. "What strengths do you bring to a team? And what strengths do you seek from your teammates?" Class members would exchange views and would participate in exercises designed to let them test their ideas. Eventually, with help from the instructor, the class would develop its own conclusions about what is needed for team effectiveness. More exercises and discussion would ensue until, at the end of the day, teams had been formed.

From then on, teams rather than individuals were the primary units for performing customer service work. Even the construction of work schedules was done at the team level. The domestic airline used, for a time, a lottery system to award monthly schedules. A team that drew a good lottery number had much more choice about its schedule than did a less lucky team. A good number was not necessarily a blessing, however. Would the team select a schedule that had interesting destinations and many nights away from home, or one that permitted members to sleep, most nights, in their own beds? If a team included some members who sought adventure and others who liked to be home as much as possible, then negotiation was required. It was the team's responsibility to work things out—rarely was there a manager around to help members with these sometimes difficult trade-offs.

Teams also had to decide about their own composition and leadership. Federal air regulations require that there be at least three flight attendants aboard a 737 aircraft, one of whom is designated the "lead" flight attendant. But the CSM teams had four members, not three, and no permanent leader. It was the team's responsibility to decide, after looking at the weather and passenger loads, whether all four members were needed on a given trip, or whether one could remain at the company offices to do other work while his or her colleagues were flying. Moreover, it was the team's responsibility to decide which member would be the lead that day.

The CSM teams also had significant authority for deciding how to carry out their in-flight work. In sharp contrast to practice at the international carrier, company managers refrained from specifying and insisting upon any "one best way" to provide on-board service. Instead, crews were given extremely thorough training in the company's objectives, the direction for their work. They were told clearly what the outer-limit constraints on their behavior were. And, finally, they were given a diverse set of tools to use in pursuing the airline's service objectives. Beyond that, the teams were on their own.

Direction

The airline's service objectives derived directly from six guiding precepts that its officers had specified as the core values of the enterprise. They were (1) service, commitment to the growth of the individual, (2) best provider of air transportation, (3) highest quality of management, (4) role model, (5) simplicity, and (6) maximization of profits. As useful as the precepts were for organization-wide decision making, the chairman decided that the implications of the second precept for customer service needed to be spelled out in more detail. He eventually summarized the company's aspirations for how it would deliver its product in what he called the Three C's: complete, clean, and communicate. Senior managers reinforced the importance of the Three C's at every opportunity.

Most important, the chairman explained, was that each customer's flight be *complete*. Without question, a safely completed flight was the ultimate sign of good customer service, and the airline was proud of its splendid safety record. Yet the "complete" concept included much more: trying never to cancel a scheduled flight, departing and arriving on time, and making sure that each and every suitcase arrived at the same airport and at the same time as the customer who had checked it.

Clean was something of an obsession with the chairman. He insisted that the airline, and its people, sparkle—and he was willing to spend money to make it happen. The paint job on company planes, for example, cost far more than was really necessary. And planes were washed on a regular, frequent schedule, whether they needed it or not. Tray tables, most of the time stowed out of sight in seatbacks, became a symbol of cleanliness. "What does a customer think if one of our tray tables is dirty?" the chairman would ask. The answer eventually became so well learned that the exchange was something of a litany: "That if they can't even keep their tray tables clean, how well do they do at taking care of their engines," someone would say. "Right!" he would roar back. "Those tray tables have to be spotless!" "Clean" also applied to the people of the company and to their dress. Those who slipped from the highest standard of appearance were noticed—and, more often than not, nudged gently back into line by their colleagues.

Anyone who has experienced a "creeping delay" at an airport gate knows how important it is for airline staff to *communicate* with their passengers.

As frustrating as such delays are, they are not part of a plot to inconvenience passengers. Most times airline staff cannot know exactly how long it is going to take to fix a broken piece of equipment, or when a line of thunderstorms will clear the area, or when Air Traffic Control finally will release the aircraft for departure. Even so, passengers want to be told the truth, and the whole truth, about what is going on. At the domestic carrier, it was a key part of the work of CSM teams to do just that. If they themselves did not have the information, then it was their job to seek it out and pass it along.

Best provider of air transportation. Complete, clean, communicate. The direction for CSM teams at the domestic carrier was clear, and it was their responsibility to do whatever needed to be done to achieve it. Sometimes that meant doing some extra work themselves. Other times they had to persuade other people to take the needed action. Still other times, they had to lend a hand with work not officially their own to get things moving. It was up to them to decide.

Constraints

Although flight attendants at the domestic airline had enormous discretion in pursuing the company's service objectives, their freedom of action was not unlimited. For one thing, the technology with which they worked implicitly constrained their behavior. There were, for example, many technology-specific techniques for operating the on-board equipment that crews used. In addition, the chairman placed two explicit restrictions on crews' latitude in deciding how to proceed with their work. One was that each crew must, without fail, comply with all Federal Aviation Administration regulations. These regulations, which are quite detailed, address such diverse matters as the content of safety announcements, the stowage of cabin baggage, and even where crew members are to sit or stand at specific times on the ground and in the air. Crews were to take no shortcuts with safety-related matters even if, in a given circumstance, the federal requirements seemed unnecessary or irrelevant.

The other constraint was that crew members were never to give away liquor. Aside from the financial consequences of passing out free drinks (the cost of those little bottles adds up fast), the chairman was concerned that cabin crews would be tempted to use liquor to resolve service difficulties.

"I don't care whether it's our fault or an act of God," he would explain. "When there is a problem, look your customers in the eye and deal with them person to person. Explain to them honestly what the problem is and what you are doing to take care of it. Don't try to buy their goodwill with free booze."

Except for these constraints, the crews had a wide-open playing field. They were allowed—indeed, encouraged—to do whatever was required to provide service so pleasing that customers would queue up, if necessary, to fly with the airline again.

Tools

To assist crews in achieving company service objectives, management provided a diverse set of resources for crews to draw on in serving customers. These resources included ideas about ways to resolve common service problems, an open-door policy that made it easy for crews to seek the advice of company managers, access to marketing and performance data that in many airlines are considered proprietary and withheld from front-line employees, and so on.

Cabin announcement scripts are a good case in point. Many airlines give their crews scripts for every eventuality, from safety announcements to pitches for new company services, and insist that crew members memorize or read these prepared announcements. The worry, according to a manager at another carrier, is that "If we don't tell them exactly what they are supposed to say, they'll get it all wrong." Although it may reassure managers to know that every crew member's flight bag contains copies of company-approved announcements, the scripts actually provide little protection against crew members getting it wrong anyway. One way to get it wrong, for example, is to recite the announcement by rote using a tone of voice that says "I'm telling you this only because I have to, and it isn't really very important." Another is to read the script verbatim, pausing in strange places and stumbling over words.

I encountered a rather creative way to get it wrong on a flight (on another carrier) that was plagued by mechanical glitches. Three times we were pushed back from the gate only to return because of problems discovered during taxi. Finally, as we were reapproaching the gate for the third time, the captain announced over the public address system that the flight was being canceled. The aircraft came to a stop, and as the jetway was approaching the door, a flight attendant took the microphone. "Welcome to St. Louis [not the actual city]," she intoned. "We know you have many airlines from which to choose, and we appreciate your deciding to fly with us. We hope the next time you travel, you will choose us once again. Have a good day in the St. Louis area." It was the standard gate arrival script, competently delivered. The only problem was that the gate was the one from which we had been trying unsuccessfully to *depart* for the last hour.

There are, indeed, many ways to get it wrong, whether or not one has the aid of a company-provided script. At the domestic airline, CSM teams did carry scripts in their flight bags—but they also were encouraged to improvise as needed to get their message across. They were expected to use the scripts in the same way that they used all the other tools the company supplied—as resources, not as requirements.

How It Worked

When the domestic airline's customer service teams clicked, they performed superbly. Team members were fully engaged with their work, they exhibited both ingenuity and good judgment, and their customers received superb service.

I happened to do an observational flight with the same CSM team on two different occasions, about two weeks apart. The first flight was from New York to Florida. It was late winter, the weather was good, and the plane was booked about half full. After the captain finished his briefing, the cabin crew made its way to the gate. Members immediately noticed an unusually high number of children, tennis racquets, and festively dressed passengers in the boarding area. "Looks like we have a vacation crowd today," the lead CSM observed. "Shall we make it a fun flight?" Her teammates liked the idea, as did the captain when she told him what the cabin crew had in mind. "I'll get out my *Captain's Atlas*," he added. "We'll do a couple of contests." (The *Captain's Atlas* is a standard road atlas overprinted with jet airways and with notes about places visible from aircraft that fly them. It is, in effect, a crib sheet for pilots who like to entertain and, perhaps, impress their passengers.)

As the crew welcomed people aboard, members occasionally took a little extra time to chat with a passenger or to give special attention to a child. Once everyone was seated, the lead took the microphone to make the required safety announcement. "We have a surprise for you," she began. "This has been designated as one of our airline's special 'safety award' flights. There is a twenty-dollar bill tucked into one of the safety folders on this aircraft. When I give the signal, look inside the folder in the seatback in front of you, and let's see who has won the safety award!" She then counted down from five, and at zero most passengers did indeed extract and examine their safety folders. The lead looked around expectantly, as if waiting to identify the lucky passenger. Then, with exaggerated disappointment, she again lifted the microphone. "Well, it seems we have no winner today after all. [pause] But since you already have the safety folder out, let's take a moment to review some very important information it contains. . . ." It was all done in good humor, and passengers seemed to enjoy rather than to resent the fact that they had been duped into paying attention.

About half an hour after departure, the captain announced over the public address system that Mount Trashmore soon would become visible from the right side of the aircraft. Mount Trashmore, he explained, is a landfill in Virginia Beach that has been covered with soil, planted, and turned into a playground. Whoever spotted it first was to pull the flight attendant call button and would be awarded a small prize. As a flight attendant, with great ceremony, delivered a soft drink to the winning passenger, the captain came on again to reassure passengers on the left side of the plane that they, too, would have a chance to compete when the plane approached the coastline of Florida.

The friendly, high-spirited service continued throughout the rest of the flight. When the plane finally pulled up to the gate, the passengers spontaneously applauded—something that, in my experience, tends to happen only when one is relieved to be back on the ground with body and soul still connected. On this flight, the applause was not an expression of relief. It came because passengers' Florida vacations had begun two and a half hours sooner than they had expected.

The same crew, two weeks later, worked a late afternoon flight from Newark to Boston. Booked nearly full, the flight already was over an hour late because of a snowstorm and indefinite gate holds. The crew had waited out the delay in the briefing area. As boarding time approached, members walked together to the gate and surveyed their customers. It was an easy group to read—mostly businesspeople and students impatient to get where they were going. No tennis racquets, children, or festive clothes were to be seen, but there was lots of pacing and nervous watch-checking. "Business mode?" asked one crew member of her colleagues. The others nodded. They knew exactly what she meant. The crew had, after all, been working together for months.

Businesslike is what it was. The crew greeted boarding passengers with a word of welcome and a professional smile, but refrained from any chatting that might slow things up. The lead delivered the safety announcement concisely and crisply, and then the crew waited for the plane to begin its taxi. Only then did they walk though the cabin to check that baggage was properly stowed, seat belts secured, seatbacks forward, and tray tables up—thereby holding off as long as possible the moment when passengers had to forgo comfort for safety.

Shortly after takeoff, the captain cycled the No Smoking sign, the signal that cabin service could begin. The crew immediately swung into action, moving drink and ticketing carts simultaneously in both directions from mid-cabin. They hoped to move through the cabin so quickly that they would be able to offer a second drink service prior to the start of the approach into Boston. There were no jokes, no offer from the captain of a free soft drink to anyone who could discern through the murk the lights of Providence, and, when the plane finally did land, no applause.

It was, nonetheless, another fine job by the crew. On both flights I observed, the crew had tailored its service to that day's special circumstances. This crew did precisely what the officers of the airline, in giving cabin crews a large playing field, had hoped and expected they would do.

Not all crews did. Indeed, when a crew at the domestic carrier decided to take it easy, or to get back at the airline for some real or imagined wrong, it could do real damage. One crew we studied, for example, decided that it was inadequately supported in its work and not appropriately recognized for its contributions to the airline. Thereafter, members did the absolute minimum that was required of them. Since crews were self-managing and not monitored by supervisors, this crew's shortcuts went undetected by everyone but their passengers for months. Another crew, not in our study, used members' considerable intelligence and ingenuity to divert portions of their ticket and food service revenues into their own pockets. Again, it was months before the crew's larceny was detected.

There also were inefficiencies in the use of the airline's human resources, as each crew developed and fine-tuned its own way of doing things. It was not uncommon for a crew to invent and test a service strategy that other crews had already tried and abandoned as a bad idea. Indeed, it sometimes seemed as if each crew was intent on becoming its own little airline—which, of course, meant that the face the company presented to its customers varied from day to day and from crew to crew. At the domestic carrier, the creativity seen so rarely at the international airline occasionally was present in excess, or was used to benefit the team itself rather than the airline and its customers.

EFFECTIVE WORK TEAMS

Let us now return to the question with which the chapter began. Given the experiences of the international and domestic airlines, what would *you* do to ensure that teams of flight attendants consistently provide the highest possible quality of service to passengers?

The international airline's answer to the question was to engineer and preprogram the work to the fullest extent possible. It achieved predictability and protection from excessive downside risk, but at a considerable cost: Both individual flight attendants and cabin crew teams were significantly underutilized. Managers at this airline left a significant amount of talent on the table. The domestic airline had the opposite problem. Its customer service teams brimmed with energy and innovation and were ready to turn on a dime to solve the problems and exploit the opportunities they encountered. But there was a pervasive worry at the company that some team somewhere in the system might be just about to fly out of control. Managers at this airline, one suspects, did not rest as well at night as did their counterparts at the international carrier.

Is it possible to eat one's cake and have it too? Can one achieve creativity, agility, and learning while still maintaining reasonable levels of consistency, control, and alignment with collective objectives? The message of this book is that, with wise and assertive team leadership, that is indeed possible. It is not a matter of threading carefully between the poles of creativity and control. As we will see, superb leadership can make it possible for teams, in their everyday work, to operate as well as the domestic airline flight attendant team did when it instantly adapted its performance strategy to the different circumstances of the Florida and Boston flights, and as well as the international airline team did when it got into gear and took such good care of its customers after the emergency landing.

The very best work teams always serve their customers well, of course. But they also become increasingly capable performing units over time, as members gain experience and discover new and better ways of working together. And, finally, they provide settings in which each individual member can find in his or her teamwork a good measure of personal learning and fulfillment. An effective work team does all three of these things. Because the main purpose of this book is to identify what leaders can do to help teams achieve and sustain a high standing on all three of these criteria, we will take the next few pages to deepen our understanding of them.[3]

Serving Clients

The productive output of the team (that is, its product, service, or decision) meets or exceeds the standards of quantity, quality, and timeliness of the team's clients—the people who receive, review, or use the output. Those of us who study team performance in the experimental laboratory often can finesse the problem of deciding just what *effective* means. We can, for example, construct a task that has a clean, reliable performance measure—such as the number of puzzles a group solves in a given time period, or whether a group comes up with the one right answer to the problem we asked them to solve. And then we can proceed to investigate experimentally the factors that enhance or depress a team's score on that measure.

Effectiveness criteria are not so straightforward for teams that perform work in organizational settings. Few organizational tasks have clear right-or-wrong answers, for example. Nor do they lend themselves to simple, unidimensional numerical measures that validly indicate how well a group has done its work. Even for teams whose performance can be timed or counted, such "objective" measures rarely tell the whole story (or, in many cases, the most important part of the story) about how they are doing.

As part of our *Groups That Work* project a few years ago, Mary Lou Davis-Sacks and I studied a number of teams in the Fiscal Analysis

Branch of the federal Office of Management and the Budget (OMB).[4] Among the teams in the branch were some whose work was to perform economic analyses for the director of OMB and his staff. How should the reports prepared by these teams have been assessed?

One possibility was to obtain judgments of the "objective" quality of the reports, using generally accepted standards for economic research, the kinds of criteria that editors of economic journals use in deciding whether to publish an article. Team members, all of whom were civil servants and many of whom held advanced degrees in economics, knew and respected these standards. They would have been quite comfortable having the standards used to assess their products.

Yet what actually *happened* to the teams' reports—and, ultimately, to the teams themselves—depended mainly on the views of the OMB political officials for whom the work was done. These officials sought bulletproof analyses because the findings were certain to be carefully scrutinized by political opponents. Even more important to the political officials, however, were the timeliness of the reports and their usefulness in promoting the president's political and policy agendas. A publishable-quality report that arrived the day *after* the director testified in Congress, or one that focused mainly on issues of interest to the team itself, would be ignored. Worse, if the team's reports came to be viewed as useless or self-serving, the political staff might well arrange to do its own analyses—in effect, freezing the civil servant teams out of the policy-making process.

It is the client's standards and assessments that count. Not those of the team itself, except in those rare cases when the team is the client of its own work. Not those of outside researchers or evaluators, except when they are engaged to do an assessment by those who *do* have legitimacy as reviewers. And not even those of the team's manager, who rarely is the person who actually receives and uses a team's output. Rather than serve as a surrogate client, the manager's job is first to help the team identify the standards that are used by its real clients, and then to do whatever can be done to help the team meet those standards.

A large number of "But what if . . ." objections flow immediately from this view. What if the client has bad judgment? What if the client's standards are far too low or too high? What if the client wants something inappropriate or even illegal? What if the client doesn't even *know* what he or she wants? What if there are multiple clients, and they want incompatible things? In such questions lie real opportunities for a work team and its leaders—opportunities that might never surface were the team to focus mainly on self- or manager-defined performance criteria. Explicitly addressing the fact that different clients have different views of what *good* means (or views that differ from the team's own), for example, can break a team out of its usual routines and, sometimes, result in innovative performance strategies.

Professional symphony orchestras can be viewed as large teams whose clients are audiences. Orchestra musicians like to play music that stretches and challenges them, but many audiences prefer music that is melodic and familiar. The imperfect alignment between team members and clients about the definition of a "good" concert has become increasingly consequential in the last decade as the economic situation of many orchestras has worsened. These times require that most concert hall seats be filled and that people pay substantial sums of money to sit in them.

The ensembles that Jutta Allmendinger, Erin Lehman, and I assessed in our research on professional symphony and chamber orchestras responded to this challenge in a variety of ways.[5] One orchestra succumbed to the wishes of its audience and, in effect, converted itself into a full-time pops ensemble. The concert hall brimmed with people who were enjoying themselves hearing old favorites, but neither the orchestra nor its audiences were being stretched. A self-governing orchestra took almost the opposite tack. To challenge themselves musically, members decided to play what *they* wanted to play. Audiences dwindled as patrons stayed away from concerts dominated by unfamiliar, strange-sounding music. By focusing on the wishes of team members to the near-exclusion of those of its clients, this orchestra came perilously close to going out of business.

A third orchestra attended to *both* musicians' and audience members' views of what a "good" performance is—but also took initiatives to bring audience members' criteria more closely into alignment with its own. Programming at this orchestra had the feel of a sandwich: Some meaty new music was performed in the middle of the program, between an engaging opening number and the major concluding work. The top and bottom slices of the sandwich provided the incentive to get people into the hall, where they also were exposed to (and, one hopes, gradually came to enjoy) serious contemporary music.

Through its artistic programming, supplemented by other educational initiatives such as preconcert discussions, this orchestra altered its clients' views of what "good performance" means. But what if a legitimate client knowingly asks a team to do something that is wrong or inappropriate? In the heat of the budget season at OMB, the fiscal analysis teams began to get cues from their political clients that it would be helpful if the team's reports were more directly supportive of the administration's position. Might it be possible to omit certain projections about the possible implications of the administration's proposals on the national debt? These extrapolations, after all, are almost certainly unreliable. Besides, including them could distract attention from the many positive features and short-term benefits of the proposals. Might the team be willing to orient its analyses and reports just a bit more in the president's direction?

David Mathiasen, the chief of the Fiscal Analysis Branch, felt it was time for an informal tour of the political side of the house to see if he could reduce some of the pressure on his teams. He reminded the team's clients why it was in their own best interest to have reports that were as complete and trustworthy as the analysts could make them. Mathiasen also met with his own manager, the head of the Budget Review Division, to suggest that he reaffirm with the director himself the importance of civil servant staff not becoming politicized.

These initiatives did appear to reduce the number of inappropriate requests made of the fiscal analysis teams—for a time. But the process of shaping clients' views of what good performance meant was, for these clients, never ending and never sufficient. Therefore, Mathiasen also worked directly and extensively with his analysis teams, making sure that members had a deep understanding of their ultimate purposes and norms of conduct that were consistent with those purposes. These leadership initiatives strengthened the teams' ability to deflect political pressures when teams did encounter them, and helped ensure that they could continue to make their unique contributions to the inherently political budget-making process.

Some teams are fortunate in that all relevant parties—the team, its managers, and its clients—agree on the criteria by which the team's work will be assessed. Less fortunate teams still have many options. They can educate their clients. They can apply political pressure. They can try to replace recalcitrant clients with others who are more amenable to the team's own aspirations for its work. Or they can succumb and do exactly what the clients want. All of these approaches, in various circumstances, can be appropriate.

What is never appropriate is to say, when the client finds the group's work wanting, "The group did great; it was just that the client was dumb." The group produced a wonderful new software package, but users were not perceptive enough to buy it. The team created a fine treatment regimen, but the patient would not cooperate. The staff came up with an elegant transportation plan, but the bureau chief wouldn't have it. All of these are group failures, and all of them stem from the team not taking seriously the fact that what good performance *means* is whatever the group's clients think it means.

Good teams know that, and meet their clients' expectations. Great teams actively shape those expectations, and then exceed them.

Growing as a Team

The social processes the team uses in carrying out the work enhance members' capability to work together interdependently in the future. Printed across the front of a T-shirt worn by a bearded, professorial-looking individual near Harvard Square: "The older I get . . ." On the back: ". . . the better I get." That may or may not have been true for the professor, but, as we will see in the next chapter, it is true for lots of teams. Over time, members come to know one another's special strengths and weaknesses and become highly skilled in coordinating their activities, anticipating one another's next moves and initiating appropriate responses to them even as those moves are occurring.

Other groups show the opposite pattern, as was illustrated by a two-person Boeing 737 cockpit crew I observed. The crew had gotten off to a bad start the previous day and things had deteriorated ever since. Now it was the crew's last leg together and the tension was palpable. The captain was flying, which meant that the first officer would operate the radios, manipulate the landing gear and flap levers, and keep an eye out for conflicting traffic. As the aircraft lifted off the runway, the captain glanced over to the first officer and nodded his head almost imperceptibly. That was his signal for the first officer to raise the gear. There was no response; the first officer kept his eyes outside the cockpit looking for other aircraft.

After a few seconds, the captain took his right hand off the control yoke and made a thumbs-up gesture in his teammate's direction. Still no response from the first officer. Finally, the captain exploded: "Gear up, dammit!" Slowly, deliberately, the first officer turned to his captain and said, "I believe the correct phraseology, Captain, is 'Positive rate of ascent, gear up.'" The captain's response was to grab the gear lever himself and slam it into the up position. The rest of that last leg was flown in almost complete silence.

As I held my breath hoping that nothing would go wrong on that flight that would require the crew to operate as a real team, I reflected on a less dramatic but otherwise similar experience of my own. A few years before, the president of the university where I then worked had asked me to serve on a committee to identify candidates for a deanship that had become vacant. According to the first of the three criteria of team effectiveness, our committee was a success. The president liked the candidate we recommended and appointed him as dean. By the time that happened, however, I already had made my vow: Never again, no matter what, would I do *anything* that required me to work with the other members of that search committee. If the president wished to consider additional candidates, he would have to appoint a new committee. Ours had destroyed itself in the process of doing its work.

Effective work teams operate in ways that build shared commitment, collective skills, and task-appropriate coordination strategies—not mutual antagonisms and trails of failures from which little is learned. They become adept at detecting and correcting errors before serious damage is done, and at noticing and exploiting emerging opportunities. And they periodically review how they have been operating, milking their experiences for whatever learning can be had from them. An effective team is a more capable performing unit when its work is finished than it was when work began.

Individual Members' Learning

The group experience, on balance, contributes positively to the learning and personal well-being of individual team members. Work teams have much to offer their members. Teams are, for example, wonderful sites for learning—for expanding one's knowledge, acquiring new skills, and exploring perspectives on the world that differ from one's own. Teamwork also can engender feelings of belonging, providing members a secure sense of their place in the social world. And, of course, working with others on a shared task can spawn satisfying interpersonal relationships, some of which may flower into friendships that extend well beyond the group setting where they were formed.[6]

Why, then, when I announce on the first day of class that students will do a group project for which members will get a common grade, does the classroom fill with barely suppressed groans? The answer, of course, is that my students have done group projects before, and they know how awful it gets when a team does not work. Being a professor who aspires to empathy, I always acknowledge that some project groups do turn out to be more frustrating than fulfilling, more a source of angst than of learning. But the groups in my course, I assure them, will be different.

In fact, the students' previous experiences mirror my own. Membership on teams such as the deanship search committee has left me dispositionally disinclined to work in teams, preferring instead to work by myself whenever I can. Like the students, I have felt the frustration that comes from trying to craft a group product that all members find acceptable. And I know from research, but also from experience, that teams can stress their members, alienate them from one another, and undermine their confidence in their own abilities. Many work teams, perhaps even most of them, provide their members with significantly less personal learning and satisfaction than they could.

While not denying the inevitability of rough spots in the life of any group, I nonetheless do not count as effective any team for which the impact of the group experience on members' learning and well-being is more negative than positive. If the group prevents members from doing what they want and need to do, if it compromises their personal learning, or if members' main reactions to having been in the group are frustration and disillusionment, then the costs of generating the group product were too high.

Using the Criteria

Although it can take some effort to think through just what "effective" performance would mean for a given work team, it invariably is worth the trouble. For one thing, it forces us to be clear and explicit about our values, about what it is that we are hoping for and trying to promote when we create work teams. It lessens the likelihood that we will thoughtlessly use whatever performance indicators happen to be available or easy to obtain. It makes salient the fact that teams must continuously manage trade-offs among the three different aspects of overall effectiveness rather than focus exclusively on any one of them. And, finally, explicit effectiveness criteria provide a standard for testing and choosing among various structural or managerial interventions we may be contemplating. "If we did that," one can ask, "how would it affect the team's standing on the criteria that we care most about? Why do we think so?" Asking such questions promotes thoughtfulness of the type that can lessen the number of times that well-meaning interventions turn out to yield unexpected and unfortunate consequences.

The three criteria—a team product acceptable to clients, growth in team capability, and a group experience meaningful and satisfying for members—can be used to assess the effectiveness of any work team, regardless of task or setting. The relative *weight* of the three criteria, however, does vary across circumstances. If, for example, a temporary self-managing team were formed to perform a single task of extraordinary importance, then the second and third dimensions would be of lesser relevance to that team's overall effectiveness. On the other hand, tasks sometimes are created mainly to help members gain experience, learn some things, and become competent as a performing unit. During the startup of an engine manufacturing plant, for example, management created a special "core skills" production unit specifically to build team members' skills and experience for the work they subsequently would do in metalworking teams.[7] The task in such cases may be as much an excuse for the unit as the reason for it, and assessments of team effectiveness would depend more on the second and third criteria than on the first.

Including social and personal criteria in a definition of effectiveness is a departure from tradition in small-group research, as is my emphasis on system-defined (rather than researcher-defined) assessments of a group's productive output. Yet the criteria themselves require neither extraordinary accomplishment nor exemplary social processes. All that is necessary for effectiveness is output judged acceptable by those who receive or use it, a team that winds up its work at least as capable as when it started, and members who are at least as satisfied as they are frustrated by what has transpired. The challenge is to generate ways of understanding, designing, and managing teams that help them meet or exceed these modest criteria.

CREATING CONDITIONS FOR EFFECTIVENESS

This book identifies and explores the five conditions that leaders can put in place to increase the chances that a team will, over time, achieve and sustain a high standing on the three criteria just discussed. Specifically, the likelihood of effectiveness is increased when a team (1) is a *real team* rather than a team in name only, (2) has a *compelling direction* for its work, (3) has an *enabling structure* that facilitates rather than impedes teamwork, (4) operates within a *supportive organizational context,* and (5) has available ample *expert coaching* in teamwork.

Each of these conditions, depicted in figure 1-1, is addressed in turn in the five chapters that follow. The first three of these chapters address the three core conditions for effectiveness—namely, creating a real team with a compelling purpose and an enabling structure. The next two chapters discuss the two conditions that can help a team harvest the benefits of a good basic design—namely, a supportive organizational context and expert coaching in teamwork. Finally, the concluding section of the book explores the implications of this way of thinking about work teams for larger questions about group and organizational leadership and change.

To view team leadership as creating conditions that increase the chances that a team will evolve into an effective performing unit is somewhat unconventional. Both practicing managers and writers about management commonly view the actions of leaders as "causes" and the responses of teams as "effects." In cause-effect models, particular leader behaviors and styles are viewed as strongly determining team behavior and performance. By contrast, I view the main responsibility of leaders as creating and maintaining the five conditions that increase the chances that a team will, over time, become increasingly effective in carrying out its work.

FIGURE 1 - 1

The Conditions for Team Effectiveness

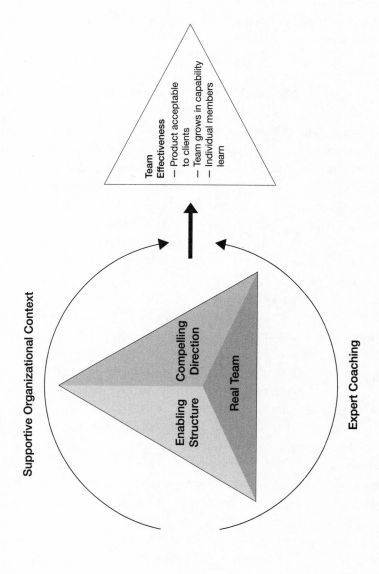

Supportive Organizational Context

Enabling Structure

Compelling Direction

Real Team

Expert Coaching

Team Effectiveness
— Product acceptable to clients
— Team grows in capability
— Individual members learn

No one person has sole responsibility for team leadership. Leadership is provided by anyone who helps create and maintain the performance-enhancing conditions, regardless of whether that person happens to hold a formal leadership role. Nor is there any one right way for leaders to behave. Instead, they use whatever expertise they have and whatever resources they can corral to get the five key conditions in place and keep them there. This book explores what is involved in doing that, how it can be done well, and what those who would lead teams can do to build their own leadership capabilities.

PART II

ENABLING CONDITIONS

2

A Real Team

I t can be inspiring to watch a superb team in action. One wonders, as members of a jazz ensemble pass solos back and forth without missing a beat, how they *do* that. The same feeling can come while watching a great basketball team. A player feints in one direction, moves three strides in another, and, at the precise moment she has broken free, the ball reaches her outstretched hands. The subsequent shot is anticlimactic; the awesome part is how it happened that the player and the ball arrived at the same place at the same instant.

The other side of the coin is the empathic embarrassment one feels when watching a team that does not work. The ball is passed but no one is there to catch it and it bounces untouched out of bounds. There was *supposed* to be someone there of course, but the play fell apart and the passer, who actually did what he was supposed to do, looks like a fool. Or the amateur jazz group finishes one passage, the drummer keeps on beating out the rhythm, but no one picks up the solo line. Members of the audience look away as the players signal one another with their eyes to try to recapture the music that they somehow lost.

Anyone who has logged much time working in teams, or watching them work, has experienced both kinds of feelings. Our job is to figure out what makes the difference between teams that inspire and those that embarrass—and to do so in a way that invites constructive action. Accomplishing this requires that we transcend the common human tendency to assign credit (and, especially, blame) for collective performance to single individuals. When a team has performed superbly, for example, credit often goes to the leader—or, for some tasks, to the one individual whose performance was both exceptional and salient, the "star" player. And when a team has performed poorly, we often ask, almost without thinking, "Whose fault was it?" Again, the most common answer is the person who served as team leader or, perhaps, the individual who dropped the ball at a critical moment.[1]

This tendency to assign credit and blame to specific people is seen in the individualistic orientation of interventions intended to improve team performance. The goal of many such interventions is to help group leaders and members become more aware of those aspects of their personalities, attitudes, and behavioral styles that change agents think are key to team effectiveness. The hope is that improved team functioning will come about more or less automatically if each member understands his or her personal style and recognizes the need for good communication and coordination. I know of no evidence that supports this assumption.

The opposite may be closer to the truth: The best way to get individuals to behave well in a group is to do a good job of setting up and supporting the group itself. A healthy group promotes competent member behavior; a sick group invites all manner of bizarre individual behaviors—which, ironically, can then be used to explain the problems of the group as a whole.[2] To understand what makes a team effective, then, requires that we become comfortable thinking and acting at the *group* level of analysis. Because that is not something most of us routinely do in our daily lives, it can take some learning and practice.

EXPLAINING GROUP BEHAVIOR

Here is a question sent to "The Ethicist" column of the *New York Times Magazine*.[3] How would you respond to it?

My son's lacrosse team was being bussed home from a game. When a rival school's women's lacrosse team pulled alongside, two boys in the back of the bus mooned them. The coach ordered the entire team to sign a letter of apology. I have encouraged my son not to sign: he was not responsible for the deed or even aware it was occurring.

Randy Cohen, who writes the column for the *Times,* responded as follows:

Your son ought not confess to something he did not do. One should lie neither to deny nor to avow wrongdoing. What he and his team-mates could sign, however, is a letter of regret that honestly describes the epidermal transgression, noting that many may have contributed to the rowdy atmosphere but few actually depantsed. All members of a group can honorably take responsibility for something done in its name and embodying its function . . . [but] your son need not apologize for the antics of two teammates.

Randy Cohen balances delicately and appropriately between individual- and group-level explanations for the event. On the one hand, two specific individuals did the deed, and the letter-writer's son certainly should not apologize for an action he personally did not perform. But another way of viewing the incident is as an intergroup event, as an exchange between one team and another as their buses passed. The "rowdy atmosphere" in the mooners' bus may have been all that the two least inhibited team members needed to initiate action *on behalf of the group.* I suspect many readers of Cohen's column (and perhaps readers of this book as well) would not go even as far as he did in concluding that what happened may have been, at least in part, the act of one intact group vis-à-vis another.[4]

To further explore the implications of group-level thinking, let us move from the lacrosse team bus to the flight deck of commercial aircraft, where two- or three-person teams share responsibility for flying the aircraft safely and efficiently to its destination. The extremely low accident rate in commercial aviation testifies to just how well cockpit crews perform day in and day out. When an incident does occur, however, more often than not it is because the team broke down. Analyses of the causes of accidents and incidents have documented that, in the great majority of cases, the *crew* got itself into trouble even though the aircraft was mechanically capable of flying out of the situation and all crew members were highly skilled, well trained, and in good health.[5] Despite these findings, explanations of why an accident occurred—explanations offered by trained investigators as well as by laypersons—generally assign responsibility to individual crew members. Even pilots themselves, who have grown exceedingly weary of hearing the words "pilot error," rarely use the language of groups in talking about their work.

To illustrate, here is how a pilot described to me the final approach of a flight that did not go well.

> There was this flock of geese having a tea party right over the end of 22 Left [a runway designation], so the tower switched them to 31 just when Charlie [the copilot] was getting lined up on the ILS [Instrument Landing System]. Well, the weather was a mess, they were vectoring old Charlie all over the place, and he got confused and got behind. Three times Phil [the captain] had to remind him about something, and eventually Phil got so frustrated that he took the airplane and landed the damn thing himself.

And here is a different way of telling the same story. See what differences you notice.

> After they got ATIS [recorded airport information] they just assumed it would be a routine ILS approach to 22 Left and they started chewing the fat. They didn't hear the talk on the radio about the geese over the runway, so when the tower switched runways at the last minute it was scramble time. Charlie was flying, and he had his hands full because of weather and the new vectors he was getting. Phil started changing the radios to set up for the new approach, but he didn't tell Charlie what he was doing, and Charlie couldn't quite figure out what was going on. Nobody got things organized, everybody got confused, and eventually Phil got so frustrated that he took the airplane and landed the damn thing himself.

The two versions of the story offer two quite different ways of understanding what happened on that flight. In the first, the one most likely to be heard, it was Charlie who had a problem. He let a situation that was not all *that* demanding get the better of him and had to be bailed out by Phil, his captain. The attributions made are all to individuals.

The second account invites a group-level interpretation: The *crew* got itself into trouble by not paying attention to changes in the situation, by not planning and organizing the team's work, and by poor coordination between members. Focusing on the crew also highlights the captain's team leadership—not so much his behavioral style, but the kinds of expectations about behavior that he had established and enforced. Such matters are unlikely to be revealed by the first account, which implicitly casts Phil in the role of savior. The second version of the story also raises questions about the airline's overall strategy for structuring and supporting its crews. Might there have been something about the way crews were set up and staffed at that airline, or about the amount of authority they had for managing their own affairs, or about company-specified performance routines that could have contributed to what happened to Charlie and Phil?

To answer such questions requires that we move beyond explanations of team performance that rely mainly on the attributes or behaviors of individuals, and instead focus on how the teams themselves are designed and supported. It may sound silly to say, but if you are going to lead a team well, you must first make sure that you actually have a team to lead—and that you then deal with it as a *team* rather than as a set of individuals.

ESSENTIAL FEATURES OF REAL TEAMS

Real work teams in organizations have four features: a team *task,* clear *boundaries,* clearly specified *authority* to manage their own work processes, and membership *stability* over some reasonable period of time.[6] The first and perhaps most important task of those who create or lead work teams is to make sure that these four essential features are in place.

Team Task

Everybody would agree that a string quartet is a team. Its work simply cannot be accomplished without all four members present and playing. Everybody also would agree that a collection of people on a street corner waiting for a traffic light to change is not. Beyond such extremes, however, the terms *group* and *team* are akin to projective tests: People read into them what they wish, and conversations about teams can be frustrating because people have different things in mind when they talk about them.[7]

The first group I encountered in my research career was in the central office of a telephone company. My colleague Ed Lawler and I were being shown around the company in preparation for some research we were planning. One group we visited was introduced to us as "Supervisor Szczarba's team." Arrayed before us were a dozen or so telephone operators, each at her own console (there were no men in the group), each talking to her own customers, each taking her break at a time negotiated with Ms. Szczarba. Members of the group did perform their work alongside one another. But the only thing they actually shared was Ms. Szczarba.

Such teams are called *co-acting groups*. It is easy to tell who is in a co-acting group because members usually work in proximity to one another and have the same supervisor. But each member has an individual job to do, and that job's completion does not depend on what the others do. Co-acting groups are barely groups at all, and they are not what we are concerned with here. Our focus is on groups whose task requires them to work *together* to produce something—a product, service, or decision for which members are collectively accountable and whose acceptability is potentially assessable. The kind of outcome produced is not critical; it can be a physical product, a service, a decision, a performance, or a written report. Nor is it necessary that the outcome actually *be* assessed; all that is required is that the team produce an outcome that can be identified as its product and that it be theoretically possible to measure and evaluate that product. If Ms. Szczarba's team had been assigned collective responsibility for handling all service requests for, say, a specific part of the company's service area, and if members had been held collectively accountable for how quickly and well those requests were processed, then it would have been a real work team.

A great deal of organizational work is performed these days by sets of people who are called "teams" but who really are co-acting groups. Managers in organizations where this is done may harbor the hope that they can harvest the widely touted benefits of teamwork while continuing to directly manage the behavior of individual members. That hope is misplaced: If you want the benefits of teamwork, you have to give the *team* the work. So there is a choice here: Either design the work for a team, or design it for individuals. If done well, either strategy can yield fine results.

What is not fine is to send mixed signals: to use the rhetoric of teams when the work really is performed by individuals, or to directly supervise individual members when the work really is a team's responsibility.[8]

Sometimes managers' choices about work design are constrained because some tasks can only be done by teams (such as the string quartet mentioned earlier, or carrying out a multiparty negotiation) whereas others are inimical to teamwork. More often, however, the work could be carried out either by an individual or by a work team. In such cases, wise managers do not rush to assign the work to a team. Instead, they carefully weigh the advantages and disadvantages of using a team to perform the work, and take care not to assign to a team work that actually would be better performed by an individual.

Creative writing is one type of task that is often assigned to a team but should not be. So far as I know, not a single great novel, epic poem, or symphonic score has ever been written by a team. This kind of work involves bringing to the surface, organizing, and expressing thoughts and ideas that are but partially formed in one's mind (or, in some cases, that lie deep in one's unconscious), and these tasks are inherently better suited for individual than for collective performance. Even committee reports—mundane products compared with novels, poems, and musical scores—invariably turn out better when written by one talented individual on behalf of a group than by the group as a whole working in lockstep.

The same is true for many aspects of executive leadership. For all the attention being given to top-management teams these days, my reading of the management literature is that successful organizations almost always are led by a single talented and courageous human being rather than by a team, no matter how many well-qualified members the team contains. As numerous senior managers have discovered, bucks rarely stop at teams. Moreover, the most engaging and powerful statements of corporate vision invariably are the product of a single intelligence, set forth by a leader willing to take the risk of establishing collective purposes that lie just beyond what others believe to be the limits of the organization's capability.

Beyond creative writing and executive leadership, there are many other kinds of tasks that are better done by individuals than by teams. It is a mistake—a common one and often a fatal one—to use a team for work that requires the exercise of powers that reside within and are best expressed by individual human beings. A manager's first responsibility in creating a work team, then, is to make sure that the work to be done is appropriate for team performance and that it requires members to work together interdependently to achieve an identifiable collective outcome. If that cannot be done (and many times it cannot), then the wise choice is to design and manage the work for individual performers rather than for an interacting work team.

Bounded Team

To work well together, team members need to know who they are. Members are sure to run into difficulties if there is so much ambiguity about who is actually on the team that they cannot reliably distinguish between the people who share responsibility and accountability for the collective outcome and others who may help out in various ways but are not team members. Having a clearly bounded team does not mean that members must do all their work in the same place at the same time, nor does it mean that membership cannot change as circumstances change. It merely means that members know who is actually on the team—a seemingly simple matter but one that trips up a surprising number of teams.

A task force at a financial institution where I once did some research got in trouble for exactly this reason.[9] The team's task was to develop a plan for standardizing certain policies and practices across multiple locations that had, over time, developed their own ways of doing things. The team was formed by a senior vice president who also was its primary client. To ensure that all major points of view were represented, the vice president appointed to the team representatives of several key functional areas in the organization, including a few individuals he knew and trusted from other countries where the company did business. He further specified that the team could recruit to its ranks members from additional functions or locations if they would bring useful perspectives to the team's work, and he encouraged the team to work closely with professionals from a consulting firm who were on site to help the firm focus and streamline its offerings.

The first meeting of the task force was held at company headquarters and was attended by most of the functional area representatives but no one from a nonheadquarters location. Subsequent meetings, also at headquarters, were attended by different subsets of members, sometimes including

overseas representatives who happened to be in town. These meetings were
frustrating to the task force leader and to other regular attendees because
members who were attending for the first time invariably suggested new
ideas or raised for consideration possibilities that had been considered
and dismissed in a previous meeting. On a couple of occasions, a senior
officer not on the team came to a team meeting to advocate a particular
idea. One or two of the outside consultants also occasionally attended,
although they behaved more as observers than as active participants. About
a month into the work of the task force, the team leader took a trip to
Europe to talk with overseas members whose contributions up to that
point had been made mainly by telephone or e-mail. He returned with yet
another set of new ideas and perspectives for the headquarters-based
members to consider.

The task force never jelled as a performing unit. Members never
developed the specialized roles and shared norms of conduct that characterize real work teams, nor did the team develop the collective momentum
that would have enabled it to generate a high-quality proposal satisfactory
to the team's client. Eventually, the team leader got so frustrated that he
went off by himself and, with input from a couple of other members, personally wrote the proposal and submitted it to the senior vice president.
There never actually was a team product because there never actually
was a *team*.

The difficulties encountered by this task force are common when a
team's boundaries are so unclear that its membership is uncertain, or when
they are so permeable that there is a never-ending flow of people in and
out of the group. Organizational psychologist Clayton Alderfer refers to
such systems as "underbounded." The primary threat to underbounded
systems, Alderfer shows, is that they "become totally caught up in their
environmental turbulence and lose a consistent sense of their own identity
and coherence."[10] It is virtually impossible for an underbounded team to
develop and implement a coherent strategy for carrying out a piece of work.

The reverse state of affairs also can occur. A team with tight, imper-
meable boundaries is what Alderfer calls an "overbounded" system. An
overbounded team is something of an island unto itself. Although membership and team identity are completely clear, the team is closed off to its
environment. Members risk overlooking significant environmental changes,
they have limited capacity to respond appropriately to such changes even

if they are noticed, and they do not engage in the kinds of cross-boundary exchanges that can be critical to team performance.[11]

The risk of overboundedness is real, especially for geographically isolated teams such as a new plant startup far from headquarters or a consulting team that operates for an extended time at a remote client site. Underboundedness, however, is the more common problem for organizational work teams. The dysfunctions that stem from unclear or excessively permeable team boundaries are especially prevalent for professional and managerial teams such as the financial institution task force described earlier. Curiously, managers generally give less attention to clarifying the boundaries of teams made up of their peers or immediate associates than they do to creating clear, moderately permeable boundaries for front-line teams composed of rank-and-file organization members.

A few years ago, for example, I was invited to meet with the top-management team of a large insurance company. The team consisted of about two dozen senior executives, each with his or her own part of the business to run or staff support function to lead. The chief executive officer (CEO) told me he was getting increasingly frustrated as he tried to get his team to take on collective responsibility for the well-being of the company as a whole. Team members, for their part, were just as unhappy with the team's once-a-month meetings as was the CEO. Everyone wanted to know what it was that was keeping this collection of highly talented and committed individuals from pulling together as a team.

But were these senior managers actually a team at all? From one perspective, they were merely co-actors: Each member's main responsibility and accountability was for the performance of his or her own organizational unit. Although it surely was a good idea for the firm's senior managers to get together regularly, it was not clear to any of them just why they were meeting or what they were supposed to *do* as a team. One thing was certain: The CEO did not want them to actually run the company. Although that assuredly would have turned the group into a real task-performing team, running the organization was *his* job.[12]

Nor was it clear exactly who was on the team—there were so many members that it was hard for them to keep track of one another, especially since some members would send deputies to meetings they could not personally attend. This top-management team had neither a clear identity nor a shared and coherent view of its purposes and processes. It was an underbounded set of people who had meetings rather than a real team that performed work.[13]

Teams of managers and professionals are at special risk of under-boundedness because their main work invariably involves extensive and often intensive engagement with a variety of other individuals and groups. That necessity can blur the boundaries of the core group, as Martine Haas discovered in her research on project teams that performed knowledge-intensive work for a large international development organization.[14] When Haas asked managers for membership lists of the teams she would be studying, she often would get a response along the lines of "Well, that's not entirely clear—it depends on how you want to define the team." Even individuals who held team leader roles frequently could not give her a definitive list of members. That there were certain individuals who were "core" members of the team was clear to everyone. But beyond the core, membership was ambiguous because some individuals were partial members, others provided information or resources to the team but were (perhaps) not actually on it, and still others were clearly not members but just as clearly were critical to its work. It was as if there were an undifferentiated gradient extending out from the core of the team to all manner of other organization members whose participation was, in varying degrees, important to the team's performance. Haas eventually solved her research problem by distinguishing between the core members and everyone else, but the organizational problem she inadvertently surfaced remained a potentially significant impediment for some of the teams she studied.

Teams of many different sizes and durations dot the managerial and professional landscape of almost every purposive organization. Managerial and professional work does not lend itself to the formation of single teams whose members work only on those teams for extended periods. Instead, one person is likely to serve simultaneously on a variety of different teams that form, reform, and disappear as frequently as sand dunes on a windy beach. In one financial institution, for example, almost all professionals served on multiple teams, some of whose expected life spans extended indefinitely into the future, some of which were created to accomplish a particular task and would disband when that task was finished, and some of which were created on the fly to solve an unanticipated but pressing problem immediately. That is as it must be when teamwork is performed in uncertain or fast-changing environments. But even temporary teams whose members serve simultaneously on others are not immune from the requirement that they be thoughtfully composed and appropriately bounded. Sand-dune teams, as much or more than permanent teams, need the advantages of having clear and moderately permeable boundaries.

Managers and professionals sometimes talk and act as if they do not require the level of clarity about team boundaries that they would insist on for rank-and-file teams in their own organizations. "We're experienced at this kind of thing; it's what we do every day," one senior manager told me, "so we don't need to have all the i's dotted and t's crossed." It may be true (although I doubt it) that people who do managerial and professional work are better than others at handling ambiguity and uncertainty. But the underbounded character of many such groups makes it harder than it need be for them to demonstrate how good they really are at teamwork.

Ironically, many senior teams could learn a great deal about establishing and maintaining clear team boundaries from teams that carry out front-line work. Recall, for example, the teams of flight attendants at the domestic airline described in chapter 1. The four-person teams formed during training had clear boundaries and stable membership. When passenger loads were light, however, not all four members were required for in-flight work. On those days, one member could stay at company offices to perform other work while his or her teammates handled the team's in-flight duties. The team's boundaries remained clear despite the fact that members were flexibly deployed as circumstances changed.

A production team in a semiconductor manufacturing plant, by contrast, had to contend with constant changes in membership that were entirely out of the team's control. The number of people needed for the work was a direct function of the number of orders the company received for the team's product, and that varied widely (some would have said wildly) from month to month. When the backlog of orders got large, management would hire additional staff; when production capacity was greater than needed, less senior team members would be laid off or furloughed. Life on the team was a yo-yo of expansion and contraction separated by occasional periods of relative stability of membership.

An opportunity to establish clearer team boundaries developed when the production manager decided to give teams in his area increased responsibility for managing their own work. One of the team's new responsibilities was the management of its boundaries. The manager determined the number and mix of members who were needed to accomplish the team's work when production requirements were at an absolute minimum, and he designated those individuals as "core" team members. Core members were given employment security in that they would not be laid off unless the entire production area was shut down. In exchange, they were required to manage the expansion and contraction of their team as business needs changed.

After some initial resistance (adding and subtracting staff is emotionally demanding and always had been a management responsibility), members stepped up to the challenge and handled it well. The team gradually developed its own pool of people who would be invited to augment the team when production demands increased. Core team members invested time and energy to develop the skills of these individuals so they would be able to join in the work quickly and smoothly. And, over time, the temporary staff came to identify with the team and develop a measure of loyalty to it.

There was nothing this organization could have done to eliminate the fluctuations in demand that frequently required that the team expand or shrink in size. But by giving the team control of its own membership, the production manager clarified and affirmed the boundaries of the team and thereby reduced significantly its vulnerability to the dysfunctions of underboundedness.

Making music is about as different from making memory chips as it is possible to get. Yet the Orpheus Chamber Orchestra, a self-governing orchestra based in New York City, had much the same problem as the semiconductor production team and solved it in much the same way. The orchestra consists of twenty-six members. Few pieces in the chamber orchestra repertoire call for exactly that number of instrumentalists, however. Pieces that require fewer players pose no problem since the orchestra can use the same strategy as the flight attendants and let members who are not needed do other things. But pieces for larger ensembles require that the orchestra use additional players, who are recruited from the ranks of New York–area freelance musicians. Many of these additional players also serve as substitutes when an Orpheus member will be unavailable for a performance or tour, and over time members have come to know the best of them quite well. Although the substitutes have neither any guarantee of future employment nor the right to participate in orchestra decision making, a number of them have become de facto associate members of the ensemble. Moreover, on those rare occasions when there is an opening in the core orchestra, the substitutes invariably are among the prime candidates to fill it. Like the semiconductor team, the orchestra maintains a clear membership boundary, but does so in a way that provides both the flexibility that the work requires and a pool of reserve members who are well known by the core team, familiar with the team and its work, and usually ready to pitch in when needed.

The three teams just described—the flight attendants, the semiconductor production teams, and the chamber orchestra—all performed front-line work in their organizations. Although the nature of that work could hardly have been more different, each of these teams faced and overcame a significant challenge in establishing and maintaining clear team boundaries. Many management and professional teams, by contrast, have similar challenges but are less inclined to step up to them. Those who lead or serve on high-level teams in organizations would be well advised to notice and learn from those front-line teams that manage to achieve, simultaneously, both clear team boundaries and flexibility in obtaining and deploying human resources as task demands change.

Delimited Authority

Once it is clear what a team's work is and who is on the team, the two features just discussed, the next item of business is to determine the extent of the team's authority. It almost always is a good idea to do this explicitly. Otherwise, team members will do it implicitly as they proceed with their work—and, in the process, run a significant risk of either excessive timidity in making decisions or overstepping the actual bounds of their authority. The only way to avoid such miscalibrations is for managers to specify when a team is formed just how much authority the team initially will have and to make sure that members understand clearly what decisions are and are not theirs to make. There are many aspects of teamwork for which ambiguity is a good thing (such as leaving room for members to bring their own meaning to the team's purposes, as we will see in chapter 3), but the extent of a team's authority is not one of those aspects.

Both leaders and team members typically experience a measure of anxiety, angst, and ambivalence when authority is transferred from management to a work team. To say "This is now *your* team's responsibility, and you are fully accountable for how you handle it" is virtually to guarantee that interesting social and emotional juices will begin to flow, both between the team and its manager and among team members. For this reason, there is no guarantee that the team will exercise no less, but also no more, than the full amount of authority it has been assigned. I have observed numerous instances of both underuse of the authority a team actually has and inappropriate exercise of authority the team does *not* have. The former is more common early in the life of a team, when managers may be overoptimistic about members' readiness to decide about matters that previously were someone else's responsibility and therefore give the team too much authority too soon. The latter is more common after a team has gained some experience and logged a series of successes, at which point members may decide (especially if they are located far from headquarters) that they can just go ahead and run the whole show. For all of these reasons, the process of helping a team come to terms with both the extent and limits of its authority requires leaders to exercise significant leadership skill and to exhibit no small measure of emotional maturity (see chapter 7).[15]

In deciding the extent of a team's authority, it is helpful to consider deliberately and thoughtfully who is in the best position to handle each of four functions that must be fulfilled by any organizational unit that has work to accomplish. The first and most basic function, of course, is to *execute* the work—applying physical or mental energy to accomplish tasks. The second function is to *monitor and manage* the work process—collecting and interpreting data about how the work is proceeding and initiating corrective action as needed. The third is to *design* the performing unit and arrange for needed organizational supports for the work—structuring tasks, deciding who will be involved in performing them, establishing norms of conduct for work behavior, and making sure team members have the resources and assistance they need to carry out their work. The fourth is to *set direction* for the team—specifying the collective objectives and aspirations that spawn the myriad of smaller tasks that command the attention and energy of members of any purposive group or organization.

There is great variation across teams and organizations in how many of these four functions are assigned to teams themselves and how many are handled by managers. (In this book, *manager* refers to any individual whose main responsibilities have to do with directing and structuring the work of others.) As is shown in figure 2-1, four levels of increasing team self-management can be identified, depending on who has the authority for each of the four functions.[16]

Members of a *manager-led* team have authority only for actually executing the task. As seen in the left-hand column of the figure, it is managers who monitor and manage team performance processes, structure the unit and its context, and set overall direction. In such teams, managers manage, workers work, and the two functions are kept as separate as possible.

Next come *self-managing* teams, whose members have responsibility not only for executing the task but also for monitoring and managing their own performance. This type of unit is often seen in new, high-commitment plants and is commonplace in professional work—for example, a team of service providers who share responsibility for promptly and efficiently

FIGURE 2 - 1

The Authority Matrix

FOUR LEVELS OF TEAM SELF-MANAGEMENT

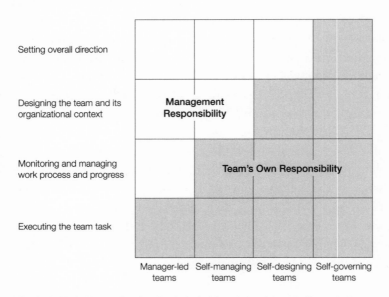

Source: Copyright (c) 1986 by the American Psychological Association. Adapted with permission.

handling requests from clients, or a construction team whose members track their progress and make any adjustments in their work strategy that are needed to get the job completed on time and in accord with the project plans.[17]

Members of *self-designing* teams have the authority to modify the design of their team or aspects of the organizational context in which they operate, or both. Managers set the direction for such teams but give members full authority for all other aspects of the work. Management task forces often are self-designing units, such as the four-person team of senior bank managers studied by Connie Gersick who were charged with creating a new kind of money market account. Individual members of this team began talking with one another informally as soon as legislation was passed that allowed banks to offer this type of account. After consulting with the bank CEO and managers of those departments whose work would be affected by the new product, the team settled on its own composition and defined its own task—which was to do whatever was needed to get the product ready for market by the first day the bank would be permitted to offer it. The team's overall direction was prespecified by the terms of the legislation authorizing the product, but members had control of virtually everything else. Moreover, Gersick reports that the CEO personally affirmed the task force's self-designing character by informing the team that "It [the product] had better be good!" but refraining from issuing any instructions whatever about how the team should organize itself or carry out the work.[18]

Finally, *self-governing* teams have responsibility for all four of the major functions listed in figure 2-1. Team members decide what is to be done, structure the unit and its context, manage their own performance, and actually carry out the work. Examples of self-governing units include some legislative bodies, corporate boards of directors, advisory councils of community service agencies, worker cooperatives, and professional partnerships.

The flight attendants at the international airline described in chapter 1 are located near the lower boundary of the self-managing category. Although they did have responsibility for monitoring and managing many parts of their work, that was only because the work was performed out of management's sight. The management strategy of their company, clearly, was for cabin service teams simply to execute work that headquarters managers had conceived, designed, and engineered in detail. Flight attendants at the domestic airline, by contrast, were self-designing. These teams not only executed and managed their customer service work but also had the authority to make decisions about their own structure. Members selected their own teammates when groups were formed, they decided whether the day's flying required the presence of all four members, and they chose which team member would serve as team leader each day. So long as their decisions were consistent with the company's overall direction (and stayed within the bounds of the handful of "must do" and "must never do" constraints that management specified), teams were free to structure their work as they saw fit.

The levels of authority held by flight attendant teams at these two airlines roughly bound the scope of this book. We do not spend much time on manager-led teams, the leftmost column in figure 2-1, because such teams invariably waste human resources. For managers to specify and control all aspects of a team's work in real time is but a group-level version of scientific management—the dysfunctions of which, for both people and organizations, have been amply demonstrated over the last several decades.[19] Nor do we analyze in depth the special decision-making dynamics that occur in self-governing groups, the rightmost column in the figure.[20]

Self-managing and self-designing teams, the middle two columns of the matrix in figure 2-1, are found in great numbers throughout all sectors of society—in businesses, in public agencies, and in nonprofit organizations. When well designed and well led, they can be a self-correcting and renewable collective resource, an organizational feature that builds rather than expends human capital. But when they go sour, they can do real damage both to organizations and to people. Managers who clearly specify a team's authority, and who make certain that team members understand both the extent and the limits of their responsibilities, go a long way toward making the former outcome more likely than the latter.

Stability over Time

We already have seen that teams whose boundaries are so unclear that it is impossible to know for sure who is actually in the group are almost certain to encounter difficulties in carrying out their work. But how about groups whose membership is reasonably clear at any given moment but likely to change at the next moment? The answer to this question is clear:

Teams with stable membership perform better than those that constantly have to deal with the arrival of new members and the departure of old ones.

The evidence documenting the validity of that assertion is, as I read it, incontrovertible. That is why, as I board a commercial airline flight, I occasionally have the impulse to stick my head into the cockpit and casually ask, "First trip flying together?" The impulse is as silly as acting on it would be embarrassing, and I never actually would do such a thing. But the reason the thought comes to mind derives from some analyses performed by the National Transportation Safety Board (NTSB) that have profound implications for both airlines and their passengers. NTSB staff combed the agency's database to identify the circumstances under which aircraft cockpit crews are most likely to get into trouble. They found that 73 percent of the incidents in the NTSB database occurred on a crew's first day of flying together, and 44 percent of those took place on a crew's very first flight.[21] Crews are most vulnerable to mishaps when they are just starting out, before they have had the chance to learn through experience how they can best operate as a team.

This NTSB analysis reinforced earlier findings obtained at NASA's Ames Research Center in a project intended to assess the effects of fatigue on pilot behavior but that unexpectedly wound up showing the benefits of keeping members of task-performing teams together. The NASA researchers recruited a number of crews as they returned from several days on the line, and compared their performance on a moderately demanding scenario in an aircraft simulator to that of crews whose members had just completed several days off duty. As one would expect, the pilots returning from multiple-day trips were indeed tired—and individual members of those crews did make more mistakes than did the rested pilots. The surprising finding was that the fatigued crews, *as crews,* made significantly fewer errors than did crews composed of rested pilots who had not yet flown together. Having experience working together as a team more than overcame the debilitating effects of individual fatigue.[22]

There are many reasons why reasonably stable teams perform better. Members develop familiarity with one another, their collective work, and the work setting, so they are able to settle in and focus on working together rather than waste time and energy getting oriented to new coworkers or circumstances. They develop a shared mental model of the performance situation, one that, with time and experience, is more integrative than the individual models with which they began. They develop a shared pool of knowledge, accessible to all, and build what social psychologist Dan Wegner calls "transactive memory" (that is, members themselves serve as memory aids to one another, providing the possibility of collective recollection that exceeds the capacity of any single individual). They learn who is especially knowledgeable or skilled about which aspects of the work and thereby build the team's capability to actually *use* what members know and know how to do. They learn how to deal appropriately with those of their members who may be less skilled, either in teamwork or on the task itself, without excessively disrupting the team's progress toward achieving its objectives. And, gradually, members are quite likely to build shared commitment to the team and a measure of caring for one another.[23]

These are all positive features of well-functioning teams, but none of them by itself is the main or only mechanism responsible for the superior performance of stable teams. Instead, the features come in a package, with each process reinforcing the constructive impact of the others. There is no specific action a leader can take to ensure that these processes will develop; like all other human and social systems, work teams develop in their own, idiosyncratic ways. Research does suggest, however, that training team members *together,* rather than as separate individuals, can jump-start the development of performance-enhancing team processes.[24] A team whose members learn together how to work together, and who then stay together to further build their collective competencies, is almost certain to develop into a more effective performing unit than otherwise would be the case.

The research findings summarized earlier have clear implications for management policy and practice. In commercial aviation, for example, crews should be trained together and then remain intact for a considerable period of time, giving members the opportunity to develop themselves into the best-performing unit that they are able to become. Moreover, on any given trip they should fly the same aircraft and work with the same cabin crew. And the leader of the crew, the captain, should conduct a team-oriented briefing before each trip to reduce as much as possible the crew's exposure to the liabilities of newness.

Yet in most airlines, crew members are trained as individuals and crew composition is constantly changing because of the long-standing practice, enforced by labor contracts, of assigning pilots to trips, positions, and aircraft as individuals—usually on the basis of a seniority bidding system. In one airline my colleagues and I studied, for example, a normal day's flying could involve two or even three changes of aircraft and as many different cabin crews. In another carrier, it was not uncommon for cockpit crews themselves to have one or two changes in composition during their one- or two-day life spans. Perhaps the most vivid example of crew instability that I have observed occurred when a crew lost its first officer for personal reasons while members were setting up the cockpit prior to departure. During the wait for a reserve pilot to appear, I asked the captain if he was concerned about the last-minute change in crew composition. "No problem," he responded. "Every pilot in this company knows his job, and the new first officer will pick up right where Bob left off." Because we were already late departing, the captain called for pushback and the prestart checklist immediately after the reserve pilot arrived. Engine start, taxi, and takeoff proceeded normally, and only when we were well into the climb were introductions made all around.

Why have airline managements, pilot unions, and federal regulators, all of whom are deeply committed to improving the safety of flight, not jumped to implement policies and practices based on the research findings just summarized? My conversations with representatives of these groups suggest two reasons. First, they do not want to believe the findings. Everyone knows that if a team stays together too long members will become too comfortable with one another, lax in enforcing standard procedures such as checklists, and too ready to forgive teammates' mistakes and lapses. Yes, teams may become better at working together as they move through the early phases of their lives. But that learning happens quickly, then plateaus, and then, at some point, overfamiliarity sets in and dominates members' subsequent interaction. It is better, therefore, to have a constant flow-through of new members to keep teams on their collective toes.

Everyone knows such things—but they are not true. Members of competently designed teams do learn fairly rapidly how to work together, as claimed. But, except for one special type of team, I have not been able to find a shred of evidence to support the view that there comes a point at which the learning stops and the positive trend reverses, when compositionally stable teams function decreasingly well the longer members stay together. (The exception is research and development teams. Organizational researcher Ralph Katz found that the productivity of such teams peaked when members had worked together for about three years, and then began to decline. It appears that research is a type of teamwork for which a moderate flow-through of new members really does help, probably because the new arrivals bring with them fresh ideas and perspectives to which the team might not otherwise be exposed.[25]) The very best teams get better and better indefinitely, like a great marriage that is stronger on the couple's fiftieth anniversary than it was on their first, or like the Guarneri String Quartet, whose members have continuously improved their music making over more than three decades of playing together.[26]

A second reason managers and policy makers do not take the benefits of team stability as seriously as they might is that doing so often would disrupt traditional organizational practices, constrain members' choices about their schedules and assignments, and cost a great deal of money. The bidding systems that are in place at most U.S. carriers, for example, provide individual pilots, especially senior pilots, with far greater latitude in choosing their work schedules than would be possible under any system that promoted crew integrity and stability. Moreover, it is much more efficient in making work assignments to treat each crew member as an individual than it would be to deploy crews as intact units—especially if one adds the constraint that each crew must remain with a particular aircraft for some period of time. The financial benefits of this scheduling strategy can be computed, and they are substantial. (An analyst at one airline did a back-of-the-envelope calculation for me and reported that keeping crews together would cost his company several million dollars a year; that, he said, made the idea a nonstarter in the industry's highly competitive environment.)

Keeping teams together does not inevitably increase costs, however. For digging tunnels, for example, the use of intact teams has been shown to generate significant financial benefits. Journalist Fred Hapgood interviewed Howard Handewith, an analyst for the American Underground-Space Association, about the matter. According to Handewith, intact teams were able to construct a mile of superconducting supercollider tunnel for $5 million, about a third of the typical cost of big-tunnel construction. Hapgood goes on to report that "the tunneling teams arrived fresh from working on the Chicago water system and the Dallas subway. They came already tuned to one another and to their tools. Handewith believes that these results suggest the kind of returns that can be expected as the opportunity to work steadily, as part of a team, becomes more common."[27]

Even when keeping work teams together would be costly, those costs must be weighed against the also real costs of substandard team performance that are incurred when scheduling and rostering practices make it impossible for members to become established as a stable work team. Our research suggests that this also is a substantial cost—albeit one that is harder to compute in dollar terms. Indeed, when the team's work is important enough and when money is no object, intact teams *are* used in aviation operations. The Strategic Air Command (SAC), whose aircraft would have delivered nuclear bombs had that become necessary during the Cold War years, did train and schedule crews as intact units. Aircraft maintenance crews also were intact teams, and both the flight crews and the maintenance crews were assigned to particular aircraft. Fortunately, SAC crews were never called on to perform their ultimate mission. But they did fly frequent training missions that were scored on objective criteria such as bombs on target. A colleague who helped train those crews reports that their performance was, with rare exceptions, superb. Inertial forces are powerful, however, and traditional practices persist in both civilian and military aviation despite the accumulated evidence that they almost certainly underutilize the enormous pool of talent and motivation present in the pilot workforce.[28]

Is all of the above relevant only to teams that fly airplanes? No; unclear team boundaries and instability of membership is a pervasive and pernicious problem for many different types of organizational work teams: project task forces, senior management teams, sales teams, and, increasingly, virtual teams whose membership may be as fluid and uncertain as it is dispersed. As we will see throughout this book, the most important contribution that leaders can make to the teams they create is to establish and maintain the handful of organizational conditions that foster and support competent teamwork. Doing that, however, requires that there be a team in place to create those conditions *for*. A reasonably stable team gives members the opportunity to accumulate shared experiences and to learn from them, to be sure. That in itself is sufficient reason for keeping teams together. But even more important, it is team stability that makes excellent team leadership possible.

LAYING THE FOUNDATION FOR EFFECTIVENESS

Creating real work teams is akin to laying a solid foundation for a building. If the foundation is well conceived and solid, the builder can proceed to erect the rest of the structure with confidence. If it is not, the building will never be as sturdy as it could have been. Neither an eye-catching above-ground design nor elegant interior finishings can ever compensate for a flawed foundation.

The same is true for work teams in organizations. Real teams can be small or large, can have wide-ranging or restricted authority, can be temporary or long-lived, can have members who are geographically co-located or dispersed, and can perform many different kinds of work. But if a group is so large, or its life is so short, or its members so dispersed and out of touch with one another that it cannot operate as an intact social system in carrying out its work, then prospects for effectiveness are dim.

Wise leaders therefore lay the foundation for team effectiveness by making sure they have created a real work team. As we have seen in this chapter, this means making sure that the task actually is appropriate for teamwork and that it requires members to work together interdependently. It means establishing clear but moderately permeable membership boundaries. It means providing the team with substantial but clearly delimited authority for managing its work. And, finally, it means ensuring that the team will be reasonably stable over time as members carry out that work.

Creating a real work team establishes the first of the five performance-enhancing conditions discussed in this book. Moreover, a real team is the prerequisite for the other conditions. Managers who establish real teams have more choices, and better choices, about setting a good direction for the team (chapter 3), creating an enabling team structure (chapter 4), arranging organizational supports for the team's work (chapter 5), and providing hands-on coaching that helps members work together productively (chapter 6). To give insufficient attention to getting the essential features of real work teams in place not only puts the team and its clients at some peril but also makes the team leader's own job harder than it need be.

3

Compelling Direction

We have arrived at our climbing camp at the base of the Big Horns, ready to attack one of the several peaks stretching across the horizon before us. As we sip our coffee, maps of climb routes laid out before us, our leader poses the Big Question: "All right then, which one shall we go for? Cloud Peak? Bomber Mountain? One of the others? What do you think?" Opinions are ventured, objections raised, and alternatives proposed. By the time we bed down for the night, some members of our team have become more committed to their prior preferences than they were before the discussion. The feelings of others, including the leader, range from frustration to irritation. And we still have not decided which peak we will ascend the next day.

Have you ever spent most of a holiday weekend deciding how the family will spend that weekend? Or come dangerously close to the deadline for a task force report with members still debating the report's purpose? Or switched approaches to a work problem again and again trying to find a way to frame the task that is agreeable to all group members?

We all have experienced such frustrations. They are among the reasons many of us avoid working in groups whenever we can. But it does not have to be that way. See how this feels: "I'm getting a group together for a climb in the Big Horns next weekend. There's a bunch of interesting mountains in that range, but I thought we'd have a go at Cloud Peak. It's a challenging climb and the afternoon weather up there can get real nasty. Probably we'd have only a fifty-fifty chance of making it. But they tell me the view from the summit is just amazing, and at the very least it should be quite a day making the attempt. How about you joining us?"

It's a wholly different experience. This time the leader's direction is clear ("*This* is the mountain we'll climb"). It is engaging ("It's challenging, we may not make it, but success will be exhilarating"). And it offers choice ("Will you come?"). This invitation is far more likely to energize, orient, and engage team members than is any open-ended discussion about what the group should do. At the risk of offending those of my colleagues who believe that the only way to "empower" teams is full participation by all involved parties until consensus is reached, let me extrapolate from this little example to a bald assertion about self-managing teams in general:

Effective team self-management is impossible unless someone in authority sets the direction for the team's work.

The assertion may seem to contradict itself. One is, after all, issuing orders to the very team members who are supposed to manage themselves. Doesn't self-management by a team require consensus decision making about team directions? No, it does not. Those in authority can indeed consult widely with team members and other constituents about alternative aspirations, and draft statements of direction can be circulated, tested, and revised many times. Such consultations and revisions are well advised because they increase the chances of getting the direction right— and they do foster its acceptance by team members. But at some point those who have the legitimate authority for the enterprise must step up to their responsibility and clearly designate the mountain to be climbed.

Who properly sets direction for a team varies from situation to situation. Sometimes it is the team leader, as for our mountain-climbing team. Other times it is someone outside the team, as when a manager appoints a committee to review an organizational issue and make a recommendation for action. And sometimes it is the team itself, as for self-governing groups such as partnerships and boards of directors. The key is to identify who has the legitimate authority for direction setting and then to make sure that that person or group exercises it competently, convincingly, and without apology. Team performance greatly depends on how well this is done.

THE MULTIPLE BENEFITS OF GOOD DIRECTION

Authoritatively setting direction about performance aspirations has multiple benefits: It energizes team members, it orients their attention and action, and it engages their talents. These are significant benefits, but, as we will see, the challenge of harvesting them also is significant—far more demanding of leadership skill than making an inspiring speech or posting on the wall a statement of collective vision.[1]

Energizes

John F. Kennedy did not assemble a committee and take a vote back in 1961 when he articulated the goals of the U.S. space program. Instead, he exercised the authority of the presidency by standing before Congress and, with the nation watching on television, declaring that the United States "should commit itself to achieving the goal, before this decade is out, of landing a man on the moon and returning him safely to earth." Nor did Martin Luther King, Jr., hold a national referendum to determine the aspirations of African Americans for the next stage in the struggle for racial equality in this country. Instead, he exercised his considerable moral authority by standing before his people at the Lincoln Memorial in 1963 and delivering the "I Have a Dream" speech—a statement of direction that still inspires those who view it on film.

We all seek purpose and meaning in what we do and how we live. When someone articulates a set of aspirations that elevates our purposes or deepens the meaning we find in our lives, motivational juices flow. That is what Kennedy and King accomplished. Even people who might have chosen other directions for the space program or the civil rights movement found themselves energized by the visions these leaders articulated. Great political and religious leaders are masters at doing this, at creating and communicating collective aspirations that align and excite others. When leaders' visions do not inspire, however, people quickly turn away from them. In almost every U.S. presidential election, some campaigns falter early in the primary season because the candidates are unable to articulate an engaging vision for the nation.

Establishing a clear and engaging direction is just as important for organizational and team leaders as it is for leaders with broader constituencies. The way David Mathiasen surmounted the considerable leadership challenge he faced as head of the Fiscal Analysis Branch of the U.S. Office of Management and the Budget (OMB) illustrates this point. David's branch had the job of conducting economic analyses of the federal budget for the president's budget director. Ronald Reagan had just defeated Jimmy Carter for the presidency and had appointed David Stockman as budget director. Shortly after the new administration took office, Stockman met with Mathiasen and other senior OMB managers and told them that the agency would proceed immediately to dismantle the Carter budget and replace it with one that expressed the political philosophy of the new president. Achieving this, Stockman told the managers, would require extraordinary commitment by everyone at OMB. He made it clear that he expected nothing less.

How, David wondered, could he engender sufficient commitment among members of his fiscal analysis team? They had worked terribly hard on the Carter budget and had finished up not long ago. Now it was to be unceremoniously discarded. How could he get members fired up to restart a task they had just completed—especially since the Reagan budget was certain to be distasteful to at least some team members? The fiscal analysis team was composed entirely of civil servants rather than political appointees, and their personal politics ranged from strong liberalism to committed conservatism. How much conflict would develop among team members as they worked together to help prepare a conservative federal budget?

David's solution relied mainly on the direction he provided to team members. He was not one to call everybody to a big meeting and make a charismatic speech. Instead, he went around from person to person, from team to team, on no special schedule, making sure that everybody understood what the mission of the fiscal analysis team really was. The essence of what he said on his rounds was this:

As corny as it may sound, what we are here for is to *serve democracy*. We don't make policy, but we make sure that the people who do have available to them absolutely the best information that they can have. Some of you applaud the priorities being set by Reagan and Stockman; others of you are certain that their proposals will lead the country to social and economic disaster.

As a citizen, I too have some opinions about what they are doing. But my personal views don't matter in our work here and neither should yours. We are the only people on this planet who are in a position to provide the president and his director with comprehensive and valid analyses of the likely effects of their policies. The PADs [political associate directors of OMB appointed by the director] can't do it—they don't have the time or the expertise and, besides, they have to keep passing political litmus tests. The director cannot do it himself—although this particular director, if we don't do our job right, is likely to try with who knows what consequences. And the Congressional Budget Office works for that other branch of government; they have a different job to do.

So there's nobody else, it falls on our shoulders. Those of you who love what Reagan is doing can take pleasure from knowing that your analyses will give him the information he needs to implement his policies promptly and decisively. And those of you who detest what he is up to can take pleasure in the fact that, with complete and accurate data, he'll probably do less damage than he would if he didn't have those data, or they were distorted.

No matter what your personal politics, it all comes down to the same thing: Our democracy will work better if the president and the people he appointed to advise him have complete and trustworthy data. Frankly, I don't know whether we can get it all done in the time that we have. It will be quite a stretch. But we're all professionals, so let's pitch in and show them what we can do.

It worked. Even staffers who had unhesitatingly pulled the "Carter" lever in the voting booth found themselves coming in evenings and weekends, when needed, to work with their teams to do their part in rebuilding the national budget. That is the energizing power of good direction.

Orients

It is Cloud Peak on which all members of our climbing team have their eyes fixed. Once we know which mountain we will climb, we have a collective focus—and we have protected ourselves from that special kind of anarchy that can come when each member of a group or organization heads off in whatever direction is personally most agreeable. Perhaps most important, however, is that our choice of mountain has given us a shared criterion against which to test alternative ways of proceeding. When we get to a fork in the trail, we ask ourselves which branch is more likely to take us toward our objective. There will still be ambiguity, of course. Sometimes the trail that looks as if it goes directly to the base of the mountain actually doesn't. But even under ambiguity a clear and shared sense of purpose helps team members sort among options for how they should proceed. As David Campbell titled his book on career decision making, a personal activity surely as uncertain as even the most ambiguous of team tasks, *If You Don't Know Where You're Going, You'll Probably End Up Somewhere Else.*[2]

For careers, ending up "somewhere else" sometimes turns out to be a happy surprise. The same can be true for task-performing teams. In research and development work, for example, focused teamwork in pursuit of a particular objective sometimes unexpectedly results in an important finding about an entirely different matter—such as when Pfizer scientists who were assessing sildenafil citrate as a possible blood pressure medication serendipitously discovered its efficacy in treating erectile dysfunction and, without having set out to do so, created Viagra.

A good orientation comes to some teams virtually automatically. Members of an athletic team need not have a group discussion before the start of each game to figure out what they are supposed to accomplish. They are there to win—or to come as close to winning as they are able. Nor do members of the systems team at a computer facility have to debate purposes when a server goes down. They are there to get the server back up and on line as quickly as they can. But for many work teams, perhaps most of them, getting agreement among members about which mountain to climb is far from straightforward.

This problem is especially pernicious for management teams whose main work is to organize and oversee work that actually is performed by others. Management teams always have multiple mountains to climb, most of which are not only legitimate but also important to the long-term well-being of the enterprise. Moreover, such teams regularly have to deal with their equivalent of a server crash: acute problems that appear to require action both immediate and well considered. How can such teams establish and maintain an orientation that helps members to choose wisely among the multiple options that invariably are open to them?

Some management teams solve the orientation problem by focusing exclusively on but a single aspiration, such as "maximizing shareholder value." This choice may help keep members' anxieties low and even guide them in charting a reasonable course through uncertain waters. But there always are multiple paths that could be followed to achieve any one overriding aspiration, and it may be far from clear which path has the greatest chance of success. Something more concrete is needed, something that is more useful to teams in their day-to-day decision making.

This was the challenge faced by Don Burr, the founder of People Express Airlines, early in the life of his company. Burr aspired to create an organization that engaged a far greater proportion of members' talents and energy than was, at the time, typical of other airlines. People Express employees, all of whom would be called managers and treated as such, would have to make decisions and judgment calls continuously in their day-to-day work—regardless of whether they were flying aircraft, taking reservations, or paying bills. Burr recognized that they would need some kind of template to use in their decision making and, moreover, that any global vision statement would be too general to be of much practical use to them.

His solution was to convene the officers of the company months before operations began and ask them to generate a list of the main precepts that everyone in the company, from himself to the newest employee, should consider as they made choices about how to proceed with their work. After extensive discussion, the officers settled on the six precepts listed in chapter 1 (service, commitment to the growth of the individual; best provider of air transportation; highest quality of management; role model; simplicity; maximization of profits). Everyone was intensively and repeatedly trained in the meaning and application of those precepts, and people did internalize and rely heavily on them in making decisions under uncertainty—such as when a team of gate agents had to decide what to do with a planeload of customers whose flight, the last one of the day, had just been canceled. Precisely because there was no single aspiration that drove all decisions at the company, teams of managers at People Express had to be thinking all the time about how to decide among alternative courses of action. Even when the precepts seemed to be in conflict with one another, a not uncommon occurrence, the proper way to proceed often became apparent after a few minutes of discussion. The precepts were a reasonably concrete implementation of collective direction that provided a tool that teams at the company could actually use in developing or selecting appropriate task performance strategies—and in revising them when circumstances changed.[3]

Business organizations such as People Express are subject to the economic discipline of the market, which can help focus team direction setting even for management teams whose work may be less clearly defined than that of front-line teams. Setting an orienting direction can be tougher in public and nonprofit organizations, especially those that have lofty but abstract aspirations and values. As we have seen, David Mathiasen was able to make a highly abstract value ("to serve democracy") meaningful and operational for his OMB teams. Direction setting was considerably more problematic at a small cooperative newspaper I once visited. The newspaper had two main aspirations: to serve its community by providing information and perspectives not available in the mainstream press, and to provide meaningful work experiences for its members. The problem came as members of the cooperative, all of whom were personally committed to the ethic of democracy and to full participation by everyone at the paper, strove to operationalize those aspirations. What kind of information and perspectives were to be provided, and to whom? Just what was meant by meaningful work? Were all to share equally in all the work activities involved in running a newspaper, or were certain individuals to have more interesting or fulfilling work than others? Despite the considerable time and energy expended debating issues such as these, co-op members did not succeed in affirming a collective direction that was concrete enough to guide their work behavior. And, partly for this reason, the newspaper never was able to get itself established as a viable alternative source of news and employment in its community.

Good direction orients team members and thereby provides them a template they can use to assess options for how they might proceed with their work—that is, with their task performance strategies. If the work itself does not automatically provide a clear orientation, as it did for the athletic and computer teams mentioned earlier, it is incumbent upon those who have leadership responsibilities to create something that does. To let a team keep on keeping on without a clear sense of where it is going deprives members of the clarity they need to manage themselves efficiently and well. It invites endless discussions and debates about the team's main purpose, such as those I observed at the cooperative newspaper, that divert member time and energy from the team's real work. And, over the longer term, it can engender the kind of personal disillusionment and collective incapacitation that comes when well-intended exchanges among well-meaning people serve mainly to bring to the surface and highlight the things about which they disagree.

Engages

It's our team's big game, the one for the championship. It's the day the visiting committee comes to review and, we hope, approve our new curriculum. It's the meeting at which we make our final pitch for the million-dollar contract. It's our one chance to convince the Senate subcommittee of the merits of the bill we support. In all of these cases, our team's purposes are highly consequential. And, in all of them, there is no question about who we ask to act for the team: We put forward our most competent members, and they, buoyed by our support, give their all to accomplish the team's purposes.

It is instructive to notice how differently member talent is used by professional athletic teams, college teams, Little League teams, and teams in pickup games played over the lunch hour at work.[4] The first-listed teams are likely to rely as heavily as possible on their very best players. If the outcome of the game is important enough, second-tier members really do sit willingly on the bench for the good of the team. The ethic for pickup games is the opposite, since the final score is of no consequence to anybody and the main aspiration is for everybody to get some exercise and have some fun. Little League games, of course, are supposed to be more like the latter than the former, providing opportunities for kids to play and learn and have a good time—although sometimes, driven by coaches or parents who do not understand that, they wind up operating as if they were professional teams whose win-loss record actually counts for something.

When the work is important, we use all of the knowledge, skill, and experience we can marshal. We hold nothing in reserve. We defer until less consequential times putting our newer or less competent members on the front line to give them developmental experience. And we temporarily set aside any team norms that give all members the same amount of say about the team product or equal time on the court or at the lectern. Yes, we all contributed a great deal in doing the analyses and interpretations for our task force report. But now it is time to present our findings and recommendations to the mayor, and we only have twenty minutes. Do each of the four of us take five minutes to present one part of the report? Or do we ask the one member who has the best presentation skills to give the report on behalf of the team, with the rest of us present and prepared to answer any questions the mayor may have? If the issue we are addressing is important enough, we just may face up to our differences in presentation skills and subordinate our individual needs for prominence to our overriding objective of getting the mayor to consider seriously what we have to propose.

Making within-group distinctions generates strong feelings among members. As a high school basketball player, I was taller than I was good. But at one tournament game it seemed I couldn't miss—virtually anything I tossed at the basket went in. The game was a cliffhanger: We were one point down and had the ball out of bounds with just seconds to play. Coach Hillman told us what to do: "Get the ball in, and then loft it to the big guy on the baseline. Richard, catch the ball and shoot it." Nobody had ever said that to me before. I glowed. Decades later, I was playing bass trombone in a community orchestra. The opening bars of one piece we were preparing included a moderately difficult and frighteningly exposed solo line for my instrument. I practiced and practiced those few bars and thought I had them in pretty good shape. Then, during one of our rehearsals, the conductor turned to the superb tuba player who sat just to my left and said, "Sam, why don't you double with the bass trombone on that passage?" I shriveled up in my seat.

Those were small matters, but my feelings were surprisingly strong. That is what happens when people get feedback from their teammates, even indirectly, about their competence. Precisely because feelings run so high when members' talents are at issue, teams often turn to the leader—the coach or conductor or chairperson—to handle such matters on the team's behalf. Only the most mature self-managing teams are consistently able to manage differences among members frontally and competently, resisting the temptation either to off-load that responsibility to the team leader or to resort to subterfuge to get the right people in place while still "protecting the feelings" of those whose offerings are declined.

The Orpheus Chamber Orchestra, which is one of the finest ensembles of its kind in the world, deals with differences in members' expertise about as well as I have seen it done. The option of off-loading the issue to the conductor is not open to this orchestra for a very good reason: It doesn't have one. There is nobody other than the members themselves to decide how to weight the diversity of ideas and opinions that invariably flood the hall when a piece of music is being rehearsed. Because orchestra members have played together regularly over the years, they know one another's special strengths and weaknesses extremely well, and they are not reticent about using that knowledge in an open, matter-of-fact way. Members listen especially intently to what certain of their colleagues have to say when a Mozart piano concerto is being prepared, but to others when the piece is a Rossini overture, and to still others when it is new music by a contemporary composer. Because Orpheus players share a commitment to perform at the highest possible level, each of their concerts and recordings is for them highly consequential. That fact, coupled with their deep knowledge of their colleagues' musical tastes and strengths, has resulted in an ensemble that wastes very little of its members' knowledge, skill, and experience.[5]

Great direction fully engages team members' talents. It is not just that members work harder when what they are doing is important. It is more than that—it is that they pursue collective purposes using every scrap of knowledge, skill, and experience that the team can scoop up. When a team has consequential purposes, one rarely sees some members smugly watching while others struggle to get their tasks done right. What one sees instead is each member doing those parts of the work that he or she can do best, and, on occasion, one sees more talented or experienced members reaching out to assist and teach those of their colleagues who are still learning.

Words Are Not Enough

Good direction has multiple benefits that significantly increase the likelihood that a work team will perform effectively. Compelling direction is *challenging,* which energizes team members and generates strong collective motivation to perform well. It is *clear,* which orients members toward their common purpose and thereby facilitates their developing and using work strategies that are fully appropriate for accomplishing that purpose. And it is *consequential,* which engages the talents of members and encourages the team to identify and use well the full complement of members' knowledge and skills.

As is seen in table 3-1, each of the three attributes serves a special function and brings a certain kind of benefit to a work team. Moreover, each attribute can reinforce the benefits of the other two, as when a challenging purpose engages members' talents in addition to heightening their motivation, or when clarity of purpose provides an energizing focus for members' motivation as well as a tool that helps them develop and execute appropriate task performance strategies. It is the constellation of the three attributes of compelling direction that brings the greatest benefits to a task-performing team.

To harvest the benefits of compelling direction, a team's purposes actually have to *be* challenging, clear, and consequential. Words alone do not suffice, not even if they are inspiring words personally delivered to the team by a charismatic leader. It can be tempting to use rhetorical devices to try to make a team's direction seem more compelling than it really is, as in the old story about the crew leader who motivated his brick carriers by

TABLE 3 - 1

The Functions and Benefits of Good Direction

Attributes of Good Direction	Functions	Benefits
Challenging	Energizes	Enhances motivation
Clear	Orients	Aligns performance strategy with purposes
Consequential	Engages	Fosters full utilization of knowledge and skill

convincing them that they actually were building a cathedral. If such devices work at all, their effect is temporary because it becomes clear soon enough that what one *really* is doing, day after day, is carrying bricks. It is impossible to articulate team purposes that energize, orient, and engage members for work that is essentially trivial.

DIRECTION ABOUT WHAT?

Having a compelling direction is a key condition for team effectiveness, but just what should be specified when direction is set? Should direction be mainly or only about the team's ultimate purposes, or should it also include some specification of the means the team is supposed to use in pursuing those purposes? Or, perhaps, should direction be mainly about means, on the assumption that if a team proceeds with its work in the right way, good outcomes are almost sure to emerge?

The answer to these questions is shown in figure 3-1. To foster self-managing, goal-directed work, those who create work teams should be insistent and unapologetic about exercising their authority to specify end states, but equally insistent about *not* specifying the details of the means by which the team is to pursue those ends—the upper-right quadrant in

FIGURE 3 - 1

Setting Direction about Means versus Ends

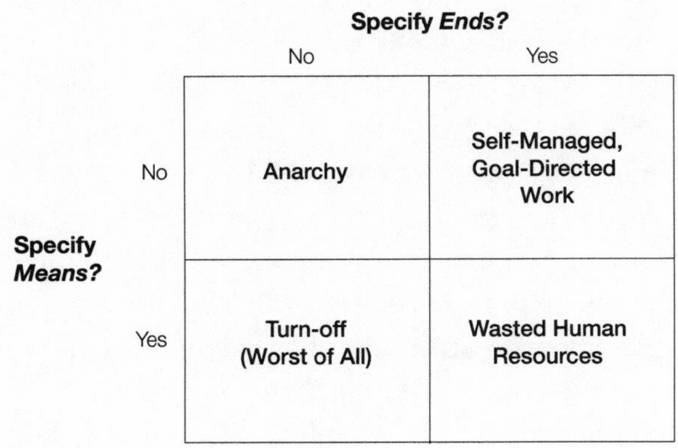

		Specify *Ends?*	
		No	Yes
Specify Means?	No	Anarchy	Self-Managed, Goal-Directed Work
	Yes	Turn-off (Worst of All)	Wasted Human Resources

the figure.[6] As we will see, to be in any of the other three quadrants is to invite significant performance problems or substantial underutilization of the team's resources.

Ends but Not Means

The way David Mathiasen set direction for the OMB budget analysis team (described earlier in this chapter) placed the team squarely in the upper-right quadrant. He insistently exercised his authority in articulating the team's main purposes, but refrained from specifying the details of the analytic methods members were to use in achieving those purposes. Team members were, after all, trained and highly professional economists, people who surely knew more about state-of-the-art techniques of economic analysis than did Mathiasen himself. Many, if not most, effective self-managing teams in industry also turn out to fall in the same quadrant.[7]

When ends are specified but means are not, team members are able to—indeed, are implicitly encouraged to—draw on their full complement of knowledge, skill, and experience in devising and executing a way of operating that is well tuned to the team's purposes and circumstances.[8] Moreover, as members work together to develop a good performance strategy, they necessarily will have to revisit their overall objectives. "No, that wouldn't work," a member may assert, "because it wouldn't give us close enough tolerances." "But we don't really *need* that level of precision in this particular subassembly," another may respond. In the discussion that ensues, members review, refine, and deepen their understanding of their collective purposes, of the ends that they are to achieve, and thereby lessen the chances that they will head off in a direction that may have seemed right at first but that actually is not what is needed.

The kind of mindful processing that characterizes teams in the upper-right quadrant benefits almost any task-performing team but is especially important for teams whose work demands high reliability, such as operating teams at nuclear power plants, aircraft flight deck crews, and surgical teams in hospitals. Mindful processing also increases the probability (but of course does not guarantee) that a team will come up with an idea or a solution that is genuinely creative, one that could never have been programmed ahead of time and, indeed, that may not even have occurred to those who created the team and set its initial direction.[9]

To specify ends but not means is a more demanding leadership responsibility than merely articulating a compelling purpose for a team and then walking away, leaving members entirely on their own to try to achieve that purpose. As subsequent chapters will show, there is much that leaders can and should do to support the team along the way, including providing an enabling structure for the team (chapter 4), ensuring that organizational systems and practices support the team in its work (chapter 5), and providing well-targeted and well-timed coaching interventions (chapter 6).

Analytic teams in Total Quality Management (TQM) programs illustrate the importance of supplementing compelling direction with an enabling structure, a supportive context, and competent coaching. Under TQM, cross-functional teams undertake research projects to develop or identify "best" work practices, those that bring work processes under the greatest possible control. Although it is left up to the teams how best to accomplish this, members are trained in good analytic techniques and are provided with a diverse set of tools to use in identifying or developing improved and simplified work practices. The tools, and the training that organizations provide teams in how to use them well, significantly increase analytic teams' prospects of success.[10]

Beyond tools and training, it usually is advisable for managers to clearly specify the outer limits of a team's discretion, thereby lessening the risk that members' enthusiasm for achieving their collective purpose will result in their taking actions that are organizationally unacceptable or ethically questionable. The overall charge to in-flight customer service teams at the domestic airline described in chapter 1 was to do anything and everything possible to provide such a good in-flight experience that customers would clamor to fly the airline again. This global direction was operationalized in terms of the Three C's (complete, clean, communicate) that every member of the in-flight staff had committed to memory. However, management also placed explicit limitations on crews' latitude in deciding how to achieve that overall purpose by requiring that they follow prescribed safety regulations and practices without fail and that they refrain from giving away liquor to please or pacify passengers. Customer service teams at that airline enjoyed an expansive playing field on which were scattered many potentially useful tools and resources, but it was a clearly bounded field. That is as it should be, even for teams in the upper-right quadrant who have wide latitude for deciding how to go about achieving their prescribed purposes.

Both Ends and Means

When work is especially important—for example, if errors have the potential for catastrophic consequences—the upper-right quadrant is where you want to be. Teams in that quadrant are able to respond immediately and flexibly to unexpected problems, information, or opportunities. They don't have to follow to the letter detailed rules of procedure or hope that prescribed processes make adequate provision for any surprises that occur along the way. It is ironic, therefore, that managers of teams that perform highly important work often drift down toward the lower-right quadrant, specifying both teams' main purposes *and* the details of the means by which those purposes are to be achieved. Such teams have more in common with a professional symphony orchestra, whose members' responsibilities do not extend beyond playing well what the score and the conductor dictate, than with a self-managing string quartet whose members have broad latitude for deciding both what and how they will play. They are like a football team whose coach has so little confidence in the team's player-leaders that each and every play is sent in from the sidelines.

Teams in the lower-right quadrant can perform superbly, of course, but when they do it has more to do with the quality of the strategy dictated by the leader, coupled with his or her skill in motivating members to do exactly what they are told, than with the capabilities or potential of the team itself. To specify in detail the means as well as the ends does consolidate a leader's control of the team, which can keep that person's anxieties within a comfortable range. But the leader's personal comfort is obtained at considerable cost in wasted human resources—not harnessing the full array of members' talents and experience, eliminating the possibility of on-the-spot team improvisations that sometimes spell the difference between disaster and triumph, and running the risk that members will become more invested in asserting control over their activities than in accomplishing well the team's main purposes.[11]

TQM teams again are instructive. As noted above, cross-functional analytic teams that scrutinize work processes and recommend ways to streamline and simplify them generally have direction that is explicit about purposes but that also provides members with considerable latitude to figure out how best to carry out the analytic work. Once improved work practices are identified and documented, however, they are standardized and diffused throughout the organization. The front-line teams that actually use them may wind up with sharply reduced discretion for managing their own work. The potential for overspecification of work procedures under TQM is so great that one is reminded of industrial engineering during the heyday of scientific management, when it was the job of process designers to identify the "one best way" to perform the work and the job of front-line producers to do the work precisely that way.[12] As noted in chapter 2, the costs of this approach are well documented, both in the quality of the work produced but also in the underutilization of an organization's human resources.

Airline flight deck crews, surprisingly, sometimes fall victim to the dysfunctions of the lower-right quadrant of figure 3-1. Until relatively recently, crews of commercial aircraft were fully in charge of their flights, doing whatever they needed to do to get the aircraft to its destination safely, economically, and (if possible) comfortably. Crews were assisted in their work by increasingly sophisticated technological and informational aids. The role of the crew changed, however, with the advent of what are called "glass cockpit" aircraft (the name reflecting the fact that data used by crews are processed digitally and presented on computer-like screens). Formerly, the technology served the crew, who flew the aircraft. Now, in state-of-the-art aircraft, the crew programs the technology, the technology actually flies the aircraft, and crew members monitor to make sure that everything is going well. Some contemporary fly-by-wire aircraft, in which pilot commands are transmitted digitally (by wire) rather than hydraulically or mechanically, even are programmed so that pilots are literally unable to exceed parameters, such as angle of bank, that have been predetermined by designers. Although with the best of intentions, designers and managers have significantly restricted the latitude of crews to manage their own flights.[13]

The increasing sophistication of cockpit technology has been accompanied by increased standardization of cockpit procedures—driven in part by the technological imperatives but also by new policies and practices put in place by airline managers and regulators to increase the safety of flight. Although standardization unquestionably has enhanced safety, we may now be starting to see some unanticipated negative effects of a very good idea. Consider, for example, what happens after an aircraft accident or serious incident. The National Transportation Safety Board invariably identifies one or more proximal causes of the event and recommends changes to minimize the likelihood of the same thing happening again. This often involves introducing a technological safeguard (such as a warning signal or a guard on a switch), a new component of initial or recurrent training, or an additional procedure that crews subsequently are required to follow. Each of these actions by itself invariably is a good idea. But no one ever examines their *collective* impact on crews and their work.

All the well-intentioned additions to procedure manuals, together with all the automated devices that have been introduced into cockpits and all the management directives intended to promote efficiency or passenger service, may be having what policy analysts call *perverse effects*. Public programs to reduce poverty, for example, sometimes can unintentionally encapsulate poor people in a state of poverty rather than help them work their way out of it.[14] It certainly is true that too much latitude for flight crews can result in a poorly disciplined cockpit in which members are unable to predict who is going to take what action next. But it also is true that too much standardization, even in the interest of safety, sometimes can perversely result in crews monitoring systems and executing procedures less attentively and deliberately than would be ideal—especially when, as usually is the case, the flight is routine and everything seems to be proceeding normally.

When a good balance is achieved between standardization and autonomy, all crew members tend to be alert and proactive in managing the aircraft and its systems. And the likelihood increases that, when extraordinary teamwork is in fact required—that is, in circumstances when standard procedures are inadequate—the crew will be both ready and able to work through the difficulties to a successful outcome. It is a significant leadership challenge to achieve balance between laissez-faire management that can invite chaos and relentless standardization that erodes leaders' ability to develop and lead their teams. Team leaders, whether their teams are operating at 30,000 feet or in an office or a plant on terra firma, need from their managements a clear and engaging statement of direction—but also sufficient latitude to take the actions that are needed to meet those expectations and confident knowledge of the outer-bound limits on their authority.

Neither Ends nor Means

The late 1960s was a time of student unrest in the United States, when even professorial authority was suspect. Bill Torbert (then a doctoral student and now a professor at Boston College) and I were slated to teach an under-graduate course on the psychology of administration at Yale University, and we were worried. How, we wondered, could we get the students involved in what we viewed as some fascinating intellectual material when there probably would be even more fascinating things, such as student protests, happening outside the classroom? Our strategy, consistent with our own values as well as with the times, was to develop a pedagogy in which we would use what went on in the class, our collective process, as a vehicle for exploring the substantive course content. The main learning would take place in small work groups of about eight members, which would devise innovative and engaging ways of exchanging with each other what they learned about their topics. One member of each group would serve on a course-wide steering committee that would work with Bill and me to monitor and fine-tune the course as the semester progressed. Once the course developed some momentum, we would serve mainly as resources for the students, using our expertise, experience, and contacts to help the work groups locate whatever they needed to pursue their learning projects. The students, we felt, could and should have as much say as we did about what would be covered, how it would be taught, and how their performance would be assessed.[15]

On the first day of class, we described the topics that generally are covered in a course on the psychology of administration, retraced in conversation the development of our ideas for the course, and finished up by saying, in essence, "This is where we are right now. Would you like to join us?" Almost everyone did, eagerly and vigorously. Course enrollment jumped substantially as word got around about what we were doing. At last, more than one student told us, some professors had gotten it right, had figured out how to provide genuinely student-directed education. We felt like heroes.

The last session of the course was held in my office rather than the classroom. Present were Bill, me, and a handful of our most ideologically committed students. Most of the others had either dropped the course or psychologically disengaged from it. Although students reported that they had not learned much about the psychology of administration that term, a number of them reported they had gained some unsettling insights about themselves. One wrote that he felt so guilty about not working in the course that "I even tried to do a little independent reading. I failed miserably. Thus, everything seems to point to the fact that I had deluded myself about my motivation." Another said, "I am bitterly disappointed because what happened has been so much less than what I told myself I was going to do that I feel I have not lived up to my promise. . . . How much less chance, I find myself feeling, is there for a liberal philosophy hoping to have an effect on the events of the world or on the U.S. government."

These students were too hard on themselves. In fact, Bill and I had failed to provide the work groups, which were the central pedagogical device of the course, with direction about *either* the ends they were to seek or the means they were to use in carrying out their educational work. As one student wrote in his end-of-course assessment, "The groups were [too much] on their own. Because of the aimlessness of the group, I found I had nowhere to channel my desire to do work in the field. As a result, my enthusiasm dissipated in this vacuum."

Although the spirit of the late 1960s is long gone, the dynamic that occurred in our course continues to be seen in contemporary organizations. Sometimes the responsibility for insufficient direction lies with managers who believe, as Bill and I did, that "empowerment" can best be achieved (or can only be achieved) when teams are given complete autonomy for deciding both what they will do and how they will do it. Other times, especially for teams and organizations with strong egalitarian values, members may be so committed to obtaining agreement about collective purposes and processes that they talk and talk but never settle on what they are going to do. Or, perhaps, members eventually do decide on something but it is so bland and innocuous that no member could possibly be offended—or engaged. In all of these cases, the failure to establish a compelling direction runs two significant risks: that team members will pursue whatever purposes they personally prefer, but without any common focus; or that they gradually will fade into the woodwork, as did so many of the students in our psychology course.[16]

Means but Not Ends

The only thing worse than failing to specify either ends or means is to dictate the latter, the procedures to be followed, without providing any sense of the former, the overall purposes of the work. The lower-left cell of the matrix in figure 3-1 is unquestionably the worst of the four quadrants, as illustrated by the following story told by George Seegers, who at the time was a vice president at Citibank responsible for stock transfer operations:

> When I first came to the bank, I wanted to find out what all the people did in my department. The first person I came to was an elderly lady, and I sat down next to her, and I said "What do you do?" And she said, "I do the yellows." I said, "Well, what is that?" And she said, "Well, it's the yellows. I take this yellow piece of paper and I stamp it and I put it over here." I said, "But what is it? What happens? What are the yellows?" I was an assistant vice president at the time, which is still a respectable officer here in the bank, and she looked at me and she said, "Excuse me, sir, but are you stupid? This is a yellow. I take the yellow piece of paper and I stamp it and I put it over here. It's the yellows. That's what it is." That lady had no idea what part that played in what we are doing.[17]

George, who eventually succeeded in reorganizing and reenergizing the stock transfer department of his bank, had his work cut out for him. His predecessors had set up the stock transfer operation as an assembly line that processed paper, with each step of the process simplified and routinized to the greatest extent possible. One floor in the bank building, he reported, was occupied by workers who did nothing but open envelopes. They passed the envelopes on to workers on the next floor who extracted the contents, and so on down the line. In theory, a paper-processing assembly line can operate smoothly and well—but only if everything works exactly as it is supposed to. In George's bank, it often did not. Worse, glitches could not be corrected on the spot because each group of workers had neither comprehension of the overall purpose of what they were doing nor the latitude to alter their prespecified work procedures.

The management strategy of George's predecessors invited both managers and group members to focus so intently on procedures that their collective purpose, the real reason they were there, dropped from awareness. When that happens, one generally sees teams at their worst: Their products or services do not satisfy those who receive them, team capabilities atrophy or erode over time, and individual members do not find in their team experiences either professional learning or personal growth (recall the team effectiveness criteria discussed in chapter 1).

The lower-left quadrant of figure 3-1 (means specified, but not ends) is the opposite of the upper-right quadrant (ends specified, but not means). The dynamics of teams that occupy these two cells differ as sharply as do the cells' defining attributes. Clear purposes with plenty of latitude to decide how to pursue them is the recipe for empowerment; the opposite, as we have seen, is a recipe for collective failure.

Walking the Authority Balance Beam

Setting direction for a team always involves the exercise of authority. For that reason, direction setting is an inherently anxiety-arousing activity. When a leader exercises authority, team members are likely to react in one of two ways: They may view the leader as an omniscient figure on whom they can depend *or* as an overcontrolling person who must somehow be repelled, subverted, or replaced. Worse, groups sometimes initially adopt the first view and then move to the second when they discover, as inevitably they will, that the leader actually is flawed and imperfect.[18]

Such dynamics are especially likely when the leaders balance, as I have argued they should, between assigning a team authority for some parts of the work and withholding it for others. To minimize anxieties and discomfort in such circumstances, managers and team members may collude to "clarify" who is really in charge of the work. Sometimes the result is the assignment of virtually all authority to the team—which, as we have seen, can result in anarchy or in a team heading off in an inappropriate direction. Other times, as in the lower-right quadrant of figure 3-1, managers retain all authority for themselves, dictating work procedures in detail to team members and in the process losing many of the advantages that can accrue from teamwork. To create and maintain an appropriate partitioning of authority between managers and teams requires that anxieties be managed rather than minimized and that people be willing and able to live with (and sometimes even temporarily increase) uncertainties and ambiguities as they seek to create a work system that works.

Few leadership choices are more consequential for the long-term well-being of teams than those that address the partitioning of authority between managers and teams. It takes skill to accomplish this well, and it is a skill that has emotional and behavioral as well as cognitive components (see chapter 7). Just knowing the rules for partitioning authority is insufficient; one also needs some practice in applying those rules in situations where anxieties, including one's own, are high. The management of authority relations with task-performing groups is much like walking a balance beam, and it takes a good measure of knowledge, emotional maturity, and perseverance to keep from falling off.

TRADE-OFFS IN SETTING DIRECTION

Even leaders who are intently focused on providing teams with both compelling purposes and wide latitude about means have many options for *how* they do that. Among the many trade-offs leaders must manage in setting good direction are those having to do with (1) how clear and complete to be in specifying purposes, (2) how challenging performance targets should be, and (3) how best to align the direction of one's own teams with broader organizational purposes.

Clarity versus Incompleteness

Good direction for a task-performing team is clear—but also incomplete. Direction that is unclear or highly abstract can waste members' time and embroil them in needless conflicts as they try to figure out what it is that they are really supposed to do. Direction that is *too* clear and complete, on the other hand, can lessen members' commitment to the work and sometimes prompt unwanted and even unethical behaviors. The challenge for those who set direction for teams is to balance between giving the team too little and too much guidance about what is to be accomplished.

Here is a statement of direction that I copied from an attractive poster on the wall of an employee cafeteria (I have changed it very slightly to disguise the company):

> Our mission is to provide quality products and services that meet the needs of individuals and businesses, allowing us to prosper and provide a fair return to our stockholders.

Another company stated its mission simply as "to create value." It is, perhaps, understandable that organization-wide mission statements such as these are abstract and general. Like the platforms of political parties, they invariably are the result of much debate and many compromises as leaders struggle to erect a tent under which everyone can comfortably sit. But, also like political platforms, abstract statements of direction are subsequently ignored by just about everyone, including those who helped write them.[19]

Statements of direction for work teams often have the same problem as those of corporations and political parties, and sometimes for the same reason: High-sounding language covers many compromises. More often, however, the direction given work teams is vague or ambiguous simply because nobody has taken the trouble to think hard about group purposes. "Why don't you get some people together and look into that?" the senior manager asks. Or, "I'd like you people to figure out how we can cut some significant costs out of our operations." Or, very popular these days, "Do what you need to do to satisfy your customers."

To energize teams, there needs to be some clarity, some bite, some specificity. David Mathiasen at the Office of Management and the Budget did not sit around with his lieutenants and generate an abstract vision statement for his teams. As pointed out earlier in this chapter, he did indeed underline the overriding purpose of the work ("to serve democracy"), but he followed that up by explaining what those high-sounding words actually meant operationally—that is, to complete the analyses required for the new budget by the deadline the director had set, and to make sure that the analytic products were trustworthy, informative, and uncolored by the personal political views of those who prepared them.

But David did not go too far. He left enough room for people to project their *own* meanings and interpretations into the overall direction he had set. That, too, is necessary to energize team members.[20] When a leader specifies every detail of what is to be accomplished, team members understandably may view the group's purposes as the leader's rather than as their own. They have little room to add their own shades of meaning to those purposes or to develop their own collective interpretation of what they are supposed to do. Collective sense-making is a natural and essential process that occurs when a team is coming to "own" a piece of work, and an overly explicit statement of direction can preempt that process.[21]

The problem with overly complete direction runs even deeper in situations in which there is but a single primary objective. There are few motivational devices more potent than having a challenging, specific performance

objective.[22] Unfortunately, well-specified objectives also can induce unin-
tended and unwanted consequences if they are too specific or if teams
become excessively focused on them. One manager of field service at Xerox,
for example, specified that field service teams should, without exception,
appear on customers' premises no later than four hours after a service call
was received. Teams accepted and generally met this challenging objective.
In doing so, however, they lost the flexibility to respond differently to different kinds of calls—for example, dealing immediately with an urgent
problem but merely letting a customer with a nonessential service request
know that the problem had been logged and would be taken care of in a day
or two. It would have been better for the manager to specify a more global
objective for customer service and leave it to the teams to balance among
considerations of response speed, cost, and quality in figuring out how best
to achieve it.[23]

The downside risks of completely specifying challenging performance
objectives are especially great when highly significant rewards (or punishments) are contingent upon their achievement, because they tempt performers to compromise their normal ethical standards.[24] During the Vietnam conflict in the early 1970s, for example, overall military objectives were
operationalized, in part, by body counts. Field commanders were required
regularly to report the number of enemy dead, and it was made clear to
them that big numbers were what was wanted. So big numbers were what
got reported back to Washington, where policy makers based strategy
decisions on data that at best were unreliable and that occasionally were
entirely imaginary.[25] The same kind of thing occasionally is seen in sales
organizations when managers set and powerfully reward specific, challenging sales objectives. The temptation to do whatever has to be done to
meet the target, even if that involves misleading customers or fudging
data, can be hard to resist. Although it always is appropriate to fault those
who lie, cheat, or steal to achieve performance targets, responsibility for
such ethical lapses must be shared by managers who use the power of
challenging direction in ways that invite these lapses.

Good direction statements have both specificity *and* a little fuzz around
the edges. Scientists call the fuzz *surplus meaning* and try to avoid it when
defining concepts in their research. Great leaders, by contrast, embrace
and exploit surplus meaning—both because it helps energize members
and because it lessens the likelihood that teams will fall victim to the

pathologies that sometimes are elicited by highly specific performance objectives that have substantial rewards attached.

Great leaders use a variety of tools to balance between clarity and completeness on the one hand and ambiguity and generality on the other. One such tool is language.[26] Leaders' words about team direction are always just a bit ambiguous. They are more likely to use stories and examples to illustrate what they mean than to set specific quantitative targets. And they use lots of analogies and metaphors to triangulate what they are after. These linguistic and narrative devices invite team members to project their own interpretations onto what is being said, and thereby enrich the meaning that members find in the work. Even more important, however, is that members develop rich and detailed images of the end states that the team is to pursue. It is images of end states, far more than any other way of representing performance targets, that engage and focus team members' motivation to perform.[27]

Another strategy that some leaders use to balance between clarity and incompleteness is to supplement statements about the team's overriding objective with explicit discussion of the multiple and sometimes conflicting second-level objectives that contribute to its achievement. One airline in our research program accomplished this in a way that surprised pilots who had just been promoted to captain. At their upgrade seminar, a senior manager welcomed the new captains to the "partnership" at the airline and congratulated them on their accomplishments. Then the head of flight operations took the podium to describe what was expected of them in their new role. Their main job, he said, was to maximize simultaneously three outcomes: safety, efficiency, and passenger comfort and service. All three aspirations struck the new captains as worthy and appropriate, and many of them began to nod in agreement. Then, gradually, furrows began to appear on brows as captains realized that they were being asked to do the impossible. No crew can simultaneously maximize safety *and* efficiency *and* passenger comfort. Instead, a crew must constantly make trade-offs among these three aspirations as they carry out their flying duties. And that, of course, was the point the manager wanted to make. To promote the overall well-being of the airline, its employees, and its customers, captains must understand the critical importance of all three aspirations, accept the fact that trade-offs must be made among them, and expertly mobilize their teams to manage those trade-offs well in real time.[28]

The direction that the captains were given, like that which David Mathiasen gave his teams of economic analysts, was simultaneously clear *and* incomplete. Teams whose direction is clear but incomplete can neither profess ignorance of what they are supposed to accomplish nor escape the challenge of online self-management by focusing exclusively on any single outcome.

Modest versus Challenging Aspirations

Let me invite you to play an imaginary game of darts. Mounted on one wall of an otherwise empty room is the target with a red bull's eye about four inches in diameter. I give you ten darts and tell you that your task is to get as many of them in the bull's eye as you can. Then I stand aside to watch and record your score. Your initial act, most likely, will be to ask me a question: "Where am I supposed to stand?" My answer: "Anywhere you like."

So where *do* you stand? Do you move right up to the target where you are virtually certain to get all ten darts in the bull's eye? Or do you stand near the far wall of the room to give yourself the greatest challenge possible? If you are like most people, you will do neither of these things. Instead, you will position yourself at whatever distance from the target will give you about a fifty-fifty chance of hitting the bull's eye on each toss. If you are a poor player, you will stand closer than will someone who is an expert. Only people who have lost the attraction to performance challenges that they were born with will choose to stand right next to the target (where they are certain to succeed) or against the far wall (where they cannot be faulted by themselves or others for failing).

The right place to be for maximum motivation is wherever it is that you have a fifty-fifty chance of success.[29] It is the same for teams: A team's performance hurdle must be neither so high as to be beyond members' reach nor so low as to be uninteresting. Recall the words of the climbing team leader: "The afternoon weather up there can get real nasty. Probably we'd have only a fifty-fifty chance of making it. . . ."

The leader's statement helped energize members of the climbing team—but only because the leader knew well the capabilities of this particular group of climbers. For a team composed of novice climbers, reaching the summit of Cloud Peak would have been an impossibility; for a team of world-class climbers, it would have been boring. To set a direction for a team that has just the right amount of challenge requires that leaders know a great deal about the capabilities of team members. It cannot be done by remote control, by leaders who sit in a headquarters office and dictate objectives to teams in the field whose work and capabilities are not well known to them. Leaders who succeed in establishing just the right amount of challenge for task-performing teams invariably are those who have taken the trouble to get to know their teams well.

Leadership versus Followership

Here are comments made by two different leaders to their work teams.[30] The first is from a leader whose unit was located far from headquarters:

> We've got to do what we've got to do to make things work here. I don't know if they'd approve what we're doing back at headquarters or not, and frankly I don't much care. They have no comprehension, zero, of what we face out here, so we have to discount to some extent the things they tell us to do. We have no choice if we want things to go right. We just have to hope that they don't find out things they shouldn't find out, and that they won't get their noses out of joint if they do. But if we do what we need to do, and if we do it well, I know they'll like the results when they finally come in.

The second comment was made by a team leader in a different organization, whose team operated in the same facility as the organization's senior executives:

> We got some new marching orders from upstairs last week. [He summarizes the essence of what he has been told.] I don't think this all makes a whole lot of sense, to tell you the truth. But it's what they want us to do, and I guess their job is to tell us what they want and our job is to do it. So let's pitch in and give our best effort and see if we can make this thing work.

These two leaders have fallen off opposite sides of the same log, and neither is dealing very well with the fact that all team leaders are, simultaneously, both leaders *and* followers. The first leader perpetrated a covert coup: Because the executives at headquarters are unlikely ever to find out what we are doing, let's do what we want. This leader entirely failed to acknowledge both the right of those who have legitimate authority for an organization to set its direction, and the responsibility of those who lead units within that organization to follow that direction. The second leader abdicated his own leadership responsibilities. His words show that he believes his own duties do not extend much beyond delivering the mail, relaying to his teams whatever he has been told. He could hardly have been more perfunctory in passing along the new direction he had received, and the words he used implicitly undermined the legitimate efforts of senior managers to adjust the direction of the overall enterprise.

Because it can be quite difficult for a team leader to chart a reasonable course between the Scylla of the covert coup and the Charybdis of abdication, most readers probably have heard some version of both of these comments in their own organizational experiences. In fact, those who own an enterprise, or act on behalf of the owners, have the *right* to specify collective directions and aspirations—even in organizations that aspire to high member commitment and self-management. It is entirely proper for senior leaders to say, in effect, "This is the mountain we will climb. Not that one, this one. Although many aspects of our collective endeavor are open for discussion, choice of mountain is not among them." And those who lead teams within an organization have a responsibility that extends far beyond merely accepting the direction set by more senior organizational leaders. It also is their job to tailor collective direction so it fits as well as possible with the special circumstances of their own work units, and to call on the full extent of their creativity and ingenuity to make each team's direction as meaningful and engaging as possible.

What, then, is one to do when senior leaders misbehave, when they either promulgate a direction that seems clearly wrongheaded or fail to provide any meaningful direction at all? My observations suggest that the best team leaders temporarily reorient their attention from their own teams to their bosses, seeking—insistently if necessary—whatever clarification they need to be able to provide their teams with direction that is both compelling and well aligned with overall organizational purposes.

As Don Burr repeatedly reminded his managers at People Express Airlines, everyone in an organization is a leader, and everyone is a follower as well. The key to success, he said, was to learn how to be *simultaneously* both a leader and a follower, to set compelling direction for those you lead even as you are receiving direction from others. Burr was right. But it takes a large measure of skill and personal maturity to do what he said—to balance between one's leader and follower roles, to attend simultaneously both to one's teams and one's bosses, and to resist the temptation either to ignore collective directions or to mindlessly pass them along.

THE RISKS OF RELEASING ENERGY

Setting direction for work teams is about the exercise of authority and the release of energy. It involves continuously balancing between tapping into forces rooted deep in the human psyche and finding mechanisms for channeling and controlling that energy. It is the organizational manifestation of the Freudian tension between the demands of libidinal drives and the restrictions of civilization. Dealing with authority dynamics and the control of human energies is therefore a dangerous business, as was vividly brought home to me by a participant in an executive seminar a few years ago.

I had been talking with seminar participants about the direction-setting strategies used by individuals who are generally recognized as great leaders. I had described the speeches of Martin Luther King, Jr., and showed how beautifully he balanced between clarity and incompleteness. Then I quoted from John F. Kennedy's speech about the U.S. space program, and showed that he set a goal that was neither too modest to be engaging nor impossibly difficult to achieve. And then I got a little carried away. "Those of you who read the New Testament," I said, "know that Jesus did not have little team meetings to decide about the goals of the ministry. That surely would have smoothed the sharp edges of his message. Instead, in assembling those who would be his disciples, he simply said, 'Come, follow me, and I will make you fishers of men'" (Matthew 4:19). The hand of a seminar participant shot up at that point and waved so insistently that it could not be ignored. "Professor, what you're saying is right on; it fits perfectly with my experience in business," the participant said. "But are you aware of the fact that, so far, you have two assassinations and one crucifixion?"

Indeed. We see not just in organizational life but also in political history that to set a clear and engaging direction, and to hold to it, is risky to the political (and occasionally even the personal) longevity of leaders. Real direction setting is not a casual activity that generates calligraphy on the cafeteria wall, something to be pronounced, approved, and forgotten. Real direction setting, to the contrary, is an organizationally consequential activity that wise leaders enter upon deliberately, thoughtfully, cautiously—and, when they are fully ready, courageously.

Providing direction that energizes, orients, and engages teams is an important ingredient in setting the stage for great performances. But it is not all that is needed, as is illustrated by the Bay of Pigs invasion fiasco planned by the senior team of advisors to President Kennedy. The direction of the Kennedy team was, without question, highly compelling. Yet both the decision the team reached and the implementation of that decision were significantly flawed.[31] The reasons for this failure, perhaps, are rooted not so much in the team's direction as in how it was structured, in the amount and kind of organizational supports it was provided, and in the quality of the coaching it received. We take up these three additional conditions for team effectiveness in the chapters that follow.

4

Enabling Structure

In the early 1970s, feminist political scientist Jo Freeman wrote a
paper intended for her sisters in the women's liberation movement
whose main message was neatly captured by its title: "The Tyranny of
Structurelessness."[1] Freeman pointed out that feminist groups were not
impeded by the excessive hierarchy and bureaucracy that often characterize enterprises created and managed mainly by men. But if women's
groups had successfully avoided those dysfunctions, then why did they not
have a better record of getting things done, of achieving the purposes to
which their members were so deeply committed? The answer, Freeman
suggested, was that having no structure can be every bit as debilitating as
having too much. In her view, what was needed in feminist groups and
organizations was not to more adamantly eschew hierarchy and bureaucracy
but instead to invent, adapt, and learn to use well structures more consistent
with feminist values.

Freeman's paper was controversial when it first was distributed, but it
would not raise many eyebrows today. The experiences of contemporary
team managers, whether in ideologically driven organizations such as worker

cooperatives or in traditional businesses and public agencies, affirm the wisdom and the generality of her message. These days, expert team managers focus much more on identifying structural features that can powerfully and efficiently facilitate teamwork than on tearing down existing structures in hopes that teams will thereby be "freed up" to accomplish their work unencumbered by organizational red tape.

It is true that traditionally designed organizations often are plagued by constraining structures that have been built up over the years to monitor and control the behavior of individual employees. Inappropriate or over-specified task structures, personnel policies, and control systems can indeed impede productivity when work is performed by teams. The question is what leaders should do in such circumstances. We saw in the previous chapter that it usually is futile to replace the exercise of legitimate managerial authority about team purposes with consensus decision making in hopes that a sharp and finely honed direction for a team eventually will emerge. It is just as futile to dismantle organizational structures in hopes of releasing a team's pent-up power. Leaders who do that often wind up providing teams with *less* structure than members actually need to accomplish their work. Tasks are defined only in vague, general terms. Lots of people may be involved in the work, but they may be the wrong people or there may be too many of them. Norms of conduct are left entirely up to the group on the assumption, as one manager told me, that "The team will work out the details." That is indeed what members will do—but, as Freeman noted, in the absence of an enabling team structure they may wind up wasting large portions of members' time and energy on interpersonal and political issues of little relevance to the team's main purposes.

Structure, like authority, is in itself neither good nor bad for teamwork. It all depends on the *kinds* of structures that are created. The best ones provide members with a solid platform on which to carry out their collective work but also leave lots of room for them to develop their own unique ways of operating. Rather than establish up front everything that may be needed for a team to perform well, wise leaders focus mainly on the handful of structural features that establish a good basic "frame" for the team's work and then give the team plenty of room to mold that frame to their particular circumstances.[2]

In this view, structuring a team has much in common with designing a house or office. Does the architect attempt to anticipate all the uses to which the space may be put and then, in hopes of optimizing utilization of the structure, generate a design that seeks to direct and constrain the behaviors that will occur within it? Or does the designer recognize that all the ways occupants may want or need to use the space can never be known ahead of time, and therefore create a structure that is well tuned to the basic functions the space will serve but also incomplete, unfinished, and adaptable? The latter approach recognizes that organic forms are always in a state of development and are never fully finished, and is the architectural parallel of good team structure.[3]

When designing work teams, then, leaders should refrain from specifying too much—but they also should take explicit initiatives to put in place the basic structures that will foster team effectiveness and minimize the organizational obstacles to teamwork. The key to good team design is to differentiate wisely between critical and unnecessary structural features. The three structural features that our research has shown to be key in setting the stage for effective teamwork are the design of the work that the team performs, the core norms of conduct that guide and constrain team behavior, and the composition of the team. These three features are explored, in turn, in the pages that follow.

THE DESIGN OF WORK FOR TEAMS

Good work design for teams is a fairly straightforward extension of what has been learned about the properties of motivating individual tasks. Some years ago, Greg Oldham and I proposed a set of task attributes that foster what is known as *internal work motivation* for individual performers.[4] A person who is internally motivated feels good when he or she performs well, and feels terrible when the work has gone poorly, thereby lessening the need for motivational props such as performance-contingent extrinsic rewards or close supervisory scrutiny. People have internal motivation when they view their work as meaningful *and* feel personally responsible for work outcomes *and* receive trustworthy knowledge of the results of their efforts.

Even a task as inconsequential as writing a computer program to handle the routine management of one's personal finances can create the three psychological states and thereby elicit internal motivation. The task is meaningful (at least to me: I'd love to rid myself of the tedium of bill paying, and besides, I find it challenging to write good computer programs). I have full responsibility for the work (I personally make all the decisions about program logic and coding). And knowledge of results is immediate and trustworthy (either the program runs correctly, or it does not). Take any of these three features away and internal motivation disappears. I cannot give myself a pat on the back if the work is trivial or entirely routine, or if I am not the one responsible for the work procedures (e.g., if I merely type in a program written by someone else), or if I submit the program but never see whether or not it runs properly.

What Oldham and I did was identify the measurable properties of jobs that give rise to the psychological states just described—experienced meaningfulness, felt responsibility, and knowledge of results—as is shown in figure 4-1. To illustrate, consider how the work of assembling a small appliance such as a kitchen toaster might be designed. On a traditional assembly line, a worker might do but a single and simple part of the overall task, such as attaching the power cord to the toaster chassis. A more motivating job, by contrast, would involve assembling the entire device, testing it, and perhaps even boxing it up for shipment to the customer. Making the toaster is *meaningful* to the worker for multiple reasons—she does the entire job from beginning to end, the work involves use of a variety of her skills, and it is inherently significant because the product will be valued by those who eventually use it. ("What did you do at work today, Mommy?" her child asks. There is a world of difference between saying "I attached lots of power cords" and saying "I made toasters for families to use in their kitchens.") The worker feels personally *responsible* for the outcomes because she has considerable autonomy to make decisions about the work processes, rather than following to the letter a procedure that someone else engineered and that a supervisor enforces. And the worker has *knowledge of results* of the work, since she generates direct and trustworthy feedback by personally testing each toaster before it is shipped. Tasks that are designed in accord with these principles generally elicit far greater internal work motivation than do those that are simple, repetitive, and of little broader significance, that provide little or no latitude for decision making, and that rely more on supervisory assessments of how well the work has been done than on feedback built directly into the work itself.

FIGURE 4 - 1

Job Characteristics That Foster Internal Work Motivation

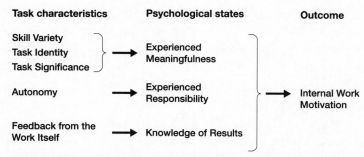

Source: WORK REDESIGN by Hackman/Oldham, (c) Reprinted by permission of Pearson Education, Inc., Upper Saddle River, NJ.

Might the same principles be applied as well to work that is performed by teams? Is there such a thing as *collective* internal motivation? The affirmative answer to those questions is obvious to anyone who has observed the differences in behavior exhibited by members of the winning and losing athletic teams immediately after a championship game, or by members of a project team who have just learned that their proposal has been accepted (or declined) by the client for whom it was prepared, or by a medical team that has just saved (or lost) a patient. The collective celebration, or shared gloom, that one sees on such occasions attests to the fact that internal motivation is just as real for teams as it is for individuals.[5]

What specific features of a team's work foster collective internal motivation? The answer is illustrated in the way the Butler Manufacturing Company structured the work of teams that manufactured large grain driers for its farmer-customers some years ago at the plant it operated in Story City, Iowa.[6] Teams were given full responsibility for constructing entire three-story-high grain driers from start to finish. It was a complicated operation, involving thousands of different parts and five types of work: assembly, fabrication, machining, painting, and shipping. Individual team members moved among these different types of work, both to provide variety and to expand each team's repertoire of skills and its flexibility. Teams had considerable latitude in how they proceeded with their work, participated in planning and scheduling meetings to ensure that the flow of completed products would meet customer requirements, and had full access to plant data about inventory, orders, and productivity. Teams also participated in the design and development of new products and tools and had the authority, in some areas and within specified financial limits, to purchase tools and materials on their own. Each team tested each drier it built, and then affixed to the device a sticker giving the team's name so that the farmers who purchased it would know who had made it and could answer questions about it. Team members even provided field service of the driers they had built. According to Larry Hayes, plant manager at the time, the field visits "teach them the impact on a farmer's business if a machine isn't working. They also learn more about the technical aspects: how the product is used in the field. And they become more in tune with our customers, our bread and butter."

The way Butler structured the task of making grain driers resulted in gains in all three of the criteria of team effectiveness discussed in chapter 1. First, the customers were well served by having driers that worked well—and by having direct access to the team that built their device if they encountered any difficulties. Second, the teams themselves became more competent performing units over time, as members learned together what assembly procedures worked best for them and became practiced in carrying them out. And third, individual team members experienced far greater personal learning from their teamwork than ever could have been obtained from performing any one part of the overall task. Given the high standing of the Butler teams on the three criteria of effectiveness, it comes as no surprise that the plant also scored high on traditional measures of quality and productivity and that profits were about 10 percent higher than comparable operations in other locations. In the words of the plant manager, "We really do produce a better product here."

The benefits of designing work for teams are substantial. But getting the team's work designed right often requires leaders to overcome powerful inertial forces in their organizations and, as will be seen in the following sections, always brings some measure of risk. Creating a teamwork-structure that fosters collective internal motivation is never as simple as just tossing the team a task and letting members run with it.

Bigger really is better . . .   Designing work for teams makes it possible to create tasks that are large and significant. No single individual could ever construct a complete grain drier because it is far too big and complex. But, as was demonstrated at Butler, a team could. No individual could possibly redesign the entire science curriculum for a secondary school because no one person knows enough. But a team could. No individual could handle all the requests for service that a computer reseller receives from a large corporate customer. But a team could. No individual could single-handedly clean the several floors of a medical clinic. But a team could.

For each of these pieces of work, those who structure the work have a choice. They could break the overall task up into pieces, assign each piece to an individual, and then devise means to coordinate the individuals' contributions and integrate them into a coherent whole. Alternatively, designers could assign the entire task to a team and give members the responsibility of coordinating their own efforts and switching subtasks as needed so that the whole piece of work gets done on time, efficiently, and in a way that satisfies the customer or client.[7]

The latter alternative almost always brings significant increases in the meaningfulness of the work. It is more meaningful to do the entire science curriculum rather than just the chemistry portion, or to be collectively responsible for all the service needs of an important customer rather than to be sent by a dispatcher from one user to another, or to share responsibility for the maintenance of an entire clinic rather than just vacuum the second-floor carpets day after day. The ability to create work that is challenging, complete, and significant—and therefore meaningful to those who carry it out—is one of the major advantages of designing work for teams.

. . . but social loafing is always a worry. As powerful as the motivational advantages of well-designed teamwork are, tasks designed for groups rather than individuals also bring significant risks. One of the most pervasive of them is the tendency of individuals to slack off when working in groups. Psychologist Ivan Steiner refers to this tendency as the "motivation decrement" and notes that it almost always is present to some extent in group work. Other psychologists call the same thing *social loafing,* and economists call it *free riding.*[8]

Just as a voter may ask, on a rainy election day, "What difference will my one vote make?" so may a member of a large work team ask how much difference it really will make to not come in to work today, or to leave unfinished work on the desk Friday rather than take it home to wrap up over the weekend. Although the motivation decrement is more pernicious when the work itself is poorly designed, it is present even for team tasks designed in accord with good work design principles.

Experienced team leaders take steps to head off the motivation decrement not just by ensuring that the work is as well designed as possible but also by making the team as small in size as it reasonably can be. (Although bigger is better for team task design, we will see later in this chapter that smaller definitely is better for group composition.) And, once the work is under way, expert team coaches watch carefully both for signs of motivational slippage and for opportunities to help members develop and sustain high shared motivation (see chapter 6).

Autonomy gives teams room to excel . . . Collective internal motivation also is fostered by team tasks that provide members a large measure of autonomy to decide how they will use their human and material resources in carrying out the work. In terms of the authority matrix discussed in chapter 2, a work team should have at least the right and responsibility to monitor and manage its own work processes (that is, to be a self-managing team rather than a manager-led team). This is advantageous not only for motivational reasons but also because team members usually have a much better understanding of the demands and opportunities in their immediate work situation than do the managers or engineers who lay down and enforce standard work procedures. Standard procedures are almost always a little "off" from the ideal way to proceed in the particular circumstances of the moment, and they invariably result in members feeling less collectively responsible for how the work turns out than would be the case if the team were genuinely self-managing.

Teams whose tasks provide ample autonomy for managing work procedures also have the opportunity to experiment with alternative ways of working together and, through trial and error, to become more competent in their work than ever could be imagined by those who determine the "one best way" the work should be carried out. It is well known among those who do shift work that the midnight shift, despite its disruption of sleep cycles, can be the best time to work because there usually is no one around to enforce adherence to standard procedures. Workers on the midnight shift commonly devise their own, better ways of getting the work done, take full responsibility for the results they produce, and feel collective pride in what they accomplish. We all should learn from the midnight shift, and give work teams in organizations the kind of autonomy about work processes that can engender a strong sense of collective responsibility among members and nurture their impulse to improvise, experiment, and learn from the team's successes and failures.

. . . but autonomous teams gone bad are very bad indeed. Work teams do not always use their autonomy in ways or toward ends that those who designed the team's work had in mind. Although a team with autonomy has the power to do wonderful things for its customers or clients, it also can do real damage. Recall, for example, how one of the flight attendant teams at the domestic airline (chapter 1) used its considerable autonomy to line the pockets of team members rather than to provide their customers with the best in-flight service of which members were capable.

Managers understandably seek to protect themselves and their organizations from the disasters that can be wrought by a work team that goes sour. Sometimes that protection is obtained at the cost of unexploited opportunities, such as Supervisor Szczarba's group of telephone service providers, described in chapter 2, who were a team in name only. Managers in that organization did not have to worry about the team going out of control because there was no team there. But neither was there any possibility that the service providers could develop into a superb work team. Another costly way to obtain protection from the damage that can be done by a rogue team is to strip the team of its autonomy by laying out in great detail all the work procedures members are supposed to follow. But by denying the team the latitude to adjust its performance strategies to deal with unanticipated problems or to invent ways to exploit emergent opportunities, this strategy trims the team's upside potential just as surely as it protects against downside risks.

Problems are especially likely to emerge when managers *tell* team members that they have the authority to manage their work and that they therefore are accountable for the results—but then specify work procedures in such detail that members have no way to actually exercise that authority. The response of the crew of the Skylab 3 space station to the restriction of its autonomy by planners and managers in Mission Control provides a vivid example of how a team can respond in such circumstances.

NASA rhetoric emphasized (indeed, sometimes came close to glorifying) the key role that the astronaut crews played in Skylab missions. Yet the actual behavior of the Skylab 3 crew was almost completely dictated by Mission Control in Houston, even to the extent of what crew members were to do during meal times. Here is how Neil Hutchinson, the lead flight director for the mission, put it:

> Back at the first mission, we weren't good enough to schedule the guys tight, but by the time the second mission ended, we knew exactly how long everything took. . . . We knew how long it took to screw in each screw up there. . . . We prided ourselves here that, from the time the men got up to the time they went to bed, we had every minute programmed. . . . You know, *we* really controlled their destiny.[9]

The crew repeatedly communicated members' frustration and irritation with how Mission Control was managing the crew's time and work, but with no apparent effect. Finally, the crew took an action that definitively asserted their own control of the mission: They turned off the radio and refused to speak with Mission Control. It was the world's first strike in space.

Although the astronauts' action was extraordinary, it reflects a more general and pervasive phenomenon. When managers view the work of a team as especially important, they often find it nearly impossible to keep from specifying all procedures in detail so that things will be done correctly. That way, managers reason, they can lower the probability of disaster to nearly zero—but in doing so they also severely restrict the team's autonomy to manage its own work. As we saw for both aircraft flight deck crews in the previous chapter and the Skylab 3 crew in this one, that can undermine the very aspiration that the procedural specifications were put in place to achieve.

Feedback makes team learning possible . . .   Learning requires knowledge of results. When a team task is structured so that trustworthy feedback about performance comes not just to individual members but also to the team as a whole, learning opportunities expand.[10] If there are others with whom members can compare their own reactions to feedback, individuals can make better sense of it and more productively probe its implications for their own work activities. Moreover, if the team has become a setting in which members feel psychologically safe to explore the reasons for team successes and failures, considerable *collective* learning can occur—learning that would be far less likely if the feedback were exclusively about the performance of individual members.[11]

Collective learning from performance feedback cannot occur, of course, unless a work team is reasonably well bounded and stable over time (see chapter 2). There was no way that teams of flight attendants at the international airline discussed in chapter 1 could have learned from postflight feedback, since crew composition at that airline was constantly in flux. By the time a customer's comments reached the airline, the team that served that customer no longer existed. All the airline could do (and did do) was put a note in each member's personnel file, which may have been helpful subsequently in individual performance assessments but was irrelevant to the improvement of the flight attendant teams.

Collective learning is not automatic even when feedback comes to a reasonably stable team whose members share a sense of psychological safety. We will see in chapter 6 that one of the most important functions a team coach serves is to help team members work through the antilearning temptations that invariably accompany both successful and failing performances, and then harvest the lessons that always are present when a team receives feedback about its work performance.

When the work provides a stable team with regular, trustworthy feedback about how it is doing *and* when the team is well coached, then the team is almost certain to evolve into a self-correcting performing unit, one whose every experience may come to be viewed by members as an occasion for continuous improvement.[12] Unless a team has data about how it is doing, however, there is no way it can learn. And unless a team learns, there is no way it can improve.

. . . but a poor team design can foster an antilearning stance. Members of poorly designed teams sometimes ignore or deflect opportunities to learn and improve even when they do receive abundant feedback about how they are doing. I once worked with a social service team in a state welfare agency whose members spurned virtually all the opportunities they had to learn from the considerable feedback the team received— from clients as well as from agency-generated statistical reports and supervisory assessments of the team's productivity and efficiency. During the several months I occasionally observed the team, members never used any feedback from any source to reflect on ways the team might improve its productivity, efficiency, or service quality. To the contrary, members constantly reassured one another that they were doing splendidly in a nearly impossible work situation. Managers who raised questions about their performance or suggested ways the group might improve were viewed as not understanding anything about the rigors of front-line work. Clients were characterized as people who just wanted "more" and who had no appreciation of the quality of the services they actually were receiving. And the statistical reports that the team received were seen as irrelevant if not actively misleading. In conversation with one another, and with me, members affirmed that they were a fine social service team, and they explicitly rejected or rationalized any data that would have implied otherwise.

This team was not composed of bad people. Most members were deeply committed to their work and their clients. They had accepted lower salaries and higher workloads than they would have had in other organizations because they believed so strongly in the importance of what they were doing. But the team was poorly designed—its direction was less clear than it could have been, and although members had a good deal of latitude in how they dealt with client families in the field, legal requirements and agency policies significantly constrained their autonomy to do what they felt was in their clients' best interests. Perhaps partly because of the flaws in its design, the team had fallen victim to a common group malady, the tendency to see one's own group as virtuous and other groups (in this case, both clients and management) as impediments to their own good efforts. Even when there is a great deal of feedback available, as there was in this case, teams that are poorly designed may develop an antilearning stance that closes members off from the very kinds of improvements that both they and those they serve would greatly value.

Balancing Benefits and Risks

There are many benefits, for organizations and for their clients or customers, of designing work to be performed by teams. As we have seen, team tasks can be structured so they challenge members and allow them to do an entire and significant piece of work from beginning to end, thereby boosting the experienced meaningfulness of the work. Teams can be given substantial autonomy, within clearly specified limits, to decide about work methods and procedures, thereby enhancing members' sense of collective responsibility for work outcomes. And performance feedback can be provided to the team as a whole, which both gives members socially verified knowledge of the results of their work and the opportunity to learn from their collective successes and failures. When present, these features almost always create a state of collective internal motivation and, in many cases, can set a team onto a course of continuous improvement.

Risks also are introduced when teams perform work, however, which can negate or even reverse the upside potential of teamwork. This is as it must be. Although well-designed work is a key ingredient in setting the stage for team effectiveness, even the best possible work design cannot ensure good performance. Only when an enabling work structure is reinforced by engaging direction (chapter 3), a supportive organizational context (chapter 5), and expert coaching (chapter 6) are the benefits of good work design realized and the risks of designing work for teams minimized. How the work is structured is an important thing, but it is not the only thing.

CORE NORMS OF CONDUCT

Group norms specify what behaviors are acceptable—and unacceptable—in a group. Behavior that is viewed as appropriate by the team is reinforced, and behavior that is seen as unacceptable or inappropriate is sanctioned. Given that the approval and disapproval of one's teammates are consequential for almost everyone, a member's behavior can be shaped readily by almost any group of which he or she is a voluntary member.

One of the great things about norms is that they can be about anything members want, although in practice they tend to focus on behaviors that members view as especially important. So if team members decide that they want to have a norm that people do not interrupt one another, or that everyone will arrive punctually at each meeting, all they have to do is obtain agreement about that. Henceforth, members who interrupt others, or who are late for meetings, are likely to experience raised eyebrows or head shakes from their teammates. When a team norm is powerfully shaping behavior, one does not observe much deviant behavior (for the same reason one does not see people putting their fingers on a hot stove to make sure it still burns like it used to). Moreover, the more members agree about what is approved and disapproved, and the stronger those sentiments, the greater the compliance with team norms.[13]

Team training courses in organizations and practical books about good team behavior invariably give a great deal of attention to the development and enforcement of group norms that are thought by the trainers or authors to facilitate effective teamwork. The norms mentioned earlier (about interrupting and punctuality) are commonly included in lists of "good" norms, as are norms about listening, information sharing, participation, respect, trust, and risk taking. I would much prefer to be in a group that has such norms than one that does not.

But does it follow that these norms are the ones that those who create work teams should explicitly build in as part of a team's basic structure? Let me propose that they are not, that norms such as these address behaviors that are secondary rather than primary enablers of team effectiveness. More fundamental are norms that are outward looking, that address the relationship between a team and its performance context. In their most general form, these norms are as follows:

1. Members should take an active, rather than a reactive, stance toward the environment in which the team operates, continuously scanning the environment and inventing or adjusting their performance strategies accordingly. (A team's strategy is simply the set of choices members make about how to carry out the work.[14])

2. The behavioral boundaries within which the team operates should be demarcated, identifying the small handful of things that members must always do and those they must never do.

The first of these two norms lessens the risk that members will charge ahead with a work strategy that is inappropriate for the task being performed, or that they will fail to notice environmental opportunities or obstacles. The second norm lowers the chances that a team will get into trouble by inadvertently violating requirements or constraints established by its own organization. Teams whose behaviors are guided by these two norms are less likely to encounter unpleasant surprises in their work, and more likely to develop performance strategies well tuned to their task and situation, than are teams whose norms exclusively address within-team interactions. Outward-looking norms facilitate competent team performance, to be sure. But they also provide a solid platform on which team members can develop, along the way, whatever additional norms they may find helpful in guiding and regulating internal team processes.

How the two basic norms that foster team effectiveness operate in practice is illustrated by the flight attendant team at the domestic airline that served the vacationers going to Florida on a sunny day and then, on a subsequent trip, staffed a weather-delayed plane full of business travelers trying to get to Boston (see chapter 1). Before each of these flights, the flight attendant team quickly scanned its work environment (the first of the two basic norms) and determined that different work strategies were required for the vacationers than for the business travelers. The strategies the team opted for could hardly have been more different for the two flights—a lighthearted and entertaining set of routines for the Florida trip, and a competent, low-profile, businesslike way of operating for Boston.

Team members also adhered to the "must do" and "must never do" prescriptions that had been laid down by their own management. On both flights, they performed each and every required safety procedure (the "must do" items). And on neither flight did they give away liquor (the "must never do" item) even though that might have further lightened the mood of the Florida vacationers and somewhat placated the delayed business travelers on the Boston flight. This flight attendant team had incorporated the two outward-looking team norms into its everyday work life, which enabled members to exploit the special opportunities the team encountered, sidestep potential difficulties (especially on the Boston flight), and do all that while staying well within the bounds of organizationally acceptable behavior. Moreover, on both flights the team adjusted and implemented its work strategy efficiently; a new flight attendant team— one that had not yet developed its operating norms—would have needed to invent its strategy from the ground up.

The flight attendants at the international carrier (discussed in chapter 1) also operated in accord with group norms. For that team, however, the norms were inward focused, aimed at minimizing disruption and confusion among members as they went about their work. Each crew member was expected to know his or her job and to follow exactly the choreographed moves that had been engineered to give the appearance of a seamless team performance. These norms were shared across the entire flight attendant workforce, which was necessary because teams did not stay together long enough to develop their own unique ways of operating.

Although a flight attendant could join any team without worrying about his or her teammates' expectations (they were basically the same from team to team and from trip to trip), the international carrier's inward-looking norms did not encourage teams to scan their work environments and tailor their performance routines to each flight's unique characteristics. Only when one team's aircraft was diverted to an unfamiliar airport and members had to find meals and accommodations for a planeload of passengers did the team break stride. And it was only then, when standard team norms had become irrelevant, that the team became outwardly focused and my colleague on the flight was able to see the level of motivation and ingenuity of which members actually were capable.

Countering Ordinary Human Tendencies

It would be convenient if the two core norms that foster team effectiveness appeared automatically, but unfortunately they do not. Instead, they almost always must be deliberately created as a feature of a work team's structure. The reason they must be explicitly created is that they operate in opposition to a pair of very ordinary human tendencies that can impede competent teamwork.

Reacting to Whatever Comes Our Way.   The first ordinary tendency is our disposition to react to whatever captures our attention and demands a response, rather than to actively scan our environment for less obvious problems and opportunities that may call for nonstandard actions. It is a stimulus-response kind of thing: A stimulus comes our way, and we respond. A student sends me an e-mail asking for an appointment (the stimulus), and I reply by suggesting a specific time we could meet (the response). Another student writes to ask me to read the draft of a research paper, and I immediately agree to provide comments. Over time, my responses become habitual: I reply without explicitly considering the request or contemplating alternative responses I might make. It is this pattern that time management books seek to break by asking readers to be clearer about their priorities, more aware of features of their environments that impede progress toward their main goals, and more deliberate about developing a behavioral strategy that really does put first things first.

The same things happen for task-performing groups. Members develop collective routines for handling common events in group life and then mindlessly execute those routines when one of those events appears. Ask members of a team with strong norms why they behave as they do and they probably will respond with something singularly uninformative such as "I don't know, that's just how things are done around here." Translated, that means the team norms are working and have become both routinized and invisible.[15]

Let me indulge myself with an example from the academy. I've participated in numerous faculty meetings in my career, and few have surprised me. Certain standard items will be brought up for consideration, we will discuss some of them at excessive length, and then we will dispense with the rest in rapid-fire order. Rarely, if ever, do we stop and reflect upon any opportunities or constraints in our environment that do not come packaged as an agenda item. A norm that supported active scanning of our university and intellectual context, and explicit planning of our strategy for further developing our department, could be very helpful to us. But we are faculty members. We do not need such artificial props. So we just keep on keeping on, letting opportunities lie unexploited and problems we could have known about surprise us.

Seeking Harmony.   A second human tendency that makes it necessary to explicitly build the two core norms into the structure of a work team is our understandable impulse to have harmonious interactions with others, to be approved rather than rejected by our teammates, and generally to keep anxieties as low as possible.[16] This tendency sometimes leads us to thoughtlessly do things that perhaps we should not do, and to go further than we ought to go in pleasing our fellow team members or our clients. By building into the structure of a work team an explicit norm that sets the outer-limit boundaries of what behaviors are acceptable, team members can have both a clearer sense of the location of the line they should not cross and a collectively enforced agreement that that line will be respected.

Building the two core norms into the structure of a work team is especially important when that team is likely to be subjected to either (1) a barrage of demands that must be responded to quickly (in which case members may feel that there is no time to do *anything* other than respond as rapidly as they can) or (2) strong political or social pressures to cross the team's outer limits of acceptable behavior to please a customer, client, or supervisor (in which case team members may be strongly tempted to abandon their own standards in order to gain the approval of valued others).

Both of these conditions were in place for the fiscal analysis teams at OMB discussed in previous chapters. These teams had to deal with an almost unending stream of incoming questions and requests. It would have been the easiest thing in the world for team members to fall into a pattern of reactivity, dealing as competently and promptly as they could with all that came their way and giving themselves a pat on their collective back when, at day's end, their collective inbox was empty. For manager David Mathiasen, that was not good enough. So he reinforced both of the core norms whenever he had a chance. He made it clear to fiscal analysis teams that although responsiveness to client requests was important, it was not the only thing—or even the most important thing—they should be doing. The most important thing, he emphasized, was making sure that the teams' clients, most of whom were political appointees, were as fully informed as possible about the budgetary implications of the president's policies and programs. And that meant that the fiscal analysis teams needed to have their antennae out at all times so that members could be aware of what was developing in the background and be on top of emerging issues well before they spawned urgent client requests.

Second, as we saw in chapter 3, David set direction for the fiscal analysis teams in a way that firmly established the bounds of acceptable behavior. Analyses were to be conducted and results reported at the highest level of professional competence—the "must always do" item. Moreover, teams were never to bow to social or political pressure from their clients or from anyone else—the "must never do" item. The clients, David noted, also had to deal with their own stream of urgent demands and, as political appointees, were appropriately partisan. For both of those reasons, they could not be expected to insist that analyses be as comprehensive and objective as possible. Responsibility for that, David said, lay squarely with the civil servants who comprised the analytic teams. If a client wanted to truncate a chart so that the long-term budgetary impact of some policy would not be seen, or stretch the *y*-axis so that an effect would seem especially large, that was the client's business. These were not activities in which fiscal analysis teams should participate.

How Norms Form

The core norms David established worked well for the fiscal analysis teams at OMB. Teams rarely were surprised by political or economic developments and they usually were ready with a strategy for dealing with emerging issues even before clients asked about them. Would these norms have developed naturally, without having been explicitly created by the teams' manager? To answer that question, we must take a brief detour to understand the three different ways that group norms can come into existence.

The first way group norms can be established is for them to be "imported" to the group by individual members.[17] Each member brings to the group, based on previous group experiences, a set of reasonably well codified expectations about the kinds of behaviors that are acceptable in groups of this kind. If members' experiences have been similar, behavior will unfold in an orderly fashion, guided by invisible norms that never are explicitly discussed. This happens all the time. We all know what one is supposed to do and not do in a wide variety of group settings, ranging from a training seminar to Thanksgiving dinner. Behavior generally is orderly in such settings without group norms ever being discussed.

A second way that norms can become established is for them to evolve gradually, as members try out different behaviors. Invariably, members discover that some of those behaviors work well and are positively valued in the group, whereas others do not have the intended effect and may even get the actor into a little trouble with his or her peers. Over time—and generally it is a relatively short time—norms come into being for those behaviors that members view as important. Some time ago, I was asked to join a diverse group of faculty and administrators to conduct a performance review of a university staff member whose contract was up for renewal. None of us had done such a thing before. We not only had to figure out a strategy for carrying out the review, but we also had to establish a set of norms about how we would work together. Although we never explicitly discussed what our norms should be, by our second or third meeting a set of shared expectations about appropriate behavior had evolved and was invisibly guiding our individual and collective behavior.

The third way to establish norms is to deliberately create them as part of the group structure, as was the case for the core norms of the fiscal analysis team at OMB. This third mechanism brings us back to our original question. Might the core norms that foster team effectiveness come naturally into being through importation by individual members or through gradual evolution in the normal life of the group? Or is the only viable way to establish these two outward-focused norms to explicitly create them? I know of no direct evidence that answers this question, but a considerable body of knowledge about behavior in social settings indirectly bears on it. That evidence suggests that it is quite unlikely that members will establish norms that support active environmental scanning and strategy planning, or that they will explicitly set and enforce specific "must always do" and "must never do" constraints on the team's task behaviors. Instead, the norms that members import or evolve are much more likely to focus on keeping interpersonal relations within the team and with clients smooth and conflict free, on keeping members' anxieties low, and on making sure that all inputs received are converted into outputs in a timely fashion with a minimum of fuss.[18]

The norms that are most likely to develop naturally, then, are likely to be good for maintaining harmonious interpersonal interactions within the group but less likely to be what is needed to foster team effectiveness and the long-term well-being of those the team serves. The two core norms are unnatural, and the behaviors they support often raise rather than lower anxieties within a work team. And that, in the final analysis, is why they usually must be explicitly and deliberately created as part of the team's structure.

How Secondary Norms Help

If the two core norms are in place, there remains a great deal of room for a work team to develop whatever secondary norms members may find helpful in guiding and regularizing their interactions with one another. I am entirely agnostic about what those norms should be, and it is none of my business in any case. Secondary norms properly cover whatever behaviors members wish to regulate, and that is certain to vary from group to group.

Certainly many groups will find it helpful to have norms about such matters as punctuality, participation, communication, and conflict management. One insurance company, for example, printed up and distributed throughout the organization an attractive card that listed a handful of norms (e.g., "accept and share responsibility and participation," "never withhold information," and "never tolerate turf issues") that senior leaders believed would foster good interpersonal and group behavior throughout the company. That is fine, but it also would have been fine if their norms had focused on standards of politeness, or even on appropriate dress, if those were matters that members cared about. Secondary norms can and should be about whatever behaviors members view as important enough to regulate.

Far more significant for the health of a group than the content or coverage of secondary norms are the benefits that accrue to a group as these norms are created and enforced. In most groups there will be quite a bit of variation in the behavior of members early in the team's life (the exception being when all members of a group have such similar experiences that they import virtually identical expectations about appropriate behavior). As members find that they wish to rein in some of the more excessive, disruptive, or unhelpful behaviors that occur, group norms begin to form. As these behaviors come under normative control, members learn what their limits really are—what they want to regulate and what they are willing to let vary freely, which is less likely to happen when everyone always behaves well within the bounds of acceptability.[19] Such knowledge is good for a team to have because it increases the likelihood that members will respond competently if the team subsequently has to deal with a problem for which standard ways of operating are inadequate or inappropriate. If a team has already established and tested its limits, it can more competently make decisions about whether and when to violate them.

Moreover, many groups include someone who regularly deviates from team norms. Because what that person says or does is so frequently "off" from mainline group behavior, he or she may gradually become identified as the group deviant. "There Vernon goes again," his teammates say, "always wanting to slow down the work until management shows it is taking our complaints seriously." Vernon actually is serving the group well. In addition to clarifying the limits of what the team views as acceptable behavior, he is providing a corrective to majority processes that drive efficient task execution but rarely prompt innovation or change. By constantly having to deal with Vernon, his team is much more likely to come up with an original way of construing its situation, or new ways of responding to old problems, than would be the case if he also behaved well within the team's latitude of acceptable behavior.[20] Deviations from group norms, and the people who so deviate, serve their teams in important ways—even though their teammates may often wish that they would shut up, get in line, or go away.[21]

Getting Priorities Right

Norms are a critical aspect of team structure because they are a powerful and efficient means of coordinating and regulating member behavior. But not all norms are equally helpful in promoting team effectiveness. A leader's first priority should be to help a team establish the core norms that foster competent task performance—those that guide how the team deals with the opportunities and constraints in its performance context and that establish the outer limits of acceptable task behavior. Having done that, the leader can then stand back and let whatever secondary norms members may find helpful emerge as the team goes about its work.

I am aware that what I am espousing here runs counter to what most of us would do when seemingly "bad" behavior is exhibited in a team. Almost everyone would choose to focus first on getting that behavior corrected—tamping down whatever seems most disruptive and bringing those who are misbehaving back into line. And it is true that genuinely out-of-control behaviors within a team can make it impossible to get anything at all done, as would be the case if no one listened to anyone else or if most behaviors were aimed at putting other group members down rather than getting on with the team's real work. It is asking too much of a team to suggest that members develop outward-looking norms that may eventually help the team perform well when there is chaos inside the group.

In the great majority of cases, however, things are not that bad. In the normal course of teamwork, to give highest priority to dealing with unwelcome behaviors by establishing and enforcing norms that inhibit them is merely to treat the behavioral manifestations of what most likely is a more basic structural malady. And it diverts members' attention and energy away from getting in place those core behavioral norms that actually will turn out, over the longer term, to facilitate achievement of the team's purposes.

The more powerful and enduring strategy for fostering competent teamwork is to focus first on ensuring that the basic design of the team is solid, and then help team members take full advantage of the positive potential of that design. The two core norms of conduct discussed in this section are a key feature of a good basic design. When these norms are in place, the probability that "bad" behaviors will occur is significantly reduced, and, moreover, team members are more likely to be able to deal competently with such behaviors when they do appear. Those who design and launch teams, therefore, should be insistent about the core norms, give the team great latitude to establish whatever secondary norms members may prefer, and then help the team learn how best to capture and use well the benefits of the "deviant" behavior that remains.

COMPOSITION OF THE TEAM

The three biggest mistakes people make when they compose a team are as follows:

1. They assume "the more the better" and therefore put too many people on the team.

2. They assume that people who are similar to one another will get along better, and therefore compose a team that is too homogeneous.

3. They assume that everyone knows how to work in a group, and therefore pay too little attention to the interpersonal skills of prospective members.

The mistake that they generally do *not* make is to overlook members' task-related knowledge and skill. We all know that a team is likely to get into trouble if members are not expert in the technical aspects of their work, so those who create teams generally take care to ensure that the team has plenty of task-relevant talent. Because that is the case, I focus here mostly on the three compositional errors just listed, and on what can be done to avoid them, rather than on the necessity to make sure that team members actually know how to do that which they are supposed to do.[22]

Size

It takes four people to play a string quartet, two crew members to fly a Boeing 737 aircraft, and twelve persons to form a full-sized jury. Not a person more nor a person less will do, so those who compose such groups can focus on matters other than the size of the performing unit. More commonly, however, managers who create work teams in organizations have considerable discretion about team size. Although managers sometimes form teams that are too small to accomplish their work well, the far more common and dangerous mistake is overstaffing them.[23]

Frederick Brooks was the manager of the systems programming effort at IBM that in the 1960s created OS/360, then the largest such effort ever undertaken. As almost always happens with large-scale projects that involve a great deal of coordination and uncertainty, the project tended to fall behind schedule. The temptation in such cases is to compute how far behind the project is and then add staff to make up time. So if the project is a dozen person-months behind, perhaps a dozen people could be assigned to it for one month to get back on schedule. That has no better chance of working in software development, Brooks says, than would a scheme to produce a baby quickly by assigning nine women to be pregnant for one month each. In fact, adding people has the opposite effect, which led to the formulation of Brooks's Law: "Adding manpower to a late software project makes it later."[24]

Psychologist Ivan Steiner reached the same conclusion in his analysis of the effect of group size on group productivity.[25] As can be seen in the three graphs in figure 4-2, the potential productivity of a group (that is, what the group theoretically could produce if member resources were used optimally) increases as size increases—but at a decreasing rate (figure 4-2a). Each new person adds something, but not as much as the previous person added. So increasing group size from two to three makes a much bigger difference in potential productivity than adding a thirteenth person to a twelve-person group.

Groups never perform at their level of potential productivity, however, because of what Steiner calls "process losses." These include the

FIGURE 4 - 2

The Relationship between Group Size and Productivity

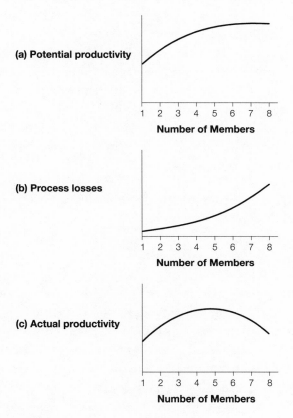

Source: From Steiner (1972), p. 96.

motivational decrement discussed earlier, coordination problems, and the myriad of other inefficiencies that develop when people work together in teams. As is seen in figure 4-2b, process losses also increase with size—but they grow at an accelerating rate.[26] The actual productivity of a group, then, is its potential productivity minus the process losses. As is shown in figure 4-2c, actual productivity increases for a while as size increases, then levels off, and then actually begins to *decrease* for very large groups. When group size becomes very large, the problems generated far outweigh the incremental resources brought by the additional members.

Is there an optimum team size, one that maximizes the human resources the team has for use in its work without running the risk of the
team getting bogged down trying to coordinate and maintain the engagement of a large number of people? A study conducted by Neil Vidmar and
myself is at least suggestive of an answer.[27] We composed groups that ranged
in size from two to seven members to assess the impact of size on group
process and performance for various kinds of intellective tasks. After the
groups had finished their work, we asked participants independently to
indicate the extent of their agreement with the following two questions.
(You might wish to respond yourself for a group of which you are a member,
using a scale from 1 ["strongly disagree"] through 3 ["neither agree nor disagree"] to 5 ["strongly agree"].)

1. This group was too small for best results on the task it was trying
   to do.

2. This group was too large for best results on the task it was trying
   to do.

We charted the average answers to these two questions on the same
graph; the results are shown in figure 4-3. Not surprisingly, few people in
the dyad thought it was too large, and few people in the seven-person
group thought it was too small. What is noteworthy is where the two lines
cross. We dropped a perpendicular line from that point to the horizontal
axis on which group size was indicated (the dotted line in the figure), and
voilà! we discovered that the optimum group size was 4.6 members.

That conclusion, of course, was just an exercise done on data from a
not-very-important study, but it does remind us that most of the time
smaller really is better. Indeed, a team may function better when it has
slightly *fewer* members than the task actually requires.[28] A few pages ago,
I noted that flying the Boeing 737 aircraft is a two-person task. In fact,
Boeing engineers designed the cockpit so it could be flown by either a
two- or a three-person crew. United Airlines was the lead customer for
the aircraft and wanted the flight deck set up for a two-person crew,
thereby generating enormous savings in labor costs. The pilots union, on
the other hand, thought the plane should have a three-person crew since
it would be flying many short hops in busy airspace. It surely would be
safer to have a third pair of hands to help with the work and a third pair of
eyes alert for potentially conflicting traffic.

FIGURE 4 - 3

Member Satisfaction with Group Size for Smaller and Larger Groups

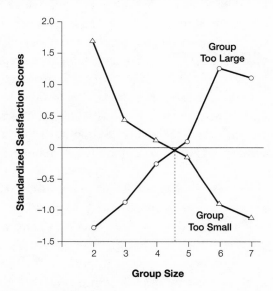

Source: From Hackman and Vidmar (1970), p. 48.

When it became clear that the disagreement could not be resolved through discussion, the company and union jointly sponsored a research study to compare the behavior and performance of two- and three-person crews in actual flight operations. You no doubt have guessed the finding of the study: The three-member crews showed no across-the-board advantage relative to the two-person crews. Members of three-person crews did leave the cockpit more frequently to visit the cabin, which may have helped strengthen the work relationship between pilots and flight attendants. But they caught no more potentially conflicting traffic called to their attention by Air Traffic Control than did the two-person crews.[29]

So what *is* the best group size? It depends on the size of the task, of course, but I do have a rule of thumb that I relentlessly enforce for student project groups in my Harvard courses: A team cannot have more than six members. Even a six-person team has fifteen pairs among members, but a seven-person team has twenty-one, and the difference in how well groups of the two sizes operate is noticeable.[30]

If the evidence is so strong that small team size is better, why do we see so many large teams struggling along in organizations? Certainly the faulty assumption that "more is better" for team effectiveness is part of the reason. But the main driver may have less to do with team performance than with emotional issues, such as using large numbers of people to share responsibility and spread accountability, and with political considerations, such as ensuring that all relevant stakeholders are represented in the group so they will accept its product. For these reasons, individuals from various constituencies may be appointed to a team one by one, or even two by two, creating a large team, a safe team, a politically correct team— but a team that can find itself incapable of generating an outcome that meets even minimum standards of acceptability, let alone one that shows signs of originality.

I once asked the executive director of a large art museum what in the world his forty-member board of directors could possibly accomplish. "Not much of anything other than to make financial contributions," he responded with a smile. "And that's just the way I want it." Sometimes those who create teams that are too large to perform well know *exactly* what they are doing. But what if one really does want one's board of directors (or top-management team, or some another team whose work requires many members) to be an effective performing unit?

There are a number of options.[31] My university has a thirty-person Board of Overseers from whom are sought (and genuinely wanted) ideas, perspectives, insights—and, of course, contributions. But the Overseers are not the governors of the university. The decision-making group is the Harvard Corporation, which consists of five outside members plus the president and treasurer of the university, just the right size to make the consequential choices and decisions that are the responsibility of any organization's directors.[32]

Another example. A startup organization I once studied became sufficiently large that the dozen founding officers of the firm no longer were able to coordinate their activities and make decisions in the informal manner that had worked well in the organization's early days. The time had come, the CEO concluded, for some kind of senior management structure. He considered devising such a structure himself, but that would have been inconsistent with the collegial and democratic spirit of the firm, which he and his colleagues greatly valued. He also considered the opposite strategy—asking the dozen officers to go off by themselves and come up with a structure that they all could accept. But he wisely realized that a group of that size, all of whose members had enormous personal stakes in how things turned out, was quite unlikely to come up with a structure that would serve the organization well. What the CEO finally did was form a reorganization task force composed of four diverse members, all highly respected by their peers, whose task was to develop a proposal for the new management structure that he would review, possibly modify, and approve. But he did not stop there. He also created a "must always do" norm for the group. Each member was assigned responsibility for staying closely in touch with each of three other officers who were not on the task force. Before each task force meeting, each member was expected to speak to each of those three persons. The first agenda item at every meeting was to be a report of the views of those nonmembers, and the last agenda item was to be an explicit review of what should be communicated to, or asked of, them. Task force members took their responsibilities as linking pins seriously, and although there were many rough spots along the way (including slippage in adhering to the norm about pre- and postmeeting communication), the team eventually came up with a reorganization plan that was accepted both by the CEO and the other officers.

One aspect of Microsoft's strategy for protecting that company from the liabilities of large size has been to create organizational devices that make it possible for core programming teams to be quite small—commonly one program manager and three to eight developers. The company takes a modular approach to large development projects, providing each team with a clear and concise statement of the vision for its part of the work, specifying a clear deadline by which the work is to be done, and then giving each team substantial autonomy for doing what needs to be done to complete its part of the project. Even the development centers within which the teams operate, and whose managers watch over the links among the separate modules, are relatively small—usually no more than 300 to 400 people for work that might be performed in a 1,000-person unit in a traditionally structured organization. According to MIT management professor Michael Cusumano, from whose research this account was taken, Microsoft has found a way to make large teams work like small teams.[33]

One final example. From its founding in 1972, members of the twenty-six-person Orpheus Chamber Orchestra have been committed to rehearsing and performing the repertoire for small orchestras in chamber music style—that is, without a conductor and with the greatest possible participation by all members in matters of artistic interpretation (see chapter 6 for more on the orchestra). But a twenty-six-person team is far too large to operate as collegially as a string quartet does. With everyone chiming in with thoughts and ideas, rehearsal could become a cacophony. So orchestra members came up with the idea of the "core," a small group consisting of the principal players for the piece being rehearsed. The core meets prior to the first full-orchestra rehearsal to work out the basic frame for the piece being prepared. Then, when the rest of the orchestra joins in, these individuals have special responsibility for helping other members of their sections understand and implement the ideas the core has roughed out. Any musician still can offer up new musical ideas for consideration by the ensemble, of course, but the starting point is the interpretive direction the core has set.[34]

I have floated the idea of the core with players, conductors, and managers of a number of full-sized symphony orchestras. If it worked so well for Orpheus, could not the same idea be adapted for a 100-person orchestra? Could not principal players meet separately with the conductor before the first full rehearsal to work through the piece being prepared? It was a modest proposal, I thought, something at least worth thinking about if not experimenting with. But absolutely no one nibbled. It would violate the labor contract, I was told. Conductors would never stand for it. Players would resist. So large orchestras continue as they always have, playing great music to be sure, but doing so in a way that leaves enormous amounts of musical talent unused on the rehearsal stage and sufficing with less engagement and commitment from musicians than they could have.

With size, as with all other aspects of team structure, there always is a choice. But it takes the courage of informed conviction, plus a good measure of willingness to innovate and experiment, to find ways to exercise that choice that can simultaneously harvest the diverse contributions of team members *and* foster efficient collective action.

Mix

A well-composed team strikes a balance between having members who are too similar to one another on the one hand and too different on the other. Members of an excessively homogeneous group may get along well together but lack the full complement of resources needed to perform well. An excessively heterogeneous group may have a rich diversity of talent and perspective but be unable to use it well because members are too different in how they think and behave. In a balanced group, members have a variety of talents and perspectives, yet are similar enough that they are able to communicate and coordinate with one another competently.[35]

A balanced group is easier to describe than it is to create and maintain. Although the dysfunctions of too much diversity are real enough, the more common and pernicious problem in work organizations is excessive homogeneity. Multiple forces, acting in concert, foster similarity among members. For one thing, the people who are attracted to a given group are likely to have numerous attributes in common. "Which project would you most like to work on?" we ask. "And who would you like to work with on that?" The people who gravitate toward a particular kind of work, or toward a particular set of coworkers, are likely to be far more similar to one another than people who prefer different projects or teammates. Given a choice, I probably would be more comfortable working on an intellectual project with other white male pipe-smoking academics of a certain age whose first language is English and whose origins are Midwestern than with teammates who differ from me on all of those attributes. Such self-selection biases often are affirmed and extended by managers who understandably prefer to compose groups whose members, in their view, are likely to get along well together. And when team members have the authority to decide who will be invited to fill an open slot on the team, similar-to-us biases can dominate the selection process—at least for teams that are not yet mature enough to appreciate the value of diversity in accomplishing collective work.[36]

Forces toward homogeneity continue to operate even after a group is formed and under way. Teams gradually but inevitably develop a shared view of reality (which means that members' perceptions of the world in which they operate converge over time) and, as discussed earlier, they import or establish norms to regulate member behavior (which means that members' behaviors usually become more similar over time). Once that happens, members' beliefs and attitudes—which have been significantly shaped by the team's shared perceptions and behaviors—gradually converge as well.[37] Finally, at some point in the life of most teams, one or more members decide to leave or are asked to. These individuals are not drawn randomly from the membership; those most likely to depart are the ones who in one way or another are viewed as, or view themselves as, different from the rest of the team.[38]

All of these forces pull in the same direction, and the result commonly is a team of rather similar people who find it easy to work together smoothly and harmoniously.[39] (We are, after all, the same kind of folks. Heck, maybe we could even have our next meeting on the links, or over a sherry down at the club.) Moreover, homogeneous teams are virtually certain to find it easier to develop the "shared mental models" that are all the rage these days in explaining what it takes for a team to perform effectively.

This is all to the good except for two troublesome facts. First, there is little evidence that homogeneous teams, for all the good relations their members may have with one another, perform better than heterogeneous teams.[40] Second, the experience of working in a homogeneous team is less likely to promote member learning (or, for that matter, learning by the team as a whole) than are experiences in a more diverse team. How much do I actually have to learn from that group of pipe-smoking white professors in whose company I am so comfortable? Not much.

In fact, the kind of task-focused conflict that is common when a diverse set of members find that they are not of one mind about how to proceed can improve decisions and even increase the chances that they will come up with something creative.[41] Diverse groups do often experience rough sledding early in their lives as members struggle to figure out how to work together (and *interpersonal* conflict definitely is not a boon to performance).[42] But if members make it through their early difficulties, they are likely to come up with products that are significantly more creative than those generated by more homogeneous teams whose interactions are smoother from start to finish.[43]

The key to having a good mix of members is to balance carefully between too much similarity and too many differences. At Butler Manufacturing, the process began well before grain drier assembly teams were formed. Prospective team members initially were trained on three of the five basic jobs in the assembly process, and then teams were composed of people who had received different patterns of initial training. This provided both commonality of skills within teams, since more than one member of each team was competent to do each subtask, as well as moderate heterogeneity, since no one person was initially competent to perform all the subtasks. This balance both gave teams some flexibility in how they deployed their human resources, and promoted interdependence and cross-training among members.[44]

The natural social forces that sand off the rough edges of teams and polish their compositional center are strong and mutually reinforcing. A good place to start in countering or redirecting those forces is to make sure that interesting differences among members are built into a work team when it initially is composed. But good composition by itself is insufficient. As we will see in chapter 6, it also takes expert coaching to help a diverse group—especially one whose diversity has to do with the personal and group identities of members, not just their task skills—find ways to constructively learn from their differences and exploit them in carrying out the team's work.

Interpersonal Skills

Some people just are not cut out to be team players. They may have a great deal to contribute to the work of an organization, but those contributions are better made as solo performers than as team members. All the teams on which such a person serves have difficulties that appear to stem from his or her disruptive or inappropriate behavior. The person may behave so abrasively as to alienate teammates. Or head off in an independent direction even after the team has decided what it will do. Or escalate conflicts far beyond their actual importance. Or regularly misunderstand what others are asking or suggesting. Or just generally behave as a nuisance, getting in the way rather than pitching in and helping move the work forward.

Without question, there is variation in organization members' interpersonal skills, in their ability to work competently with others (yes, you may call it "emotional intelligence" if you want). This variation is seen in all functions and at all organizational levels. Becoming a senior manager, for example, does not automatically confer on a person interpersonal skills that he or she did not have before. It also is unquestionably true that some basic level of interpersonal skill is required to function well on a team. Therefore, one ideally would compose a team entirely of members who have the requisite levels of interpersonal skill. If some people do not have those skills, they can be offered training to help them acquire such skills. Sometimes widespread training in interpersonal skills may be required. In organizations that have a long history of designing and managing work for individual performers, most organization members may have mastered well the skills needed for individual work, but more than a few may find that the transition to teamwork stretches their existing skill set.

What can be done with people who do not have the skills needed for competent teamwork and who are unwilling or unable to acquire them? There are only three ways to deal with such individuals when teams are formed. First, keep them at a safe distance so they can do no damage. Indeed, some firms these days try to be rid of them altogether. "Only team players at this company!" is the slogan, as if being a team player were the ultimate measure of one's worth, which it is not. Second, go ahead and put them on teams, install strong leaders to keep things under control, and hope for the best. "Everybody here works on teams. No exceptions!" is the motto, as if everybody were skilled in teamwork, which they are not.

Neither of these alternatives has much to recommend it. The first is wasteful because talent is knowingly withheld from teams. The second is dangerous. Team after team can be sunk by "team destroyers" whose brilliance is exceeded only by their incapacity for collaborative work.[45] Individuals with marginal task competence are less of a problem. If they persist in misbehaving, the team can afford to do without them. But it is hard to contemplate shunning someone whose task skills are extraordinary.

The only realistic alternative, then, is for a team to find a way to harvest the contributions of those with shaky interpersonal skills, and do so in a way that minimizes the risk to the team and its work. Teammates and the team leader, working together with such a person, often can make significant progress in helping him or her to learn the basics of what teamwork requires. This can be done in the course of the team's regular work and sometimes results in greater progress than would be obtained from his or her participation in even a well-executed interpersonal skills workshop or training course. If peer coaching does not have the hoped-for effect, then the team still has the option of isolating or working around the person so that it can get on with its work relatively unimpeded by his or her disruptions.

Working around a member whose interpersonal skills are viewed as insufficient or inadequate in effect dismisses that person from the team. That is a draconian action, to be taken only after everything else that

members can think of has been tried. Excluding a member from participation in the work of a team can be quite costly to the team itself. The
most obvious cost is that the team loses all that the disruptive member
has to contribute to the group. That may include some special talents for
task work, to be sure, but the loss of the disruptiveness can itself be
costly. As noted earlier, group members who violate the norms of a team,
who persistently suggest things that everyone else knows is wrongheaded
or who behave in ways that are coded as out of line, make their own special contributions to a team. To lose a "deviant" member often is also to
lose opportunities for fresh thinking.

A more serious risk of dismissing or ignoring a person whose interpersonal skills seem inadequate is that the attribution itself may be wrong.
We all tend to view behaviors that are disruptive or off-target as reflecting
some problem with the person who exhibited them. But sometimes those
behaviors may actually reflect the perspective of some other *group* that is
not otherwise represented in our own. If, for example, a team consists of
five marketers and one engineer who seems constantly to be acting up,
that may indeed reflect something that is not quite right about that particular person. It is possible, however, that the person is manifesting an
alternative perspective or way of operating that characterizes the other
group of which he or she is a member.[46] The person may be doing that
entirely unconsciously, without even being aware that the problems he or
she is having in the group actually reflect tensions between that group
and the engineering department. If that possibility is not explored, the
team runs a real risk of socially or behaviorally dismissing the engineer
and, in the process, avoids dealing with intergroup issues that ought to be
addressed rather than suppressed. This phenomenon is especially pervasive, and its consequences especially severe, when the other group is central to the identity of the person whose behavior is being questioned—for
example, when the person's race, gender, ethnicity, or nationality differs
from that of the majority members.

Another potentially destructive misattribution regarding the causes
of seemingly unskilled interpersonal behavior derives from a psychody-
namic phenomenon known as *splitting*.[47] In emotionally charged settings,
people sometimes deal with their uncertainties and ambivalences about
how things are going by unconsciously splitting the positive and negative
affect they are experiencing into separate parts, assigning all the former to

one person (the hero) and all the latter to another (the bum). Splitting can be especially pernicious in teams where there are only a few members with distinctive demographic attributes, because those are the ones who are disproportionately likely to be scapegoated, viewed as "unable to work in groups," and assigned most or all of the blame for collective failures. If that bad actor could just be removed, the thinking goes, the team's problems would disappear. The impulse to scapegoat someone when the going gets rough can be quite strong; even worse, the scapegoated member often starts to behave in accord with his or her teammates' expectations—thereby setting in motion a self-fueling spiral whose outcome does no good for either the team or the person.

The final reason teams should move slowly on an impulse to blame and dismiss people whom they experience as disruptive has to do with the topic of this chapter—team structure. One more time, a reprise of the now-familiar refrain: If a team's structure is appropriate, members will encounter fewer interpersonal problems than they would if the team's task, norms, or composition were ill considered. Moreover, the snags a well-structured team inevitably will hit are more likely to be resolved without resort to the kinds of dehumanizing misattributions just discussed.

Putting It Together

Good composition of a work team requires leaders to attend simultaneously to the attributes of the individuals who will make up the team and to the properties of the team as a whole. At the individual level, the main focus should be on ensuring that each member has strong task skills and, as discussed earlier, at least adequate interpersonal skills. At the group level, there are two key considerations. First, the size of the group: It should be small, perhaps even a bit smaller than seems needed to accomplish the work. Second, the mix of members: Team composition should balance between homogeneity and heterogeneity, with special attention to countering the natural social forces that tilt teams toward similarity among members and uniformity of belief, attitude, and behavior.

Herman Melville in *Typee* describes the makeup of the whaleship *Dolly*'s crew as follows: "Unfortunately, with a very few exceptions our crew was composed of a parcel of dastardly and mean-spirited wretches, divided among themselves, and only united in enduring without resistance the unmitigated tyranny of the captain."[48] With thoughtful attention to how work teams are composed, we should at least be able to do better than that.

BREATHING LIFE INTO A TEAM STRUCTURE

Those who create work teams can do a great deal before a team ever meets to get things set up right, to stack the cards so that competent teamwork will be easy rather than a struggle. The team task can be designed so it engages and motivates members for work on the collective task. Basic norms of conduct that promote active strategy planning within broad but clearly defined limits can be articulated. People with the right skills and experience can be selected for membership on the team, and care can be taken to make sure that both the size of the team and the mix of members are as good as they can be. These structural features comprise what Robert Ginnett and I call the *shell* of the team. A team's shell, like that of an egg, is the shaping structure within which an organism (in the present case, a social system) comes to life. Until an egg is fertilized, it is lifeless; until a team meets for the first time, it is lifeless as well.

Ginnett and I stumbled onto the idea of the shell, and came to appreciate the full importance of that first team meeting, in the course of our research on airline and military flight deck crews.[49] We went into the research assuming that the behavior of captains made a great deal of difference in how their crews functioned, so we were surprised to discover how many of the determinants of flight crew behavior were already in place when crews first convened and were effectively beyond any captain's control. Both the design of the flying task and crew members' roles are preengineered, for example. Basic norms of conduct on the flight deck are largely dictated by regulatory authorities and airlines' flight standards staffs. The composition of crews is determined jointly by the predefined structure of crew roles and, in most commercial airlines, by a seniority-based bidding system that, in turn, is enforced by a labor contract.[50]

The shell that has evolved for flight deck crews, happily for frequent fliers, is quite sound. What the captain does when the crew first forms is indeed consequential for future team dynamics (see chapter 6). But even if the captain does little more than help members occupy comfortably the standard structure the crew has been provided, things are likely to go fine. It's like slipping into a suit of one's own size at the clothing shop; all that is required is a little tailoring to perfect the fit. If the captain accepts the basic structure, helps members of his or her team do the same, and refrains from behaving disruptively, the crew is almost certain to get off to a good start.

Some team shells in other kinds of organizations, however, are badly flawed, with the design of the work, expectations about appropriate conduct, and the composition of the team so far off the mark that teams are doomed from the start. In such cases, there is little that any team leader can do to remedy the situation after the group has started its work—it can be difficult, or even impossible, to change the task, to redefine basic norms of conduct, or to adjust the number or mix of members on line and in real time.

That is why it is so important to get the basic structure right, to set things up so the team has every favorable chance of success. But it is only when the team first meets that life is infused into that structural shell. Those who create teams, therefore, have two quite different but equally important responsibilities: to make sure that a team has the best structure that can be provided, and to help members move into that structure and competently launch themselves onto a course of their own. To focus on either one of those responsibilities to the exclusion of the other is to significantly handicap a team even as it begins its life.

VIRTUAL TEAMS: THE END OF STRUCTURE?

It is a fantasy—a tempting and pervasive one, but a fantasy nonetheless—that it is possible to have great teams without the bother of creating enabling team structures. We hope that markets will make hierarchies unnecessary. That we can have networks rather than organizations. That boundaryless social systems can accomplish work efficiently and effectively. And, when some kind of structure actually is needed, that self-organizing processes of the kind celebrated by complexity theory will create them automatically. Both positive models, such as W.L. Gore & Associates, where there are no managers, and horrifying models, such as terrorist groups where there is no visible organization, are held up as previews of the coming of the new organizational age.[51]

Now, on wings of ever more powerful, sophisticated, and compact computational and communications technologies, comes yet another possibility that may allow us to move beyond the necessity to explicitly create team structures: virtual teams. Such teams are becoming increasingly popular these days in forward-looking organizations, especially for knowledge work but also for front-line activities that keep individual team members on the road much of the time, such as sales and service work.[52] In virtual teams, members interact mainly (and sometimes exclusively) electronically. Virtual teams can be larger, more diverse, and collectively more knowledgeable than those that rely on face-to-face interaction because members do not have to be geographically co-located. And when virtual teams work well, they can bring widely dispersed information and expertise to bear on the team's work quickly and efficiently.[53]

Do these developments mean the end of structure for work teams? Will managers no longer have to worry about the difficult decisions regarding team design that we have covered in this chapter? I may be proven wrong by the time this book is published (the virtual world is developing faster than I am writing), but I predict the opposite. I am guessing that we will see in the years immediately to come a new millennium version of the "tyranny of structurelessness" that Jo Freeman wrote about in the 1970s and with which I opened this chapter. Virtual teams will be tossed together even more casually than some organizational task forces are these days; it will be unclear who is actually a team member; norms of conduct will be set, if at all, only at the most general level (e.g., "we don't flame each other"); and although the teams will be quite diverse in membership, they will be far too large for members to work together efficiently.

Research evidence about the conditions required for virtual team effectiveness is just now beginning to accumulate.[54] My reading of that evidence is that the structural conditions that foster the effectiveness of face-to-face teams are just as critical for virtual teams—but with one caveat: *It is much harder to create those conditions in virtual teams.* It is a significant managerial task to create an appropriate team structure—let alone to bring a team to life as a real social system—if members are scattered around the region, the country, or the world. Many practitioners are realizing this, and increasingly are taking the costs in time and travel to bring all members of a virtual team together at least for a face-to-face launch meeting at which the team establishes itself as a group, comes to terms with its task, and sets the basic norms of conduct that will guide members' interactions online. In my view, that is all to the good, well worth the cost and trouble. But I probably would go even further and ask that members also come together at critical milestones in their team life cycle to debrief, to reflect on ways they might have better used their electronic resources, and to make whatever changes may seem wise in how they will carry out their collective work and operate as a virtual team in the future.

Team structure, as challenging as it can be to get it right and implement it well, will always be with us. That is as it should be, since it is a team's basic structure that provides the platform on which members do all of their work. It always is a good investment to devote time, thought, and energy to making that platform as high and sturdy as it can be— regardless of whether members will be working together around the same table or will be dispersed around the globe, communicating and coordinating their activities electronically.

5

Supportive Context

The conditions discussed in the previous three chapters—a real team, a compelling direction, and an enabling structure—provide the basic platform for competent teamwork. But work teams do not operate in an organizational vacuum.[1] Features of the organizational context, as well as the coaching behaviors of team leaders, can either make it much easier for a team to exploit the advantages of a good basic structure or so powerfully impede the team that the advantages of a fine basic design are negated. Even managers who carefully plan the design, formation, and launch of a work team sometimes then back off and say, in effect, "Good luck, kids, you're on your own now!" These managers stop too soon, since what is needed for team effectiveness is a good design *reinforced by* a supportive organizational context and expert team coaching.

If a well-designed work team is a seedling, then the organizational context is the soil in which it is planted, the milieu that provides the nutrients needed for it to grow and bear fruit. Just as infertile soil can stunt the growth of even the healthiest seedling, so can an unsupportive context limit the performance of even a well-designed work team. The reverse also is true, of course: Even the most fertile soil cannot help a fundamentally crippled plant, nor will a wonderfully supportive organizational context enliven a team whose design is fundamentally flawed—once again affirming the importance of giving first priority to a work team's direction and structure.[2]

There are so many organizational structures and systems that potentially bear on team performance that no leader could possibly fine-tune every one of them to make sure that all aspects of the organizational context support teams in their work. The leader's first priority, then, is to identify those specific structures and systems that are most critical to team effectiveness and therefore worthy of focused attention and possible intervention. Findings from research on the organizational context of work teams can be helpful in this regard.[3] In particular, my colleagues and I have found that three organizational systems have particularly high leverage in supporting teamwork: the reward system, the information system, and the educational system.

This chapter explores these three systems, as well as strategies for bringing them into alignment with the support needs of work teams. We will see that identifying the key contextual supports for teams is much more straightforward than getting them implemented in ongoing organizations. Chapter 6 addresses the last of the five conditions for team effectiveness, the provision of expert team-focused coaching.

REWARD SYSTEM

The reward system should provide recognition and reinforcement contingent on excellent team performance. When a reward system does that, it reinforces the motivational benefits of challenging direction (chapter 3) and well-designed teamwork (chapter 4). Moreover, it demonstrates to the team that others in their organization (specifically, those who designed the reward system and administer it) care enough about a team's performance that they are willing to expend organizational resources to recognize what it accomplishes. Recognition for good team performance encourages members to think of "us" rather than "me" and goes a long way in helping to sustain collective motivation.[4] The pages that follow briefly examine each component of the principle stated in the first sentence of this paragraph to develop a richer appreciation of what is required to tailor an organizational reward system so that it supports and reinforces team effectiveness.

Recognition and reinforcement . . .

It has long been known that rewards are better than punishments for shaping behavior. A reward increases the likelihood that the behavior just exhibited will occur again, whereas a punishment makes it more likely that some *other* behavior, and not necessarily one that the punishment giver will view as desirable, will be exhibited. These principles hold for shaping the behavior of animals (e.g., training a puppy to fetch), of individual humans (positive reinforcement works beautifully for teaching a child how to be polite), and of work teams. When a team receives something that members collectively value, it becomes more likely that members will do again whatever it is that they did before. But punishments (e.g., levying a fine or requiring that a team stay after closing to perform some additional aversive work) are likely to focus members' attention on how they can better protect themselves from such things happening in the future—a development that almost certainly is not what the manager who administered the punishment had in mind.

The consequences of excellent team performance, therefore, must be something that team members themselves view as favorable. Even if managers think that putting a team's name on a list of "Top Teams in Our Plant" posted in the reception area is a dandy way to recognize excellence, that listing will have no effect whatever if team members view it as silly. One kind of recognition that almost everyone cares about is money. At least in Western societies, people have learned well to "follow the money" if they want to understand what is going on or what is most valued by those in charge. Although compliments and nonmonetary rewards can go a long way in reinforcing team excellence, they cannot go all the way. At some point, people want to see some cash—or at least feel they have a piece of the financial action.

Providing financial rewards for team excellence is far easier said than done in most work organizations—in part because first-line leaders of work teams rarely have direct control of, or even influence on, organizational reward policies and practices. So some ingenuity often is required to make it happen, as is illustrated by the experience of Hank, a production manager at a Utah semiconductor plant where David Abramis and I once conducted some research.[5] Hank had started out as a production worker at the plant. Although he had no formal training in semiconductor manufacturing (indeed, he was studying at night for his high school diploma), he thought he had a better idea about how to make semiconductors. Over time, he promulgated what turned out to be something of a revolution in using self-managing teams to manufacture memory chips. Hank began to experiment with his idea shortly after being promoted to manage one of the plant's production units (called a *fab*). He converted serial production lines, the standard work design in semiconductor manufacturing, into small teams, each with major responsibility for one part of the chip. Team members learned one another's jobs, took on increasing responsibility for quality control, and were encouraged to do whatever needed to be done within the bounds of their limited authority to increase yield (i.e., the proportion of usable chips relative to the total number of starts). Although Hank had never read anything about the principles of teamwork design, he created a good one.

Initial results were encouraging. Yields increased, production workers seemed pleased with their new responsibilities, and managers of other fabs began to take an interest in what Hank was doing. Then he called me up one day and said, "I think you ought to come out for a visit. There have been some interesting developments with the teams." Whenever Hank called, I would come, as I was fascinated by what this home-taught manager was up to. It turned out that the corporate vice president for human resources happened to be visiting the plant from headquarters in California the same day that I was, and we three found ourselves having coffee in Hank's conference room talking over what he was learning from his team experiment. As if scripted, I asked, "So how are the teams going?" "Big problems," he responded. "Yields are great, but team members are noticing that *somebody* is making more money now than they used to—and it's not them." The conversation then continued along the following lines, which I later realized was just what Hank had anticipated when he arranged for the vice president and me to visit on the same day.

Me: This is serious. Unless you provide them some kind of rewards or recognition based on team performance, the whole thing could crater.

Hank: Can't do it. All I have to work with is an end-of-year bonus pool, and I can only use it to reward outstanding *individual* performers. Doing that could undermine the teams.

Me: Oh, my! Don't do that. That would be the *worst* thing you could possibly do. It probably would kill your teams.

Hank: Well, then, I guess I'm just stuck.

Vice president: Well, just a minute now. Let's think some more about this, see if we can come up with any other possibilities.

By the end of the meeting, Hank had obtained from the vice president an exception to corporate compensation policy that enabled him to use his end-of-year individual bonus funds at any time he wished to provide performance-contingent financial rewards to his teams. The only restriction was that he could not overspend the bonus budget in any fiscal year.

Given that the corporation took its compensation policy quite seriously, the special arrangement Hank negotiated was an extraordinary accomplishment. But do you think he behaved unethically, that he played a little too fast and loose with the vice president? Let us inspect his behavior a little more closely. Did he lie to anybody? No. Did he cheat anybody? No. Could he have made the decision to convert the individual bonus pool to team incentive funds on his own authority? Also no. Did he behave politically? Absolutely.

Hank's political behavior got him what he needed and did not have: the right to use corporate financial resources in a way that could promote, simultaneously, the interests of both the organization and his people on the production floor. Could Hank have used a different strategy to try to achieve the same outcome? Of course. But given his organizational role (a low-level manager in a plant distant from headquarters), his corporate clout (essentially none), and his expertise (unschooled in intervention strategies), what he did may have been about the most effective and appropriate thing he could have done. If you remain skeptical, you might want to speculate about what would have happened if instead he had sent a reasoned memo to headquarters formally requesting permission to deviate from corporate compensation policy. My guess is that he still would be waiting for a response.

Hank's success in obtaining the right to use individual bonus funds to reward teams merely gave him the resources he needed to do something. Next he had to decide what that would be, and that brought another problem. An amount of cash that might be considered a quite nice piece of change by an individual can look more like small change when divided among half a dozen team members. Research on compensation warns us that using financial rewards is not a piker's game—there is no point in doing it if the amount of money is not enough to be experienced as significant by those who receive it.[6] And the amount of money Hank had to hand out would not have made much of a difference in the lives of the members of his teams.

So he came up with an alternative way to use his limited funds. Every so often, a top-performing team was treated to a trip to Salt Lake City for dinner and theater, spouses invited. I don't recall whether or not team members were picked up at home by limousine for the ride to Salt Lake City, but if not they should have been—it would have been a nice additional touch. Dinner and theater provided an enjoyable reinforcement for his best-performing teams and was certain to catch the attention of all the other teams. The event no doubt strengthened team boundaries even as it brought members' life partners into the circle of celebration. And it did not break the bank. It was not a permanent solution to the problem of rewarding excellent team performance in the organization, however. Even after one has eaten lots of dinners and seen lots of plays, someone *still* is making more money than they used to because of the team's efforts and it still is not the team members. At some point, teams that are acting like owners deserve to be treated like owners—and, ultimately, that means having a share in the financial returns from their work.

Hank showed considerable creativity in using a rather small amount of money to recognize and reward excellent team performance, a lesson that should not be lost on others who feel that budgetary or policy restrictions keep them from doing much beyond verbally praising good-performing teams. We should not minimize the importance of verbal praise—just knowing that someone in authority has noticed your performance and taken the trouble to comment on it can mean a lot to a team. But there almost always are other, more tangible ways to supplement informal recognition of team excellence.

For example, Dartmouth organizational psychologist Ruth Wageman trained managers of service teams at Xerox to provide small spontaneous rewards on the spot to teams that were performing well.[7] I have yet to visit an organization where there is absolutely no possible way to recognize and reinforce good-performing teams. But I quite frequently have encountered managers who *think* that nothing can be done—and who therefore do not engage their ingenuity and political skills to find a way to do it.[8]

that is contingent on . . .

We all would like to have a fine salary and generous benefits—the more the better—and most of us are pleased to receive "awfully glad you're on our team" compliments and tokens of appreciation from our bosses. Such noncontingent rewards do increase the likelihood of our remaining in the organization where we get them. But they do little or nothing to motivate us to work together to accomplish our teamwork at the highest level of excellence. Indeed, they may send slightly the wrong signal, suggesting that just being here is what is valued, maybe even more than what we accomplish during our residency. For the motivational benefits of performance-contingent rewards to be realized, they must actually be *contingent*. Hank did not invite everybody to come along to dinner and a play; he invited only his best-performing teams. In doing that, he sent the right signal: Demonstrated excellence brings good things to teams.

That rewards be provided contingent upon the desired outcomes is necessary, but it is not sufficient. In addition, team members must *understand* what it is that is wanted and rewarded. There must be trustworthy *indicators* of the degree to which the desired outcomes actually have been achieved. And, finally, members must perceive that they have *leverage* on the attainment of those outcomes, that their collective behavior directly shapes the outcomes that trigger the rewards.

When these three conditions are met, teams have a good "line of sight" between what they do and what they get, and therefore performance-contingent rewards and recognition can have powerful effects on members' collective motivation. A team's line of sight is obscured if its work is but a small part of an overall project, or if there are no naturally occurring data to indicate how well the team has performed, or if exogenous factors such as market conditions so strongly determine outcomes that it is impossible to tease out the team's contributions. In such circumstances, managers may choose to base contingent rewards on how well a larger organizational unit is doing (e.g., a department or an entire plant) rather than on the performance of specific work teams. Unfortunately, the larger the organizational unit, the less the leverage any single team (let alone any individual member) has on its overall performance. If Hank had made rewards to his teams contingent on how well the plant as a whole was doing, the motivational power of those rewards would have diminished substantially.

The longer the link between a work team and the entity on whose performance contingent rewards are based, the less power those rewards have to shape team behavior. This is a major problem with most corporate profit-sharing plans. It is great that everyone benefits financially when the company does well, but members of front-line teams perceive, quite accurately, that what they do at work today will have such a small effect on the corporate bottom line as to be literally invisible. Senior managers recognize this problem, and often attempt to solve it by using rhetoric to convince people that their work really does make a difference—that they are, to draw on the old aphorism, building a cathedral rather than carrying bricks. "When you do well, we all do well," the poster reads.

Rather than make posters or hold motivational meetings, managers would be better advised to find ways to more directly link team behavior with team outcomes. And the best way to do this, in most cases, is to improve the design of the team's work. As we saw in chapter 4, good work design for teams involves having a whole piece of challenging work (rather than a small, routine part of a larger task), autonomy to decide about the methods of accomplishing the work, and feedback that provides direct and trustworthy knowledge about how well the team has done. When work is designed along these lines, a meaningful, measurable product for which team members feel collectively accountable is almost certain to exist. The line of sight to that product is short and unobscured, just what it takes for performance-contingent rewards to make a motivational difference. If those team-focused rewards are supplemented by other contingent rewards, perhaps based on overall plant or office productivity or even on corporate market valuation, so much the better. But it is the immediate rewards, those that are directly tied to outcomes that a team directly leverages, that make the most difference in work team motivation and behavior.

Is there a contradiction here? Is it not well known that performance-contingent extrinsic rewards reduce rather than strengthen individuals' *intrinsic* motivation? And does that not happen for work teams as well? If teams receive extrinsic rewards such as bonuses for doing well, won't that reduce or even eliminate the internal motivation that comes from performing well-designed work?

Not necessarily. Not even usually. To see why, let us take a look at the kind of research that has shown that extrinsic rewards reduce intrinsic motivation. A study by Stanford psychologist Mark Lepper and his colleagues is typical.[9] The researchers gave preschool children a number of colorful marking pens and invited them to do some drawing. Some of the children were told that they would receive a "Good Player" certificate for doing the drawing; others were not. A couple of weeks later, marking pens of the same kind were put in the children's classroom, and researchers noted the amount of time each child spent drawing with them. Those children who had received the extrinsic reward spent significantly *less* time drawing than those who had not. Similar results have been obtained for adults: The amount of time spent pursuing an intrinsically interesting activity drops when a person is paid for doing it.[10]

The key words in that last sentence are "doing it." The extrinsic rewards are not contingent on doing well; they are contingent on simply engaging in the activity. That makes good sense, given that most of us are constantly on the lookout for good explanations of our behavior. I explain the amount of time I spend on vacation clambering up hills in search of a pristine trout stream, for example, by saying to myself and others that fishing is an intrinsically enjoyable activity. But take me off vacation and pay me to spend time fishing, and attributional ambiguity enters the picture: Am I fishing because I enjoy it, or because I'm being paid? If the extrinsic reward is strong enough (and to powerfully shape behavior it should be), I very well may conclude that I'm in it mainly for the money. Once that explanation becomes dominant, my intrinsic motivation atrophies and it is much less likely that I will spend my free time climbing those same hills.

But what if it were already settled that I was going to *do* it, and we focused instead on how *well* I do it. Trout fishing is a well-designed task: People find it meaningful (because it is challenging), they feel responsible for the outcomes (it is hard to blame the fish for having spooked them), and there are incontrovertible data about the results of one's efforts. People who fish feel great when they've had a good day on the stream and less good when the fish get the better of them. That is internal motivation. What happens when an extrinsic reward is added in, such as acclaim from one's family, provided contingent on the number of foot-long trout brought back for dinner? Does one's motivation to fish well drop? No. Supplementing the built-in motivational incentive, the good feeling that comes from catching fish, with a performance-contingent extrinsic reward, family approval, further reinforces the motivation to fish well. The two sources of performance motivation are additive.[11]

The best state of affairs, then, obtains when an organization does not rely exclusively on either intrinsic or extrinsic rewards but instead structures the work itself to foster internal motivation (see chapter 4) and then supports that positive motivation with performance-contingent extrinsic rewards. Most of the research on the interdependencies between intrinsic and extrinsic motivation has focused mainly on individual performers. But the findings apply to work teams as well. It is entirely feasible to create work designs and reward systems that reinforce one another, thereby promoting both internal and extrinsic motivation simultaneously.[12]

good *team* performance.

Hank's instincts were exactly right when he worried that using his company's bonus funds to reward outstanding individual performers would undermine his manufacturing teams. Yet the simple principle Hank was following—namely, if a team does the work, the team should get the reward—is violated all the time, especially in organizations that have been fine-tuned over the years to recognize and reward excellent performance by individuals.

Reward systems in some such organizations actually put team members in direct competition with one another for their portion of financial rewards that are allocated from a fixed pool. Such practices divert members' attention from their work and refocus it on monitoring who is getting what when rewards are distributed. They also risk undermining relationships among team members and thereby making it harder for them to work together competently on their shared tasks. Moreover, to deal with the personal anxieties and interpersonal tensions that emerge in such circumstances, members may even develop a group norm that enforces equity in workload. In the words of one member of a service team that had developed such a norm, "Nobody sticks out here." Members of that team smoothed over or suppressed differences among themselves in knowledge, skill, and experience. Those differences potentially could have been drawn on to bring the team's best talents to bear on its work, but they were ignored in order to make sure that no one on the team was in a position to get more recognition or rewards than anyone else. What that team did to counter the effects of its individual-focused reward system on team performance may seem excessive or silly. But that kind of response is not uncommon for teams in organizations where they and their managers have to contend with individualistic compensation arrangements over which they have no control.

One strategy for dealing with such situations is to exercise a little managerial authority and require that the team itself handle the distribution of rewards among members. After all, nobody knows better than the members themselves who carried most of the freight and who was just along for the ride. I once experimented with this strategy for project groups in my undergraduate course. Each group received a certain number of points reflecting my assessment of its product and was charged with distributing those points in whatever way members felt was fair and appropriate. Almost all groups divided the points exactly evenly among all members (one group divided the points evenly among everybody except for one person, who got no points). In effect, my project groups ran at full tilt away from the distributive task I had given them, and they did so despite my exhortation that this could be a wonderful end-of-term learning opportunity. I concluded that it takes a quite mature work team to manage competently the differential distribution of rewards among members, and that one semester was perhaps not enough time for student project teams to develop maturity sufficient for such an anxiety-arousing undertaking. I did not try my experiment in team-distributed individual rewards again.

Even the very idea of team-based rewards can engender resistance in organizations where teams are not commonly used to perform work. The strength of that resistance was discovered by the faculty of Harvard Business

School (HBS) when the possibility of using graded group projects in the M.B.A. program was floated for the first time in 1986. Traditionally, students had been graded as individuals on a strict curve. So many students objected to the idea of group grades that the student education committee recommended to the administration that group projects be disallowed in M.B.A. courses. In the words of one student, "Students don't want their grades in the hands of other students."[13] That, despite the fact that upon graduation most students would find themselves in work settings in which their "grades" would depend greatly on the contributions of their teammates on consulting or project teams. (Subsequently, HBS has implemented not only group projects in M.B.A. courses, but also a number of other educational experiences specifically designed to help students learn teamwork skills.)

An unusual example of team dysfunctions stemming from individualistic rewards is provided by organizational psychologist Jack Wood in his study of a professional hockey team, the New Haven Nighthawks.[14] At the time of the study, the Nighthawks were a farm team of the Los Angeles Kings, a National Hockey League (NHL) team. As most athletic teams do, the team had a great task: playing competitively against another professional team. There is an abundance of meaning, experienced responsibility, and knowledge of results in such work, and collective internal motivation generally runs extremely high in competitive athletic teams.

The Nighthawks, however, were plagued with interpersonal tensions and conflicts that surprised and mystified sportswriters—and even the team coach. After many weeks of observations and interviews, Wood was able to solve the mystery. Although players loved the game of hockey and clearly preferred winning over losing, the team's record of wins and losses was not what mattered most to them. What really mattered for each player was whether he would be promoted to the NHL in Los Angeles, remain in New Haven, be demoted to Saginaw (a lower-standing farm team), or be sent home.

The coach was caught in the middle. Part of his job was to build the New Haven players into a winning team (the local press and fans expected that of him, and he expected it of himself), but he also was responsible for developing his players and making recommendations to Los Angeles management about who was ready for promotion and who should be sent on his way. The aspect of the reward system that was by far most salient for the players, individual promotion or demotion, was at such variance with the rewards of winning as a team that interpersonal tensions among players, both on and off the ice, were inevitable. Worse, there was little that the coach could do about them because of the conflict built into his own role.

The costs and risks of rewarding individuals rather than teams are especially great when the rewards in question are financial or, as for the Nighthawk team, consequential for individuals' careers. Because people care a great deal about such matters, they take careful note of how their teammates are doing financially and in their careers. Yet even individual-level rewards that are mostly symbolic can spawn difficulties for teams. Members care who gets chosen to present the team's report to the board of directors, for example, or whose picture is used in the brochure, or who gets approvingly mentioned in the executive director's annual report.

One of the great advantages of using teams to perform work, as noted in chapter 4, is that teams can perform tasks that are larger and more meaningful than those sized for performance by single individuals. But that advantage can be lost if performance-contingent rewards and recognition are given to individual members rather than the team as a whole. It sometimes takes ingenuity to figure out how to provide rewards to an intact team, particularly if resources are tight or if organizational policies dictate that they be used only to recognize outstanding individuals. It is worth the trouble to find a way, however, both because providing tangible performance-contingent recognition to an intact team is a powerful way to motivate members to work *together* and because differentially rewarding individuals for their contributions to team outcomes is plagued with risks and costs.

Getting Rewards Aligned

External recognition and rewards, a contextual feature, can powerfully support the motivational benefits of well-designed work, an aspect of team structure. Yet it usually is far from straightforward to tailor existing reward systems to provide such support. At minimum, the rewards must be valued by team members and be large enough to affect their behavior. They must be provided contingent on team performance, which means that performance outcomes must be readily discernible and measurable. And they must be provided to teams as intact units, not differentially to individual members, so that they reinforce members working together on their shared task.[15] We have seen that this three-part prescription can be difficult to fill, particularly in ongoing organizations whose culture has evolved to support work performance by individuals.

Team leaders and managers can and should verbally reinforce teams that perform well, of course, as well as provide them with whatever other tokens of recognition they can invent or commandeer. But when money enters the picture, things get much tougher. Indeed, the challenge of providing performance-contingent financial rewards to teams is so great that managers sometimes look for ways to escape it entirely. The all-salaried workforce is one possible escape hatch. Because every team member is a salaried employee, there are no contingent financial arrangements to worry about and try to get right. But in that seeming advantage also is a forgone opportunity, the chance to demonstrate to teams that the organization cares enough about their performance to put some real money on it. Another escape from the difficulties of performance-contingent financial rewards is provided by skill-based pay plans, in which team members (or even the team as a whole) receive additional compensation as members add to their repertoires of work-related skills. Such plans have been quite popular in organizational startups, especially in "high-commitment" organizations, where the development of a multiskilled workforce is a high and immediate priority. But once a sufficient variety of skills have been mastered at a sufficiently high level, there is little reason to continue reinforcing teams for developing even more. At that point, the escape hatch closes and managerial attention must refocus on the hardest question of all—namely, how to create an organizational reward system that reinforces excellent team and organizational performance even as it encourages the continued development of the knowledge and skills of individual members. The long-term aspiration, then, is a multitier reward system whose different components pull together to encourage excellence at multiple levels—ongoing skill development by individuals (perhaps through a pay-for-skills salary scheme), team performance effectiveness (perhaps through performance-contingent rewards for demonstrated excellence), and performance of the organization as a whole (in businesses, perhaps through profit sharing or stock ownership programs).[16]

Such a reward system, one that recognizes and reinforces excellence at the team level even while simultaneously fostering favorable individual and organizational outcomes, can never be perfected. Ongoing developmental work on the components of such a system, even though it will never be finished—and perhaps *because* it never can be finished—nonetheless provides many opportunities for organizational leaders and members to reflect together on their collective purposes and how to celebrate their achievement. That, in itself, surely is sufficient reason to attend carefully to the design and administration of reward systems that support teams in their work.

INFORMATION SYSTEM

Organizational information systems should provide teams, at their own initiative whenever possible, the data and projections that members need to competently plan and execute their work. By providing trustworthy, up-to-date data and forecasts about the performance situation, a good information system enables members to take full advantage of the other favorable features of its performance situation—such as a clear direction that orients the team toward the right organizational purposes (chapter 3), and norms that keep members on the lookout for the best ways to achieve those purposes (chapter 4).

Information is critical to the development and execution of good team-performance strategies.[17] Absent information about the performance situation, a team is in effect flying blind, an aircraft in clouds without radar or navigational aids or a basketball team trying to execute an endgame strategy without being able to see the shot clock. In such circumstances, the team's performance strategy may be more driven by chance than by informed, competent analysis. Moreover, members risk coming up with a way of proceeding that may seem quite reasonable to them but that turns out to be grossly inappropriate when executed. A team that has adequate information about its performance situation, by contrast, can navigate around the worst of weather or launch at just the right instant its special play to get the ball in the hands of its best shooter right before the final buzzer.[18]

What Information Systems Provide

When someone suggests a new or altered way a team might proceed with its work, members generally discuss its feasibility and appropriateness before deciding to implement the idea. "No, we couldn't do it that way," one member may assert, "because the people down the line need a continuous flow of output, and that approach would generate output in irregular batches." Or: "That's a neat idea, because it's extremely important that our documentation be perfect and that would let us have two different people checking the paperwork." The key phrases in those comments, of course, are "the people down the line need a continuous flow" and "it's extremely important that our documentation be perfect." When members have solid information about task requirements and about the expectations of those the team serves, they can do a far better job of formulating a good performance strategy than would be possible if they had to guess about what was wanted.

It was extremely important to the fiscal analysis teams at OMB (discussed in previous chapters) that members had ready access to information about the president's policy agenda and the status of relevant bills working their way through Congress. That information, coupled with knowledge of the standards that their clients were likely to use in assessing their work, enabled the teams to develop and implement performance strategies that minimized wasted effort and maximized the likelihood that their work could constructively influence the budget-making process.

For some teams, forecasts about the future can be just as important as information about the team's current work situation. Hank's semiconductor manufacturing teams encountered serious and continuing difficulties because they could not find out how many orders were on the books for the memory chips they made. Because demand for chips varied greatly from month to month, the teams constantly were having to revise their work strategies and staffing arrangements to accommodate unanticipated changes in workload. The irony is that the data about incoming orders did exist in a frequently updated database at corporate headquarters. With access to those data, Hank's teams could have ramped their production up (or down) in an orderly fashion when demand changed, thereby avoiding a good deal of unnecessary thrashing about. But the managers responsible for the database saw no reason why the people who made the chips should have access to such competitively sensitive information, and Hank was unable to convince them otherwise.

Also crucial to the development or invention of an appropriate performance strategy are data about the kinds and extent of resources presently available to the team and likely to be so in the future. How much money, time, space, equipment, and staff are available for the work? How is resource availability likely to change over the next few days, weeks, or months? What are the limits on the team's discretion in tapping those resources? Information about such matters helps team members assess the feasibility of alternative performance strategies ("No way we could do it that way; we'd need twice as much space as we have"), identify times when some organizational influence attempts may be called for ("But maybe we could borrow some unused space from accounting until we get through the crunch"), and eventually settle on a way of proceeding that fits well with what members actually have to work with ("So let's proceed along those lines, but keep open the option of switching back to how we're doing it now if we lose the space").

Good planning requires good information. Information systems that support teams well are those that provide members both with trustworthy data about present task requirements and with forecasts that suggest how those requirements may change in the future. Absent data about the imperatives and opportunities in the team's performance situation, members can do little more than keep on with their present way of working. With such data, members have what they need to explore alternative ways of making the best possible use of their talents and efforts.

Delivering the Informational Goods

Access to trustworthy, up-to-date information, as important as it is to the development of good performance strategies, is hard to arrange in many organizations. Here are four reasons why.

The Really Good Stuff Is a Secret. Information is a precious commodity in any organization and thus often is viewed as something to be protected from the curious eyes of outsiders. Many forward-looking firms do share with all organization members information about how the enterprise as a whole is doing. But strategically critical information often is quite closely held to keep it out of hands that senior managers view as unfriendly, such as competitors, regulators, or investigative reporters.

The airline industry is one in which traditional wisdom holds that secrets must be kept. Information about matters such as fare adjustments, marketing programs, aircraft acquisitions, and new cities to be served is shared only on a "need to know" basis. But what if an airline uses work teams whose members actually need such information to develop and execute their performance strategies? That was the problem faced by People Express Airlines, the company whose self-managing Customer Service Manager (CSM) teams were described in chapter 1. The CSM teams needed information about sensitive matters such as future book-ings to plan their work, but if that information were made available throughout the company there was a real risk that other airlines also could find out how things were going for the airline in various markets. "We cannot possibly tell our people about such important matters," one executive declaimed at a meeting about this issue. "Everybody around here has a neighbor who has a brother-in-law who works for [a competitor airline]. We tell *our* people, and it will be in *their* executive offices within a day." After a moment's reflection, another senior manager responded, "That may be true, but which would be worse, for [the competitor] to know or for our own people *not* to know?"

Put that way, the choice was clear. It was true that competitors never had much trouble finding out about the performance and plans of People Express, but it also was true that the airline's CSM teams were enor-mously aided by having ready access to that same information.[19] Support-ing work teams well sometimes requires that senior leaders take the risk of making even highly sensitive data available to teams if that is what they require to develop and execute performance strategies well tuned to the opportunities and constraints in the work setting.

Providers and Users Speak Different Languages.   There inevitably are omissions and distortions between what one person says and what another hears, a problem that is considerably exacerbated if the two peo-ple have different native languages or dialects. The informational dialect of those who analyze and summarize financial or operational data in organizations typically differs from that of the people who use those data in their work. A database generated by information professionals, for example, may come off the computer in a format that makes it difficult for end users to find and extract the specific information they need.

I once was paying a courtesy call on the CEO of a food products orga-nization where I was doing some research. He was brimming with enthusi-asm about the capabilities of the new information system that had gone on line a few days earlier. "Let me show you," he said, pushing keys on the computer beside his desk. "I can bring up anything I want to know. Financial data, operations, personnel, just anything. I don't have to ask other people to get me the information I need any more. I can do it myself." And, after a few false starts (he was just learning the system), he did indeed bring up a screen completely filled with rows and columns of numbers. I do not recall what the numbers were about, but I remember thinking that once the novelty of the new system had worn off (I gave that about a week) he would once again be asking other people to get him the information he needed. The data were there, to be sure, but in a format chosen by the programmers who wrote the code, not one that took explicit account of the needs, preferences, or cognitive style of even this Very Important Customer.

More than a few work teams in organizations have the same problem as that CEO. They are given access to information that could help them in planning and executing their work, but it is either so hard to bring the relevant data up on their computers or the data appear in a form so discrepant from what they are looking for that eventually they give up on the information system and devise alternative means to get the data they need. Some organizations do get it right, however. Managers charged with the design of a new engine manufacturing plant decided not to follow the standard production model for such facilities, in which an engine moves along a linear production line with individual workers performing specific tasks at work stations arrayed along the length of the line. Instead, self-managing work teams would be responsible for machining and assembling entire components of the engine, and some of their production "lines" would actually be circles. If one thinks of the production circle as a compass, work would enter slightly west of north, make its way around the compass, and leave slightly east of north. Team members would develop their own work strategies within broad limits, sharing tasks as appropriate, keeping track of production schedules, doing quality control, and so on. And positioned right at the center of the production circle would be the computer that would provide informational support as the team carried out all of these tasks.

The systems designers at this plant took special care to figure out what information the production teams needed to manage their work and made it easy for teams to obtain those data. The aspiration was for team members to be able to bring up, with just a few keystrokes, easily readable information about parts, schedules, or whatever other matters they required to manage their work with the fewest possible surprises or delays. These designers had taken the trouble to accommodate their own natural dialect to that of their clients, and they envisioned an information system that would put the users of information literally at the center of things.

Information: A Flood Is As Bad As a Drought.   Part of the problem the food products CEO encountered in using his new system was the format in which the data were presented, but perhaps a more significant problem was that his computer screen was so completely full of numbers. Too much information can be just as much a problem for a team that is trying to develop and execute a good performance strategy as too little. Particularly in this era of rapid advances in computer processing power and connectivity, information overload is becoming a nontrivial problem for many teams and organizations.[20]

State-of-the-art fighter aircraft are outfitted with a highly sophisticated array of electronic devices intended by their designers to provide pilots with the most complete picture possible of rapidly changing combat situations. A pilot of my acquaintance reports that his colleagues find these devices nothing short of amazing and that they love to experiment with them and explore the full range of their capabilities. But only when they have time to do so. When the going gets really rough on a training mission, he says, they start turning the devices off, one by one, until they reach the point at which they have just the information they need, but nothing beyond that, to successfully fly their mission.

I once had the opportunity to visit the emergency response center of a law enforcement organization.[21] The facility had been created so that a coordinated response to any developing crisis situation could be made quickly using the most up-to-the-moment information available. The duty chief (DC) of the facility stands at the open end of a U-shaped table. Around the table are arrayed representatives of various agencies who link the crisis team with other individuals and teams that provide the data the team needs to monitor the situation and develop a plan for dealing with it. On the wall behind the DC are several large screens on which current information about any developing situation is displayed. In a neighboring room are work stations manned by additional staff members who work their computers and telephones to feed data to the crisis team.

The facility is not filled with as much gee-whiz technology as one sees in the movies, but it really is the place where many diverse streams of data come together, are assessed, and are acted upon. How well does it work? Does the crisis team get all the information it needs, and get it quickly enough, to be able to make trustworthy assessments in real time and take appropriate action? According to one DC with whom I spoke, the team generally handles very well the training exercises that are conducted to keep the team's skills sharp. The only times when things don't go so well, he reported, is when a situation is so complex and fast changing that members find it almost beyond their capabilities to interpret and integrate into a coherent picture all the incoming information. "When we have an exercise that simulates a multipronged event," he said, "things get pretty chaotic in here." Since the main mission of the emergency response center is to deal with complex and fast-developing situations, I asked the DC how the crisis team prepares for such a contingency. "We practice, practice, and practice," he responded. "We make sure that when we have a highly demanding situation, we are prepared for it and ready to handle it."

The multiple information systems that support the crisis team can generate so much data that, in a simulated crisis, the team has to operate quite near the limit of its processing capability. To deal with that, the team does the same thing that an athletic team would do to prepare for a big game that will test its capabilities, or that an improvisational theater troupe would do before an important performance—it practices. When a real crisis occurs, members are about as well prepared as they can be, both mentally and psychologically, to process the flood of information the team receives. I left the facility impressed. But I also wondered if there might be a way to redesign or reconfigure the information systems that serve the crisis team so that, in a real crisis, members would not be operating quite as close to the upper limits of their collective information processing capabilities as they now do in the most demanding of their exercises.

Some teams are better able to handle a flood of information than others. Intact teams whose members stay together and regularly work together, for example, invariably hone their team performance strategies and become skilled at dealing with even the most challenging and information-intensive aspects of their work. (And yes, the crisis team fell into this category—it had reasonably stable membership, as did the other teams with whom members worked on their practice exercises.)

A second factor that helps a team deal competently with a flood of information has been identified by organizational sociologist Martine Haas in her research on project teams at an international development organization.[22] Because the main work of these teams was to acquire and process widely distributed knowledge, some managers in the enterprise held the view that the more information the project teams could access, the better their performance would be. But Haas found that receiving large amounts of information from multiple sources exposed teams to what she calls an "overload trap," which can result in a team metaphorically drowning in all the data with which members have to contend. It turned out that a team's vulnerability to this trap was strongly conditioned by how much autonomy the team had in devising its own performance strategy. Teams that were required to follow organizationally predetermined work procedures were at far greater risk than were teams that had the latitude to devise their own strategies for coping with their rich informational environments. Haas's findings further affirm the strong interdependence between how a team is structured (chapter 4) and how well it handles the resources, opportunities, and constraints in its work context.[23]

Information Really Is Power.   Power commonly is viewed as a resource like money in one's pocket, something that different people "have" in different amounts. It is there to be expended, but only sparingly and wisely. Managers who hold this view have sometimes been known to deliberately withhold performance-relevant information from the work teams they are supposed to be supporting, thereby preserving their informational resource. Although this may sustain a manager's feelings of personal power, it also can require a team to develop its performance strategies based on guesses rather than data about the performance situation and, ultimately, can result in needlessly poor team performance.

An alternative view of power, developed by sociologist Richard Emerson, views power as a property of a *relationship*.[24] In Emerson's way of thinking, relational power has two parts. One part is your power over me, which is the degree to which I am dependent on you for something you have and that I cannot readily obtain from other sources. The second part is my power over you, which is the degree to which you are dependent on me for something I have that you want and cannot readily obtain from other sources. A balanced power relationship is one in which we are more or less equally dependent on each other; an imbalanced power relationship exists when one party is much more dependent on the other.

The relationship between a team and its manager often is quite unequal, with the team being more dependent on the manager than vice versa. Strongly imbalanced power relations are disliked by whomever is on the short end of the power stick, and often prompt what Emerson calls "balancing operations." For example, the team might initiate a temporary work slowdown to demonstrate to its manager that dependency runs both ways. Balancing operations waste time and energy that otherwise could be used for productive work.

If a team were to gain direct access to informational resources that previously were available only to its manager, there would be two changes in the power equation. First, the team's dependency on the manager would be reduced (now members can get the information they need on their own); and second, the manager's dependency on the team would increase (he or she would have to trust members to use the information well in carrying out the team's work). The power equation no doubt would still be tilted in the manager's favor, since there are many other resources aside from information for which teams are dependent on their managers. But it would be a more balanced relationship than it was before, which usually is a far healthier state of affairs.[25] Indeed, to the extent that the team and its manager become increasingly interdependent, Emerson's equation shows that there is more total power in the system, which means that teams and their managers, working together, can get things done that otherwise might be difficult or impossible.

The Role of Information Professionals

It is tempting to hold an organization's information system staff primarily responsible for the quality of the informational resources that work teams have for use in their work. These professionals, surely, are the ones who should know how to provide teams with the data and projections that they require. It is true that it is never excusable for information professionals to provide teams (or anyone else) with an undifferentiated dump of all conceivably relevant data in a format that subordinates rather than highlights the particular information that users most need to know. But it also is true, in many organizations, that information staff have problems of their own— such as dealing with client teams who have not worked out with their managers what data and projections they actually need but who nonetheless expect the information system to magically give it to them, or handling disagreements within the providers' own organization about the proper strategy and technology for making information available to end users.

What information system designers attempted to do for production teams at the engine plant startup described earlier, for example, violated the standard ways of operating within their own functional group. Members of the system design team had to continuously manage a tension between their own aspiration to create a user-centric information system and the preference of senior information managers at corporate headquarters for a system that would maintain central control of information.[26] Moreover, since the engine production line was being designed simultaneously with the information system that would support its operation, information professionals had to deal with constantly changing customer requirements, including change requests that occasionally arrived well after they already had implemented what they thought their clients wanted.

Relationships between teams who provide information and those who use it always work better when *both* teams are themselves well designed and well led. Only then is there a reasonably good chance that providers and users will be able to work together to invent ways of getting client teams access to the right amount of the right information, presented in a format that makes it easy for the client teams to use in monitoring and managing their work. I try never to join in the chorus calling for "top-management commitment" as the key condition required for successful use of organizational work teams. (Indeed, unless I have a serious lapse of resolve that is the only time you will read the phrase in this book.) But getting information providers and users working together to create an information system that does well what it is supposed to do may be one case in which intervention is likely to be required by management that is senior to both the provider and the user teams.

EDUCATIONAL SYSTEM

The educational system of an organization should make training and technical assistance available to work teams for any aspects of the work in which members are not already sufficiently knowledgeable or skilled. As we saw in chapter 4, well-structured teams have a good mix of task and interpersonal skills—a pool of talent that members can further expand by sharing their special expertise with one another and by learning together from team successes and failures. Even so, teamwork commonly requires members to handle work-related issues for which their existing knowledge and skill are insufficient. Outside help and expertise can help a team transcend the limits of members' present expertise.

In one sales organization, for example, customer service agents were formed into teams and given full responsibility for, among other things, compiling and communicating to customers information about prices and availability of the company's products.[27] Previously, agents merely quoted data about such matters that had been prepared by a separate department. Group members were pleased that they now could manage their own database because the reports they formerly received often contained inconsistent or incomplete information. Unfortunately, members did not have knowledge and expertise sufficient for creating and maintaining a product information database. The result was frustration, impatience, and a perception by some managers that the work team idea was a bad one because "the rank-and-file people just can't handle the whole job." A few hours of training for the agents almost certainly would have solved the problem.

Providing training and technical consultation to work teams might appear to be more straightforward than revamping reward or information systems to support work teams, since many organizations already are ramped up to provide educational and consultative support to members who need it. Organizations commonly invest heavily in employee training, for example, and typically have deeply knowledgeable support staff available to lend a hand when problems of a technical nature develop. Moreover, as noted in chapter 2, merely arranging for training to be delivered to an intact work team (rather than to individuals who will work in different teams) significantly expands the team's available pool of knowledge and expertise and makes it possible for members to draw more efficiently on their peers' knowledge and expertise.[28]

Training and consultative resources are especially likely to be provided to teams as intact units when those who provide them view the consequences of mistakes and malfunctions as likely to be severe. Members of aircraft flight crews, for example, are given team-focused "crew resource management" courses in addition to their intensive initial and recurrent individual training.[29] Moreover, if a technical problem comes up on a trip, a crew can call on an impressive array of consultative resources to help members solve it in real time—crew members always can reach airline maintenance and dispatch staff by radio, who, if necessary, can patch the crew through to experts who work for other organizations, such as the aircraft manufacturer.[30]

That is how it should work for teams in any organization. A team that encounters gaps in members' knowledge or skills that are impeding its work should at least be able to tap their organization's educational or consultative resources to close those gaps and, ideally, to expand members' existing expertise. But that is harder than it sounds to arrange, especially when support staffs are unaccustomed to providing assistance directly to teams. In organizations with top-flight personnel departments, for example, training programs usually are based on systematic job analyses that identify the particular knowledge and skills needed by individuals who perform particular jobs. Members of work teams, however, need to know more things, and different things, than what individuals require to competently perform specific jobs. There is no reason why job analyses cannot also be done for team tasks, with training provided to teams based on the results of those analyses. But, in many organizations, doing this would require human resource staff both to take on some additional work and to develop strategies for carrying it out that are nontraditional in their profession.[31]

Getting Technical Help

Supporting teamwork often requires significant alterations in the ways technical support is delivered. Traditionally, those who directly generate organizational products or services do only that. When there is a problem, such as malfunctioning equipment, they are expected to inform their supervisor, who, after determining that the problem requires outside assistance, informs a supervisor or dispatcher in the relevant functional area, who in turn sends someone to take care of it.

That is how things worked in Hank's semiconductor manufacturing plant, and he was not happy about it. When the equipment used by one of his teams malfunctioned, a not uncommon occurrence in a technology-intensive production operation, teams had to wait, sometimes for what seemed to members like a long time, for someone from maintenance to show up and do the fix so they could get back to work. It felt like what happens at home when you call an appliance repair service and are told that a technician will arrive sometime between 10 A.M. and 4 P.M. the day after tomorrow. A second problem also bothered Hank, this one having to do with the relationship between his teams and the process engineers who designed and fine-tuned the technical aspects of the production process. Engineers occasionally would show up in the production area and say something like "Could you stop the process for a little while? We need to run a test batch through." These unscheduled interruptions not only frustrated team members, but also threw into disarray the production plans that Hank's teams had been given responsibility for devising and executing.

Hank wanted to do something about both matters, but there was a problem. Production workers, most of whom had no more than a high school education, ranked lowest in the plant's status system. Maintenance staff, all of whom had considerable technical training, ranked considerably higher, and the process engineers, with their master's or doctoral degrees, were the high priests of the plant. The same status hierarchy existed in managerial ranks: Maintenance and engineering managers were far better educated and better paid than Hank, and there was no way he could get away with telling them to change the way their staff members related to his production teams.

It happened that the semiconductor plant was located in a part of the country where large numbers of people go into the mountains to shoot deer for fun. And Hank was the proud owner of a four-wheel-drive pickup truck, a full complement of camping equipment, and an amazing collection of firearms. In the status hierarchy of the outdoors, Hank ranked much higher than did the heads of maintenance and engineering. So, early in the deer season one year, he invited them to join him on the mountain for a couple of days of hunting. Around the campfire on that trip began a series of conversations that extended over most of a year and that eventually resulted in a fundamental alteration of the relationship between Hank's groups and theirs.

Although the plant status system did not change, both the maintenance and the engineering groups came gradually, if wrenchingly, to understand that a major aspect of their work was to serve those who actually made the products the company sold. Each maintenance staff member became an "associate member" of a small number of production teams (the teams did not require a fully dedicated maintenance person). That person was the first one called when a problem developed with the equipment, was invited to team meetings and social events, and in many instances even tutored team members so they could handle routine technical problems themselves.

For example, maintenance previously would be called when the temperature of an oven went out of the allowable range—a common problem in semiconductor production. Once a maintenance person arrived, he or she usually could fix the problem quickly but, I observed, often did so from a position that made it impossible for team members to see exactly what was being done. After becoming affiliated with the production teams, the behavior of many maintenance staff members changed. "Usually fixing an out-of-range oven is just a matter of adjusting this control," he or she might say. "Try that yourself next time, and if it still doesn't come back into range, then give me a call."

Some of the engineers also changed how they related to the teams. They did not develop special relationships with any one team, but did refrain from descending unannounced upon a team to tell members to stop production so they could do their own work. Instead, an engineer might approach a production team leader ahead of time and ask when some tests could be run without disrupting the team's production schedule. That, too, was a fundamental change. Just as he had done in negotiating an exception to corporate compensation policy, Hank used quite nontraditional methods with the heads of maintenance and engineering to arrange supports for his work teams that almost certainly could not have been obtained through regular organizational channels.

Delivering the Educational Goods

Because work teams rarely have within their boundaries all of the knowledge, skill, and experience needed for optimum task performance, there almost always are some aspects of the work for which additional talent or expertise would be helpful. As we have seen, the educational system of an organization is critical in helping teams obtain such training or consultative support. For this to occur, however, two conditions must be met. First, the relevant resources must be identified and the people or groups in the broader organization who can supply them must be located. Second, some sort of delivery system must be put in place to make those resources accessible by teams. This second condition may not be a simple matter for front-line teams whose members previously have not had the right to call on staff assistance. Indeed, because well-designed work teams have the authority and responsibility to manage their own task performance processes, members may feel that asking for help is a sign that they have failed or that they are not willing to live up to their part of the bargain that was struck when their team was formed. It can take some time and tutoring by the team leader to help members break through this self-imposed barrier to asking for help.

The particular kind of assistance that will be most helpful to a given work team depends both on the requirements of the team's task and on its members' configuration of talents. The appropriate *form* of assistance varies as well. Sometimes a one-shot technical consultation will suffice, sometimes an ongoing consulting relationship will be what is needed, and sometimes a tailored training program can weave the relevant expertise into the fabric of the team itself. Whatever the content of the assistance or the vehicle used to provide it, the aspiration is the same: to help work teams that do not already have the full complement of knowledge and skill required for excellent task performance to obtain it.

CONTEXTUAL SUPPORTS AND INTERGROUP RELATIONS

A well-supported work team has a reward system that provides positive consequences for good team performance, an information system that provides the data and projections that members need to plan their performance strategy, and an educational system that provides any training and technical assistance the team may need. Another organizational support, not yet mentioned, also can be critical to team performance—the material resources that are available for use in carrying out the team's work.

Material resources such as equipment, money, staff time, and physical space seem mundane when compared with the power of an organization's reward, information, and educational systems to shape or constrain work team behavior. Yet resource availability can greatly smooth a team's path toward achieving its objectives—and resource insufficiency can be disastrous, even for a team that is otherwise well directed, structured, and supported.

Among the saddest of all the team failures I have observed are teams that have been wonderfully designed but whose members are unable to obtain the wherewithal they need to actually execute their work. This happens even for teams that generally are quite well supported, such as aircraft cockpit crews. Flights too often are delayed or even canceled because of problems with the availability of catering, fuel, deicing equipment, a tug for pushback, or even the aircraft itself. Some other group is actually responsible for each of these resource problems, of course, but they still weigh heavily on—and can mightily frustrate—members of the crew those other groups are supposed to be serving. For it is this crew who, at least as passengers see it (and sometimes say it), surely should be able to do *something* to get this plane off the gate.

It is no small undertaking to provide contextual supports to work teams that operate in organizations that have well-established operating policies and practices. Existing performance appraisal systems, for example, may be state of the art for measuring individual contributions but wholly inappropriate for assessing and rewarding work done by teams. Corporate compensation policy may make no provision for team bonuses and, indeed, may explicitly prohibit them. Human resource departments may be primed to identify individuals' training needs and to provide first-rate courses to fill those needs, but training in team skills (e.g., how to deal constructively with disagreements among members) may not be available at all. Information and control systems may provide senior executives with data that help them monitor and manage overall organizational performance, but teams may not be able to get the information they need to monitor and manage their own work processes.

Moreover, the finest support systems, the ones that reflect the best practice in their respective areas, often are the hardest of all to realign to support teamwork.[32] The professionals who have invested heavily in the development of such systems are, quite understandably, disinclined to toss them aside or redo them simply because somebody else has decided to use teams to perform organizational work. "Let's not rush into this," human resource, control system, engineering, or information system professionals may say to themselves. "Because if we wait it out, this too surely will pass."[33]

One cannot simply insert work teams into an existing organizational environment without also being prepared to alter that environment. But altering the behavior or preferences of other groups in an organization is fraught with risk. Especially when an enterprise is structured along functional lines, conflict can develop when a work team or its manager seeks to obtain from another group resources or support that the other group is disinclined to provide. In one organization I studied some years ago, it seemed as if the last thing members of one department wanted to do was anything that might make life a little easier for members of another department. That, of course, elicited negative reactions from members of both groups as they experienced growing frustration that another unit within their own organization seemed to be keeping them from getting on with their own organizational work. As each group became increasingly convinced of the validity of its views and increasingly vocal in expressing them, the developing conflict became self-fueling and increasingly hard to reverse.

Because such conflicts are so clearly not in the best interests of the organization as a whole, managers (unless they also have been caught up in the intergroup dynamics) usually try to smooth out problems between groups that show signs of escalation. They may take steps to ensure that everyone realizes that everyone's prosperity and continued employment depend on company-wide cooperation. They may convene meetings to improve between-department communication. Or they may issue a management edict that requires all groups to cooperate with each other.

But if an intergroup conflict stems from basic problems such as resource scarcity or an organizational design that fosters competition among groups or functions, such remedial efforts probably will be futile. Resolving emerging intergroup tensions before they spiral into flaming conflicts that defy containment requires that managers have sophisticated political and interpersonal skills, persistence and inventiveness, and a good sense of timing. How can the interests of other groups that are in a position to provide resources and support be engaged and aligned? If one strategy for getting producer and support groups pulling together toward collective objectives does not work, what other approaches might be tried? When should action be initiated, and when would it be better to lie in wait for a more opportune moment, one when usually stable organizational systems become temporarily unfrozen? Managers who have such skills and who use them well in negotiating with their peers and bosses can do much to empower the teams for which they are responsible, enabling them to give full attention to *their* special responsibilities without constant distractions and irritations from support problems that properly are someone else's concern.[34]

6

Expert Coaching

You are the coach of a high school basketball team. With just five games to go in the season, your team has a shot at the conference championship. Tonight is a must-win contest against the other championship contender. The players have completed their warm-up on the court and are now trooping into the locker room, where you will have a few minutes with them before the game begins. What do you want to accomplish in those few minutes? And how will you go about doing it?

Now it's halftime, and you are down by four points. Your team has played well, but the opponents played just a bit better—especially on defense. They succeeded in bottling up your best shooter, and toward the end of the half she was showing visible signs of frustration at her inability to get free to receive the ball. On the other hand, your defense has been almost as tight as theirs and the game looks to be one of the lowest-scoring contests of the season. While the players head for the locker room, you remain on the court briefly to check your observations about the first half with your assistant coach. What do you want to accomplish when you join the players in the locker room? And how will you go about doing it?

Now it's the day after the game, and the players have arrived for practice in a celebratory mood. Down three points with two minutes to go last night, the offense suddenly jelled. In a spurt of intense and beautiful basketball, the team racked up seven points in rapid succession while holding the opponents scoreless. The four-point win felt like a rout, and horseplay and jollity abound in the prepractice warm-up. With the four remaining games all against lesser teams, the championship looks to be yours for the taking. You signal a halt to the warm-up and call the players to the sidelines to begin today's practice. What do you want to accomplish in this session? And how will you go about doing it?

These are the kinds of decisions that coaches must make all the time, regardless of whether they aim to help an athletic team play well, a service team please its customers, or an executive team make good decisions. Coaches, like the rest of us, think explicitly about concrete problems that they encounter, especially when those problems pack an emotional punch, and craft specific interventions that they think will help.[1] If, for example, the star of your basketball team had become obviously sullen or verbally aggressive about the fact that her teammates were not getting her the ball often enough, you unquestionably would have thought carefully about alternative ways of responding before taking action.

But when there is no specific, pressing problem to be solved, the human tendency is to keep on relatively mindlessly doing what one always has done, until something pops up that clearly does demand explicit attention and planned action.[2] That is why coaches so often overlook or underexploit the special coaching opportunities that always are present at the beginnings, midpoints, and ends of task cycles. These oversights can be costly, because proactive coaching provided at the proper times in a team's life can head off team process problems that might otherwise emerge and, moreover, can increase the likelihood that the problems that *do* develop can be resolved without distracting members too much from their real work. Well-timed coaching for a team is like preventive maintenance for an automobile: We often forget to do it, but it can prevent future breakdowns and costly repairs.

WHAT TEAM COACHING IS ABOUT

Coaching is about group processes. It involves direct interaction with a team that is intended to help members use their collective resources well in accomplishing work. Examples of coaching include leading a launch meeting before work begins (which can help members become oriented to and engaged with their task), providing the team feedback about its problem analysis (which can increase the quality of its analytic work), or asking a team reflective questions about why members made a particular decision (which can help them make better use of their knowledge and experience). By contrast, a leader who personally coordinates the work of a team or who negotiates outside resources for its use is doing things that can be quite helpful to the team—but he or she is not coaching. Coaching is about building teamwork, not about doing the team's work.

Coaching can address any aspect of team interaction that is impeding members' ability to work well together or that shows promise of strengthening team functioning. In practice, however, a more focused approach brings better results. Research has identified three aspects of group interaction that have special leverage in shaping team effectiveness: the amount of *effort* members apply to their collective work, the appropriateness to the task and situation of the *performance strategies* they employ in carrying out the work, and the level of *knowledge and skill* they apply to the work.[3] Any group that expends sufficient effort in its work, deploys a performance strategy that is well aligned with task requirements, and brings ample talent to bear on its task is quite likely to achieve a high standing on the three criteria of work team effectiveness discussed in chapter 1. By the same token, teams that operate in ways that compromise their standing on these three performance processes—that is, members apply insufficient effort, inappropriate strategies, or inadequate talent to their work—probably will fall short on one or more of the effectiveness criteria.

To illustrate, consider customer service teams (CSTs) at Xerox.[4] When a photocopier stops working, the customer wants it fixed instantly. The task of the CSTs is to do just that—and to do it efficiently (spending no more time with a machine than actually is needed), inexpensively (keeping parts costs low), and well (fixing the machine so it stays fixed). Each team has a set of machines for which members collectively are responsible, usually associated with a geographical area or a single large customer such as a university or a corporation. CSTs at Xerox, under the guidance of Chuck Ray and his colleagues, generally performed quite well. But imagine, for a moment, the pattern of interaction that might have characterized one of the *worst* teams in the company.

As is common for CSTs, members of this hypothetical, poorly performing team meet at a coffee shop before launching the day's work. Members dawdle over breakfast, talking about anything but their work. The rest of the day also is leisurely, with technicians spending nearly as much time chatting up customers as working on machines. Individual technicians go through their paces, responding to the dispatcher's directives about where to go next, and calling a headquarters technical specialist if they encounter an unfamiliar machine malfunction. Any lessons learned in the course of the day are kept to one's self, and individuals rarely ask their teammates for help when a machine insists on staying broken. For this team, collective effort is low, members have no shared strategy about how they will approach their team's work, and they neither share their expertise with one another nor draw on their teammates' special skills. The customers of a team with these work processes would not enthuse about the service they receive, and company managers probably would have reason for concern about the team's speed of response and parts expenses. Nor is it likely that the team would spontaneously become stronger as a performing unit over time or that members would get much learning or fulfillment from their work experiences. This hypothetical team, then, would surely score low on all three of the criteria of team effectiveness discussed in chapter 1.

Now imagine that we have a magic wand that, when passed over members' heads while they are sipping their start-of-day coffee, completely reverses their standing on these same three performance processes. The content of the team's conversation is transformed into an informal but focused review of what went well and poorly the previous day, and what the team can learn from that. Members examine the work that is already laid out for the present day and discuss how they might get as far ahead as possible as soon as possible so they will be able to free up a member should a customer emergency arise. Given what they already know about the nature of the machine problems at various sites, about the special expertise of each member, and about their geographical area, they decide how to divide up and sequence the morning's work. As the day progresses, they are in frequent touch with one another by telephone to see how things are going and to fine-tune their strategy in response to any unanticipated problems or opportunities. When one member gets stuck on a particularly difficult job that looks as if it may require replacement of some expensive parts, the member who has the most experience with that particular machine type heads off to assist the stuck colleague. The team leader confers with other team members about how their work plans should be revised to accommodate this unanticipated (but not uncommon) development. As the day progresses, each member makes notes about things learned and problems encountered that may warrant discussion at the next morning's breakfast meeting. The application of a little magic has resulted in a remarkable turnaround in the team's level of collective effort, in the task appropriateness of its work strategy, and in the utilization of its members' talents. And, surely, this transformed team would stand high on all three effectiveness criteria.

There is, of course, no magic wand for leaders to use in shaping up a shoddy team. Still, as we have seen in previous chapters, there is much they can do when setting up a team to improve the chances that its performance processes will more closely approximate the second team than the first in the above illustration: They can provide their teams with a compelling direction, an enabling team structure, and a supportive organizational context.[5] These basic conditions provide the foundation for superb team performance, and no amount of coaching can compensate if they are badly flawed. When conditions *are* favorable, however, coaching can significantly enhance team performance processes. To see how, we need to look more closely at each of the three processes to identify the opportunities, and the vulnerabilities, a team encounters in managing member effort, in selecting and implementing its task performance strategies, and in utilizing members' talents. We do that in the next section, and then identify what coaches can do—and when they can do it—to help a work team manage the three key performance processes efficiently and well.

PROCESS LOSSES AND GAINS

All task-performing teams encounter what psychologist Ivan Steiner calls "process losses," and all potentially can create synergistic process gains. Process losses are inefficiencies or internal breakdowns that keep a group from doing as well as it theoretically could, given its resources and member talents.[6] They develop when members interact in ways that depress the team's effort, the appropriateness of its strategy, or the utilization of member talent, and they waste or misapply member time, energy, and expertise. Process gains develop when members interact in ways that enhance collective effort, generate uniquely appropriate strategies for working together, or actively develop members' knowledge and skills. When this happens, the team has created *new* internal resources that can be used in its work, capabilities that did not exist before the team created them. As seen in table 6-1, there are special kinds of process losses and process gains associated with each of the three performance processes.

Effort

There are always some "overhead costs" to be paid when groups perform tasks. Merely coordinating members' activities, for example, takes some time and energy away from productive work, resulting in a level of actual productivity that is less than what would be obtained if members used their resources completely efficiently. The most pernicious effort-related process loss, however, is social loafing—the tendency we all have to slack off a bit when working in groups, to exert less effort on team tasks than we do when performing work that is ours alone. As noted in chapter 4, social loafing occurs because individuals usually can hide to some extent in a team. Moreover, each team member may feel less personally responsible for collective performance outcomes because there are, so to speak, multiple hands on the wheel.

For very large groups with very boring tasks, such as two dozen volunteers who share responsibility for stuffing thousands of envelopes for a political campaign, social loafing can become too pervasive for members

---

TABLE 6 - 1

Characteristic Process Losses and Gains for Each of the Three Performance Processes

Effort
Process loss: Social loafing by team members
Process gain: Development of high shared commitment to the team and its work

Performance Strategy
Process loss: Mindless reliance on habitual routines
Process gain: Invention of innovative, task-appropriate work procedures

Knowledge and Skill
Process loss: Inappropriate weighting of member contributions
Process gain: Sharing of knowledge and development of member skills

to ignore.[7] When that happens, the motivational problems themselves may become the main topic of discussion in the group, distracting members from their real work and inducing conflict among them as they struggle to understand why the team isn't getting much of anything done.

The process gain for effort develops when members become highly committed to their team, proud of it, and willing to work especially hard to make it one of the best. In a phrase, they have developed "team spirit." When this happens, members may exhibit high, task-focused effort even if objective performance conditions are unfavorable—for example, when members develop such a strong "can do" attitude that each new adversity is framed as yet another challenge to be surmounted.

Leaders appear to have great love for team spirit and maintain abundant optimism about its ability to induce members to give their all to their work. For this reason, leaders sometimes encourage teams to give themselves a name, to decorate their work area, or to participate in an athletic league, all in hopes of building spirit and commitment. Such ploys are not likely to work if the team task is not inherently worth caring about (chapter 4) or if the organizational reward system does not recognize and reinforce team excellence (chapter 5). But when the task is at least moderately engaging, team spirit can indeed generate significant motivational gains.[8]

Performance Strategy

If a piece of work is familiar to a team—or even if it merely *seems* familiar—members' previously developed performance routines usually kick in and guide their behavior. Habitual routines are highly efficient in that team members do not have to actively deliberate about how to proceed with each piece of work. But reliance on routines also invites significant process losses, especially when members are so focused on task execution that they do not notice that the task or situation has changed.

This process loss may have played a significant role in the tragic crash of Air Florida Flight 90 into the 14th Street Bridge shortly after takeoff from Washington National Airport on a snowy January afternoon in 1982. The National Transportation Safety Board (NTSB) determined that "the probable cause of the accident was the flight crew's failure to use engine anti-ice during ground operation and take-off, and their decision to take off with snow/ice on the airfoil surfaces of the aircraft, and the captain's failure to reject the takeoff during the early stage when his attention was called to anomalous engine instrument readings."[9] The cockpit voice recorder for the period just after the engines were started shows how habitual routines may have contributed to the tragedy. The captain had called for the after-start checklist, a standard procedure intended to make sure that an aircraft is set up properly for taxi. As is typical, the first officer read each checklist item, and the captain responded after checking the appropriate indicator in the cockpit.

First Officer: Electrical.

Captain: Generators.

First Officer: Pitot heat.

Captain: On.

First Officer: Anti-ice.

Captain: Off.

First Officer: Air-conditioning pressurization.

Captain: Packs on flight.

First Officer: APU.

Captain: Running.

First Officer: Start levers.

Captain: Idle.

First Officer: Door warning lights.

Captain: Out.[10]

The checklist is a routine, run every time engines are started. The standard response to the "Anti-ice" query that I have italicized is indeed "Off," especially in the summer and for crews that typically operate in warm or dry climates—as was the case for this crew. The oft-repeated litany may have become so ingrained for these crew members that they did not even consider the possibility that their situation required a nonroutine response to a routine query.

The crew had a second chance to save the flight several minutes later, as the takeoff roll began. Here is the NTSB summary of that portion of the transcript:

At 1559:46, the sound of engine spoolup was recorded, and the captain stated, "Holler if you need the wipers. . . ." At 1559:56, the captain commented, "Real cold, real cold," and at 1559:58 the first officer remarked, "God, look at that thing, that don't seem right, does it?" Between 1600:05 and 1600:10, the first officer stated, ". . . that's not right . . . ," to which the captain responded, "Yes it is, there's eighty." The first officer reiterated, "Naw, I don't think that's right." About 9 seconds later the first officer added, ". . . maybe it is," but then 2 seconds later, after the captain called "hundred and twenty," the first officer said, "I don't know."[11]

Less than a minute later, the aircraft crashed into the bridge. The first officer, who was the pilot actually flying the aircraft, noted that something seemed wrong ("God, look at that thing, that don't seem right, does it?"), but the captain did not respond. When he repeated his concern, the captain provided reassurance ("Yes it is, there's eighty"). Even though the first officer was not convinced ("Naw, I don't think that's right"), he continued down the runway. The takeoff routine was still not broken, despite the availability of data indicating that it was not proceeding normally.

Although rarely so dramatic or consequential as for the Air Florida flight, mindless reliance on habitual routines results in suboptimal performance for many organizational work teams. One of its more virulent forms is seen when team members develop a pattern of interaction that makes it virtually impossible for them *ever* to implement new performance plans. Members of such teams may have ample information about the performance situation and may even have fashioned a performance strategy that would be nicely attuned to that situation. But once the plans are complete they are ignored. When members reconvene, they develop more new plans and another new resolve—and then the cycle repeats. The team's inevitable failures are driven by standard routines that are wrapped in new, better, but never-implemented performance strategies. This dynamic often is driven by unconscious forces, and it can be lethal to team effectiveness.[12]

On the positive side, teams sometimes develop ways of interacting that result in truly original or insightful methods of proceeding with the work, a synergistic process gain. For example, a group might find a means to exploit some resources that everyone else has overlooked, invent steps to get around a seemingly insurmountable performance obstacle, or come up with a novel way to generate ideas for solving a difficult problem. Developing innovative performance strategies involves two different activities. First, scanning both the team's external environment and the state of its internal resources for emerging problems and opportunities. Second, generating and assessing a variety of ways the team might circumvent the problems and exploit the opportunities, eventually choosing the one that seems to team members especially suitable. When a team gets in the habit of regularly doing these scanning and planning activities, which is especially likely when the team's norms support them (chapter 4), genuinely innovative ways of proceeding with the work often emerge—strategies that did not even exist before the group invented them.

Knowledge and Skill

One of the most common and pernicious process losses encountered by task-performing teams is the inappropriate weighting of members' contributions. The credence given to a member's thoughts and ideas generally depends far too much on that person's demographic attributes (e.g., gender, age, or ethnicity), position in the organization or broader community (e.g., rank or office), or behavioral style (e.g., talkativeness or verbal dominance). When a team gives more weight to such factors than to what the person actually knows about the work, it wastes one of its most precious commodities—the talents of its members.

Assessing which members have the special expertise needed for a given part of the collective work is not easy. What members know, and know how to do, is not nearly so apparent to their teammates as are each member's surface attributes. In the absence of clear data about expertise, the human tendency is to turn to surrogates that *are* visible. But those surrogates invite the use of social stereotypes and, almost inevitably, result in inefficient weighting of members' contributions. Everyone "knows" that women are less skilled in quantitative matters than are men, so the female member of the team who, unknown to her colleagues, has a master's degree in quantitative economics is overlooked when it comes time to decide who will take main responsibility for the part of the work that involves quantitative analyses.

Even when team members do recognize one another's differences in knowledge or skill, they may not act on that information. We all have been in teams where members defer to the views of the person who holds a position of formal authority (e.g., a boss) or who has especially high status (e.g., a prize-winning scientist or an elected official), even though everyone knows that someone else in the group actually knows more about the task at hand. To the extent a team is able to minimize the problem of inappropriate weighting of members' talents, it will take better advantage of the expertise that was put in the group when it was composed. That is much easier to advocate than to practice, however, especially in the midst of fast-paced task work in a politically charged organizational context.

The process gain for knowledge and skill comes when team members develop a pattern of interaction that fosters learning from one another, thereby increasing the *total* pool of knowledge available for work on the team task. The practice of cross-training, often encouraged in self-managing work teams in industry, is an example of such behavior, as are more informal activities that involve the sharing of knowledge, expertise, and experience among members. Cross-functional teams are especially good sites for generating process gains of this kind, since they enjoy a diverse configuration of member knowledge and skill. Yet even in relatively homogeneous teams there always are things for work team members to learn from one another and new learning to be generated that expands a team's total pool of talent.

From Process to Performance

Task-performing teams are always at risk of falling victim to process losses that compromise their potential—but they also always have the chance to generate synergistic process gains. Teams that minimize the losses and maximize the gains can turn in performances that far outstrip what could be obtained by merely stitching together the separate contributions of individual team members.

The dynamics of the customer service team described earlier illustrated just how bad things can get when process losses dominate members' interactions. Whatever motivational impulses individual members might have brought to work on a given day were swamped by the insistently social character of the team's interaction over breakfast. Rather than develop a performance strategy tailored to the day's task requirements, members took a relatively mindless and reactive stance toward the team's work, doing what they were told to do the way they were told to do it without monitoring the situation to see if any changes from service-as-usual might be indicated. And if the team's weighting of members' contributions was not noticeably inappropriate, that was only because the team mostly ignored the special skills, interests, and experience of its members.

After the application of the magic, however, that customer service team demonstrated how good things can get when team processes are managed well. The team now kept process losses to a minimum, to be sure. But beyond that, members developed pride in their team and reinforced shared commitment to it, which got them out of the coffee shop and onto customers' premises as soon as they had developed their work plan for the day. That plan, moreover, took account of both the day's work requirements and the special skills and preferences of individual members, and it had built-in flexibility so the team would be able to respond quickly to any customer emergencies. Members turned to one another for help and expertise when dealing with particularly challenging repair problems, kept personal logs of technical issues that came up during the day, and reviewed those issues together over breakfast the next morning. Over time, this team became an increasingly capable performing unit, and eventually, individual members were selected by management to seed other teams with the expertise and team skills they had developed.[13]

Sometimes teams spontaneously develop task processes as magical as those just described. More often, however, it takes competent, persistent coaching to help a team become this good. We turn next, therefore, to what it is that coaches actually do—and when in a team's life cycle they do it—to foster superb team processes.

WHAT COACHES DO AND WHEN THEY DO IT

A coaching intervention is any action that seeks to minimize process losses or to foster process gains for any of the three key performance processes. Coaching that addresses effort is *motivational* in character; its functions are to minimize free riding and to build shared commitment to the group and its work. Coaching that addresses performance strategy is *consultative* in character; its functions are to minimize thoughtless reliance on habitual routines and to foster the invention of ways of proceeding with the work that are especially well aligned with task and situational requirements and opportunities. Coaching that addresses knowledge and skill is *educational* in character; its functions are to minimize suboptimal weighting of members' contributions and to foster the development of members' knowledge and skill.

Coaching that succeeds in reducing losses or fostering gains for one or more of the three performance processes virtually always contributes to overall team effectiveness. This kind of coaching can be done by anyone (including rank-and-file team members, external managers, and outside consultants—not just a person officially designated as "team leader")—and it can be provided at any time in the course of a team's work. There are, nonetheless, three particular times in a team's life when members are likely to be especially receptive to each of the three types of coaching interventions. And, as we will see, there are other times in a team's life cycle when even competent coaching is unlikely to make much of a difference in how well members work together.

Group life cycles have been empirically explored for many years, and a number of conceptual frameworks have sought to summarize findings about group development—the most prominent being the "forming-storming-norming-performing" model proposed by Bruce Tuckman.[14] Almost all of these frameworks have viewed group development as following a fixed set of stages, with each successive stage being contingent on successful completion of the previous one (although the possibility of returning to an earlier stage to complete unfinished developmental work is allowed by some models).

In recent years, research on temporal issues in group development and performance has raised doubt about the generality and validity of stage models.[15] The findings of organizational psychologist Connie Gersick are especially useful in explaining why certain kinds of coaching interventions are uniquely helpful at different times in the team life cycle. In a field study of the life histories of a number of task-performing teams, Gersick found that each of the groups she tracked developed a distinctive approach toward its task as soon as it commenced work, and stayed with that approach until almost exactly halfway between its first meeting and its project deadline.[16] At the midpoint of their lives, all teams underwent a major transition. In a concentrated burst of changes, they dropped old patterns of behavior, reengaged with outside supervisors, and adopted new perspectives on their work. Following the midpoint transition, groups entered a period of focused task execution, which persisted until very near

FIGURE 6 - 1

The Temporal Appropriateness of Coaching Interventions

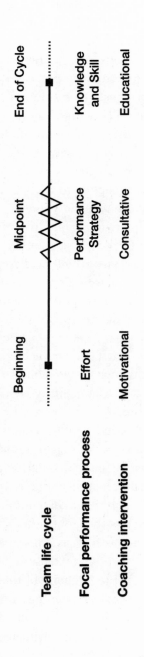

the project deadline, at which time a new set of issues having to do with termination processes arose and captured members' attention.

Gersick's findings suggest that when a team is just starting a new piece of work, members may be especially open to interventions that address their level of engagement with the team and its work. The midpoint, when half the allotted time has elapsed (or, perhaps, the work is half done), is a uniquely appropriate time for interventions that help members reflect on how well their performance strategies are working, and to change them if needed. And the end, when a work cycle has been completed, is the time when a team is ready to entertain interventions aimed at helping members learn from their experiences. The proper times for motivational, consultative, and educational interventions are summarized in figure 6-1.[17]

Beginnings

There is much on a team's plate when members first come together to perform a piece of work—establishing the boundary that distinguishes members from nonmembers, starting to formulate member roles and behavioral norms, and engaging with (and, inevitably, redefining) the group task. Members' decisions about such matters, whether made explicitly or implicitly, establish a track for the group on which members stay for a considerable time.[18] A coaching intervention that helps a team have a good launch increases the chances that the track will be one that enhances members' commitment to the team and motivation for its work.

To illustrate, we return to the cockpit to examine the behavior of airline captains during the first few minutes of a crew's life. As noted in chapter 4, the basic structure of cockpit crews, what Robert Ginnett and I call the team "shell," is already in place when the crew first meets. The aircraft to be flown, where it is to be flown, the roles of each crew member, basic work procedures such as checklists, and much more are all prespecified and well understood by each crew member. Ginnett's extensive experience as a cockpit observer led him to suspect that the behavior of captains when they first met with their crews might also have enduring effects on crew dynamics. Commercial aviation provided a nearly ideal setting in which to test this possibility, since the bidding system commonly used by airlines results in a constant flow of crews forming, working together for a limited time (often a single day and rarely more than a few days), and then disbanding.

Sure enough, what happened in the first few minutes of crew members' time together did carry forward throughout a crew's life.[19] Crews led by captains who merely took the time in their preflight briefings to affirm the positive features of the crew shell fared better than those who received no briefing at all or who received one that undermined the standard shell. Best of all were crews whose captains went beyond mere affirmation and actively elaborated the shell—identifying, commenting on, and engaging their crews in discussion of the unique circumstances of the trip that was about to begin. These captains transformed a highly competent set of individual pilots into a motivated flight *crew*. Ginnett's findings demonstrated that the initial meeting of the crew is a uniquely good time to accomplish that.[20]

Most work teams do not have structures as detailed and elaborate as those of cockpit crews. But the leader's behavior at the launch meeting of any type of work team serves essentially the same function as that of Ginnett's captains—namely, to breathe life into the team's structural shell, no matter how rudimentary it may be, and thereby help the team start functioning on its own. If the launch meeting is successful, the team leader will have helped the team move from being just a list of names to being a real, bounded social system. The official task that the team was assigned will have been examined, assessed, and then redefined to become the slightly different task that members actually work on.[21] And the norms of conduct specified by those who created the team will have been assessed, tried out (sometimes explicitly but more often implicitly through members' behaviors), and gradually revised and made the team's own.

Midpoints

If the beginning of a team's life is a good time for bounding a team and getting collective engagement with its task, would it not also be an excellent time for members to work out the performance strategy they will use in carrying out the work? That is what Janet Weiss, Ken Brousseau, and I thought, and we set out to demonstrate it in an experimental study many years ago. Specifically, we proposed that teams that took time to explore alternative ways of proceeding with a task before actually starting work on it would do better than teams that plunged immediately into their work— but only on tasks for which the most obvious and natural way of proceeding was actually not the best strategy.[22]

We devised a team task that involved the construction of fairly simple electrical devices and set up the task in two different ways. In one setup, the most obvious and natural way of proceeding was in fact optimum for team performance, but in the other, that way of proceeding would necessarily introduce some inefficiencies into the work and result in suboptimal performance. Moreover, some groups were instructed to plunge right into the work without talking over alternative ways of proceeding with the work; others were instructed to do the opposite.

Results were just as we expected: The "plunge right in" groups did better than the "discuss your strategy first" groups on the version of the task for which the obvious way of proceeding was also the optimum strategy, and the reverse was true for the version of the task for which the obvious way of proceeding was suboptimal. But perhaps the most significant finding of the study is buried in the discussion section of our research report—namely, that it was nearly impossible to get our groups to actually *have* a discussion of performance strategy at the start of the work period. Only by structuring the strategy intervention as a "preliminary task" and explicitly requiring the team to check off each step of that task when they completed it were we able to induce groups to have more than a perfunctory discussion of their performance strategy. The beginning was simply the wrong time for the strategy intervention, because strategy discussions are something of an unnatural act when a new team is just beginning work on a new task. Members need to log some actual experience with a task before they are able to have a useful discussion of how they can best go about accomplishing their work.

The midpoint of a team's life cycle, when a team is likely to experience a naturally occurring upheaval in how members are relating to one another and to their work, turns out to be an especially good time for a coaching intervention that invites them to reflect on the team's performance strategy. At such times (or at other natural breakpoints or low-workload periods), coaching interventions that encourage members to mindfully reflect on their work thus far and on the challenges they next will face can be quite helpful to them in revising and improving their plans for the next phase of their work.

Research by organizational psychologist Anita Woolley provides compelling support for this proposition. She devised an experimental version of an architectural task, involving construction of a college residence hall out of Lego bricks. Groups were informed in advance how the structures they created would be evaluated, on dimensions that included sturdiness (assessed using a "drop test" unique in the annals of architecture), aesthetics, and technical indices involving floor space, number of floors, and so on. She devised two coaching-type interventions, one intended to improve members' interpersonal relations, and another that provided assistance to the team in developing a task-appropriate performance strategy. Each team received only one intervention, which was administered either at the beginning or at the midpoint of its work period.[23]

Woolley's findings, shown in figure 6-2, confirm that strategy interventions are especially helpful when they come near the midpoint of a team's work cycle. When the strategy intervention was administered at the beginning of the work period, before members had logged some experience with the task, it did not help. Note also that the intervention that addressed members' *interpersonal* relationships rather than their task processes made no difference whatever in team performance, regardless of when it was administered—an important finding to which we will return shortly.

Let us now leave the experimental laboratory and return briefly to the cockpit. Might the research findings just summarized have any relevance

FIGURE 6 - 2

Coaching Type and Timing

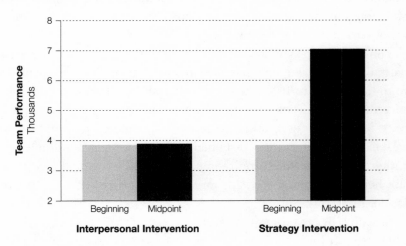

Source: Based on findings from Woolley (1998).

for captains' coaching of their flight crews? What is the equivalent of the "midpoint" for such crews? And what might captains do at such a point to build on the good team launch they provided at the initial crew briefing? There are, in fact, naturally occurring low-workload times in the life cycles of cockpit crews, such as extended cruise at altitude, and overnights on multiday trips. Although I am aware of no systematic research on the matter, my own cockpit observations suggest that there is wide variation across captains in how they use these periods. Some overlook the coaching opportunities offered by midpoints and other low-workload times, using those occasions either for personal matters or for conversations that are entirely social in character. Others, however, often raise a question or make an observation during a low-workload time that invites other crew members to join in reflecting on how the crew has been operating thus far in the trip and to consider what changes, if any, they might want to make as the rest of the trip unfolds. Even gentle coaching interventions such as these can be of considerable value in strengthening a crew and increasing the alignment of its performance strategies with the requirements of its flying task.

Coaching about performance strategy helps team members stay closely in touch with changing demands and opportunities in their environment and encourages them to find ways to implement their chosen performance strategies mindfully and efficiently. Strategy-focused coaching also can help members find or invent new performance strategies that are more appropriate to the task and environment than those they previously had been using. It even can prompt a team to engage in some persuasion or political action to try to negotiate a change in organizational constraints that may be impeding their performance.

That such behaviors would help a flight crew seems clear. I would go further and suggest that competent, well-timed coaching about performance strategy is helpful to virtually any task-performing team. The interventions that are commonly used in Total Quality Management (TQM) programs, for example, are explicitly focused on the development of improved production strategies. Moreover, a number of these techniques (e.g., Pareto analyses, control charts, cost-of-quality analyses, and fishbone diagrams) literally cannot be used until a solid record of experience with existing strategies has been amassed—once again affirming that strategy-focused coaching is more appropriately provided around the middle of a task cycle than at its beginning.[24]

Endings

People do not learn well when they are preoccupied, anxious, or hurried. If team members are thrashing about trying to figure out just what it is that they are supposed to do, or if they are in a headlong rush to get their work done on time, it is doubtful that they will make much headway in building their individual or collective knowledge and skill. Team learning requires, at minimum, some protected time and at least a moderate level of collective safety, conditions that are hard to create when members are right in the middle of task execution.[25]

Because anxieties and arousal dissipate somewhat once a piece of work is finished, postperformance periods offer an especially good time for coaching interventions aimed at helping members capture and internalize the lessons that can be learned from their work experiences. Even then, however, team members may be disinclined to exploit the learning opportunities that are available to them. When a team learns that it has performed splendidly—for example, an athletic team that has won the championship game or a task force whose project proposal has been approved—members may be much more disposed to celebrate their success than to explore what they can learn from their experience. Celebration is to be valued because it confirms that the team has done well and it fosters collective internal motivation. But if receiving positive performance feedback prompts nothing more than that, members may fail to notice those aspects of the feedback that could help them learn how to work together even more effectively in the future. It is fine for a basketball team to hoist the coach to members' shoulders to cut the net from the hoop; but in the locker room later, or at practice the next day, the team also should take a few moments to reflect on the lessons to be learned from its victory.

On the downside, members of a team that has suffered a setback may experience a pervasive sense of gloom and shared feelings of dismay about their failure. Such feelings can be helpful to the team if they serve as a motivational prod to try harder next time. But members may also experience a strong collective impulse to turn defensively away from the learning opportunities that failure always brings, to spend more energy rationalizing why the failure wasn't really their fault than exploring what might be learned from it. Helping a group work through such impulses and move into a learning mode requires considerable coaching skill. Developing a team to the point that members learn *how* best to learn from one another, and from collective failures as well as successes, is a magnificent coaching achievement.

Getting members to generate and discuss their explanations for the team's level of performance is but the first step in helping a team develop its knowledge and skill. The next and harder step is getting those explanations at least approximately aligned with reality, as organizational psychologist Richard Corn discovered in a field study of team attribution-making processes.[26] Corn identified a diverse set of task-performing teams in organizations, some of which had performed well and some of which had not, and asked members of each team to explain why the team had performed as it did. Few of their explanations addressed the kinds of team and organizational features discussed in chapters 4 and 5 that may have largely driven the team's performance outcomes. Even in a session explicitly devoted to learning from their experiences, team members often need assistance in recognizing and addressing the ways that aspects of their own structure or organizational context may have shaped their performance.

Although most of the pilots Robert Ginnett and I observed would have acknowledged that useful insights might well emerge from a few minutes of collective reflection at the end of a trip, almost none of the crews we studied actually took the time to do that. Why not? For one thing, the prospect of sitting around talking about what might be learned from their work together surely would seem to some pilots to be an unnatural act. Moreover, most flights are so routine that crews may not feel there is any pressing need to review and reflect on what has transpired. But probably the major reason why debriefings do not occur is also the most prosaic: When the aircraft blocks in at the end of a trip, a simple, three-step behavioral plan takes over. One: get the passengers off and get the paperwork done. Two: get to the parking lot. And three: *get home.* A captain who suggests that the crew delay departure for home in favor of a few minutes of reflection is a captain who likes to fight losing battles. (This does not reflect an antilearning stance on the part of pilots. College professors, whose main business is learning, would be equally incredulous if their department chair were to suggest that a faculty meeting be extended beyond the usual 5:30 P.M. ending time so that members could reflect together on the lessons to be learned from the day's deliberations.)

Yet in the right circumstances it can happen. One way to make it happen is to have some authority and use it. Military aviators, for example, are surely just as motivated to get home at the end of the day as are their counterparts in commercial aviation. But they do not leave until their crew debriefing is finished. Although crew members stay because they are required to, they invariably learn a thing or two from having participated, however reluctantly, in some collective reflection on their performance as a team. And eventually, postflight debriefings become part of the routine, just another feature of the way things are done in military aviation.

Debriefings also can become routine even when they are not formally required, as I discovered while assisting Ruth Wageman with her research at Xerox. I had occasion to sit in on many meetings with service organization managers as part of the research, but it is the first of them that sticks in my mind. We had finished our work and I was gathering my papers to depart when Tom Ruddy, the Xerox staffer who was facilitating the meeting, segued into a postmeeting review. "What did we do especially well today?" he asked. A number of items were suggested, written on a newsprint pad, and briefly discussed. "And what do we need to improve on?" Only a single item was volunteered: "The professor's social skills." We all laughed, but it had an element of truth. I'd never before been to a meeting at which postsession reflection on lessons learned was handled in such an accepted, matter-of-fact way. The professor indeed had some skills still to learn.

Other Times

Although groups are especially open to motivational, consultative, and educational interventions at their beginnings, midpoints, and ends, respectively, that does not mean that coaches should be silent or absent at other times in the team life cycle. Teams may indeed fend off attempts to make major changes in their established trajectories in the periods between each of the three temporal milestones, but it still is possible for coaching to nudge team processes in constructive directions, albeit in smaller ways, during these times.

Temporally oriented coaching interventions, such as the team launch, the midcourse correction, and the postperformance review, shape team trajectories. Smaller and more specific interventions made between these times can help a team exploit the full potential of a good trajectory, but they cannot compensate for or redirect one that is taking a team in a futile or wholly inappropriate direction. A student project team I once observed had a poor launch during which two members took responsibility for the first cut at defining the team's project and, in the process, alienated the interest and engagement of a number of other members. Once that team's work was under way, coaching could perhaps have reduced some of the damage created when the team launched. But even highly competent coaching would have been unlikely to redirect the team's basic trajectory. The opportunity to do that reopened only as the team approached the midpoint of its work.

Among the most powerful interventions coaches can make in the periods between temporal milestones are those that selectively recognize and reinforce competent team behaviors that spontaneously occur. (Coaching interventions made at the beginning, midpoint, and end of a work cycle, by contrast, seek to elicit team behaviors that usually do *not* occur spontaneously.) In the tradition of operant conditioning, coaches can keep an eye out for excellent team processes and reinforce them when they occur, thereby increasing the likelihood that they will occur yet again.[27] Wageman trained Xerox team leaders to do precisely this by showing them how to administer what she called "planned spontaneous rewards." Although some team leaders prefer to watch for mistakes and then correct them, Wageman asked team leaders to do the opposite: to position themselves in places where, based on their considerable knowledge and experience, *good* things were likely to occur and then to recognize and reinforce them when they did. The actual reinforcements were small and simple—a verbal compliment, a bottle of wine, movie tickets, or a modest gift certificate—but their impact was large and constructive.[28]

Reinforcement is an excellent way to increase the frequency of desirable team behaviors, but it is not the only thing that coaches and team leaders can do in the periods between temporal milestones. A well-framed question about why a team is engaged in some particular activity may result in members fine-tuning their team performance strategy. An observation about what seems to be happening in the team, or in its interactions with clients or other teams, may prompt some learning that otherwise would have been missed. And just being present and observant allows the coach to log data that can be invaluable when the next opportunity for a trajectory-shaping intervention comes around.

One other unique time for coaching merits special mention—namely, when a new organization is being created that will use self-managing teams as a basic performing unit. In this case, team members generally are also new employees who are only superficially acquainted with one another and who may have limited experience with the kind of work they will be doing. In a number of studies of industrial plant startups, management scholar Richard Walton found that the most effective team leaders initially positioned themselves on the boundaries of their groups—half in and half out. Leaders were far enough in to be able to provide members with technical education on a daily basis, to articulate organizational values at propitious times, and to help members develop performance strategies that were consistent with those values. But they were far enough out that members could not count on them to provide guidance indefinitely—thereby encouraging teams' development of their own self-management capabilities.[29]

Walton found that over the course of the first eighteen months of a team's life the most effective leaders gradually but inexorably removed themselves from the daily activities of their teams because many of the functions they had fulfilled were either no longer needed or were being provided by emergent leaders within the teams. Although the team leaders remained organizationally responsible for the productivity and the ongoing development of their teams, as well as for helping them deal with sometimes challenging negotiations with organizational representatives (e.g., about resources or compensation arrangements), the teams themselves assumed more and more responsibility for managing themselves. For these teams, both the *roles* and the *issues* addressed by team leaders changed over time and in predictable ways. The temporal imperatives for coaching behavior were different for these teams than they would be for, say, a temporary task force. But in both cases appropriate coaching behavior depends heavily on the waxing and waning over time of the functions that most need to be fulfilled for team effectiveness.

Getting the Timing Right

Effective coaching addresses issues that are naturally alive for a team at the particular time when the coaching is provided. Even competently administered coaching interventions will be ineffectual if they are provided at a time when the team is not ready for them, a conclusion also reached by others who have analyzed team coaching.[30] Indeed, ill-timed interventions may actually do more harm than good because they can distract or divert a team from other issues that *do* require members' attention at the time they are made.

Temporal Markers.   What about teams whose work goes on indefinitely into the future and who therefore have no identifiable midpoints or ends? The fact is that very few such teams exist, for a surprising reason that reemphasizes the centrality of time to the human condition—namely, that if time boundaries do not naturally exist, we seem driven to create them. Individuals routinely do this by setting arbitrary and wholly artificial deadlines for themselves, such as the date by which a book chapter must be drafted, a date that no one other than the particular author knows or cares about.

Teams and organizations do it as well. The academic semester, with all its seemingly natural rhythm, for example, is entirely a social creation (universities that use quarters rather than semesters have a different rhythm that seems just as natural to their students and faculty). In a wholly different institutional context, the quarters around which businesses organize and manage their financial accounting drive how managers think and act. It doesn't have to be quarters—any identifiable time marker will do. At the semiconductor manufacturing plant where Hank successfully negotiated organizational supports for his teams (see chapter 5), production periods were organizationally defined as six weeks long. There was no rational reason for that choice (the fifty-two-week year cannot even be chopped up into six-week segments—there are four weeks inelegantly left over), but everybody in the plant *acted* as if the six-week cycles were God-given. Each new period was treated as a real new beginning, production teams took stock of their progress toward performance targets around the three-week mark, and teams typically shifted into a mode of focused and intense work in the last week or so as members strove to hit their targets.

Temporal markers powerfully govern how we humans operate—biologically, for sure, but also in how we construe, organize, and manage our collective work. That fact makes team coaching easier, in that coaches can align their activities with these always-present markers, whether they occur naturally (as do the seasons) or are socially constructed (as are quarters). As we have seen, however, temporal rhythms also constrain coaches' freedom in deciding what kinds of interventions to provide at what times, since certain kinds of coaching are most helpful to teams at different points in their work lives.

Back to the Locker Room.   We now can return to the questions posed at the beginning of the chapter—what a basketball coach might most appropriately address in the locker room before the game, at half-time, and at practice the day after the game. Experience as a player supplemented by conversations with a number of coaches (*research* would be too grand a term for my data collection) affirm that the coaches' behaviors provide yet another illustration of how different coaching functions are best performed at different times.[31]

In the locker room before a game, coaches often focus mainly on matters of *motivation*. A pregame session for a prototypic coach might unfold as follows. When all the players have arrived in the locker room, any guests are excused, the locker room door is closed, and the starting five array themselves in a semicircle around the coach with the rest of the team behind them. With the team boundary established, the coach then talks a bit about the game that is about to get under way, noting that it will be quite challenging but that the team has a real chance to win if members play hard and well. The coach reviews the main points covered in practice sessions in preparation for the game, and takes any questions players have. Then hands go in, and the team heads to the court. There are no histrionics from the coach, no exhortations to "Win this one for me!" Nor does the team charge out of the locker room yelling and hooting. The pregame session is rather more businesslike than that, but it nonetheless results in a well-bounded team, well engaged with its task and motivated to play as hard and well as possible.

Halftime, back in the locker room, is a time for *consultation*, revising the game strategy for the second half of play based on how things went during the first half. The coach consults with the assistant coach, takes a minute or two to develop a plan for the halftime session, and then heads into the locker room. As soon as team members finish taking care of personal needs, the locker room door is closed and the coach reviews what went well and what did not work as it was supposed to in the first half of

play. Changes in game strategy are laid out and, if the coach has a participative bent, questions or suggestions from the players may be invited and
discussed. After the group session is finished, the coach moves among the
players, offering a word of encouragement to some and a suggestion or
correction to others. And then hands go in once again and the team heads
onto the floor for the second half of play.

Practice the next day is the time the coach focuses mainly on *education,* helping to build individual and team proficiency in preparation for
the team's next contest. If there are game films, the coach already has
reviewed them with the assistant coaches and has prepared an agenda of
learning points to be addressed. If the previous game was a win, the coach
may join in a brief celebration before practice starts; if it was a loss, the
coach may permit a bit of catharsis before getting down to business. And
if the game was an *undeserved* win, the coach may be all business from
the beginning, quickly damping any celebratory impulses team members
may have. Regardless of how the session starts, it moves quickly into a
review of the lessons to be learned from the previous game, and then to
consolidation and application of those lessons to increase the team's
capabilities as it prepares for its next contest.

That kind of coaching exploits well the special opportunities that are
built into the game of basketball (ice hockey has always seemed to me
inimical to good coaching because its three periods do not provide a ready
opportunity for a midpoint consultation).[32] It is true that many good
coaches call out corrections, instructions, reinforcements, and expres-
sions of dismay from the sidelines as play progresses on the court. These
actions, however, are process interventions at the margin, attempts to
fine-tune a trajectory that already has been established. Coaches who try
to change the basic game plan while play is under way or, even worse, try
to actually *run* the game from the sidelines usually find themselves in as
much trouble with their teams as do first-line supervisors in industry who try
to dictate every move of the work teams they are supposed to be coaching.[33]

Note that the generic account of basketball coaching just presented
said nothing about either the specific behaviors exhibited by the coach or
about the coach's characteristic leadership style. That was deliberate,
because what is critical is getting the motivational, consultative, and educational coaching functions fulfilled, not the particular behaviors or style

used to accomplish that. Beginning basketball coaches sometimes intently study great coaches such as John Wooden at UCLA or Pete Carril at Princeton in hopes of matching their success by matching their behavioral styles. It doesn't work. The best coaches—whether in basketball or in business—use those behaviors and styles that make the most sense to them personally, given the properties of the situation, the state of their teams, and their own idiosyncratic skills, preferences, and styles. There is no one right way to get the three coaching functions accomplished, no behavioral recipe to follow. But there *is* a wrong way, which is to try to enact a coaching style that is not one's own.

WHAT GOOD COACHES DON'T DO

Although I am agnostic about the particular behaviors or styles coaches should exhibit, that is decidedly not the case regarding the *focus* of coaches' activities. That focus, as by now surely is clear, should be on a team's task performance processes, not on members' social interactions or interpersonal relationships. The great majority of writing about team coaching posits (sometimes explicitly but more often implicitly) that coaching interventions should foster smooth or harmonious relationships among team members. This emphasis on harmony is misplaced and derives from a logical fallacy about the role of interpersonal processes in shaping team performance outcomes.

When we observe a team that is having performance problems, we often simultaneously see a group that is plagued with interpersonal difficulties—conflict among members, leadership struggles, communications breakdowns, and so on. It is natural to infer that these difficulties are causing the performance problems and, therefore, that the best way to improve team performance would be to fix them. As reasonable and as consistent with lay experience as this inference is, it is neither logical nor correct. In fact, the causal arrow often points in the opposite direction— how a group is performing shapes the character of members' interaction rather than vice versa. Or at least it shapes members' *perceptions* of their interaction. Social psychologist Barry Staw gave teams false feedback about their performance and then asked members to provide objective descriptions of how the team had functioned. Teams that had been led to believe that they had performed well reported that their interaction had been more harmonious and that they had communicated better (among other differences) than did groups whose members thought they had performed poorly.[34]

Doubt also is cast on interpersonal approaches to coaching by the findings from studies of the effects of interventions that seek to improve the quality of members' interaction processes. A large number of such studies have been conducted, and their findings are aptly summarized by the title of a review article by management scholar Robert E. Kaplan: "The Conspicuous Absence of Evidence That Process Consultation Enhances Task Performance."[35] Moreover, those intervention studies that *have* documented performance gains, such as the Nominal Group Technique and the Delphi method, almost always involve structuring member interactions in ways that minimize the possibility that interpersonal issues will divert the group from focused work on its task (indeed, the Delphi method eliminates face-to-face interaction among members altogether).[36] The only experimental study of which I am aware that has directly compared the impact on performance of interpersonal-focused and task-focused interventions is the research by Anita Woolley, described earlier, that found the latter to significantly outperform the former.

As tempting as it may be for coaches to jump in and try to make things better when they observe members enmeshed in interpersonal conflicts or leadership struggles, there is little reason to believe that such interventions will succeed in clearing out the interpersonal underbrush so task work can get back on track. More advisable, perhaps, would be to address the structural or contextual conditions that may have engendered the interpersonal difficulties, and to supplement those structural improvements with well-timed and task-focused coaching of the kind described in this chapter.

Yet even teams that are appropriately structured and supported inevitably encounter some rough interpersonal sledding. Despite the pain that members may feel while experiencing and trying to resolve such problems, they are not necessarily bad for a group or detrimental to its performance. On the contrary, research shows that certain patterns of interaction that often are experienced as problematic by team members and coded the same way by outside observers actually can promote team performance and member learning.[37] As we saw in chapter 4, task-based conflict is one such pattern, and the vocal presence of a member with "deviant" views is another. A skilled coach knows that it sometimes is best to leave things alone and let the tension remain high for a while, rather than to rush in and try to contain the problems or refocus their most negative manifestations.

SHARING COACHING

Throughout this chapter, I have discussed coaching as if it were done by one person, perhaps someone designated as "team leader" or "team advisor" or, for that matter, "coach." In practice, coaching often is done by a number of individuals, sometimes different ones at different times or for different purposes—including, especially in mature self-managing teams, team members themselves. What is critical is that competent coaching be available to a team, regardless of who provides it or what formal positions those providers hold.

The potential benefits of sharing coaching among team members are wonderfully evidenced by the Orpheus Chamber Orchestra, the twenty-six-person ensemble described in previous chapters that both rehearses and performs without a conductor. Although that orchestra has no leader on the podium, it has much more *leadership* than do orchestras known for their famous conductors.[38] For each piece of music the orchestra chooses to perform, one violinist is selected by his or her peers to serve as concertmaster. That person manages the rehearsal process for that piece—beginning each rehearsal, fielding suggestions from members about interpretive matters, deciding when spirited disagreements among members must be set aside to get on with the rehearsal, and taking the lead in figuring out how to handle transitions in the music that in a traditional orchestra would be signaled by a conductor's baton.

There is abundant shared leadership and peer-to-peer coaching in this unusual orchestra, but it is far from a one-person, one-vote democracy.[39] As noted in chapter 3, Orpheus members are quite discriminating about who is invited to have special say in the preparation of each piece. Only some violinists are chosen to serve as concertmasters, for example, and it is clear to all which members have earned the right to be listened to especially carefully about which musical issues. Members are not treated as equals because in fact they are *not* equals: Each individual brings special talents and interests to the ensemble and also has some areas of relative disinterest and lesser strength. Orpheus members recognize that fact and exploit it relentlessly in the interest of collective excellence. The orchestra's willingness to acknowledge, to respect, and to exploit the individual differences among its members is one of its greatest strengths as a self-managing team. It is as fine an example of shared leadership and peer coaching as I have encountered.

One of the things that helps peer coaching work so well at the Orpheus Chamber Orchestra is that those who are coaching are also playing in the orchestra, and therefore they are always *there*. It is difficult, if not impossible, for any of the three kinds of coaching explored in this chapter—motivational, consultative, and educational coaching—to be accomplished by remote control. Good coaching helps team members practice and learn the skills and rewards of being superb *self*-managers, and that is highly unlikely to happen if the coach is rarely around.[40]

It is a joy to observe great coaching. In addition to motivating, teaching, and consulting to team members, one invariably sees in great coaches' own actions the very kinds of behaviors they seek to foster in their teams. To illustrate, let me describe an event that initially may seem to have nothing whatever to do with work teams or their coaches—but that nonetheless shows the power of a coach's behavior in providing a model for others. As part of our four-nation study of professional symphony orchestras, Jutta Allmendinger and I visited Leipzig to observe the Gewandhaus orchestra and interview its players and managers just a few months before the collapse of the East German socialist regime. Late in the afternoon, an orchestra manager we were interviewing politely cut our conversation short. "I'm sorry, but we have to stop now," he explained. "It is time for me to go to the democracy demonstration." Naturally, we followed him. As we arrived, the opera plaza was filling with what seemed to be tens of thousands of Leipzig citizens, coming on that day as they did on most days to show by their presence their commitment to the democratic ideal.

Soon, half a dozen figures appeared on the balcony of the opera house, and the leader of the day's proceedings explained that each of them would briefly give his or her views of the proper political future of East Germany. The first speakers advocated democratic elections to replace the officials of the socialist regime, and their remarks were received with applause and cheers. Then a representative of that regime stepped to the microphone and tried to explain why going slowly and maintaining some continuity was a good idea. He was hooted down. He waited until the crowd had quieted, and then started again. He was hooted down again. And a third time.

At that point, the leader of the demonstration took the microphone from the would-be speaker and waited, not long, for quiet. Speaking softly and obviously from his heart rather than from a script, he said that democracy, as he understood it, meant that you listened to what others had to say, even if you already knew you were going to disagree with them. That was about all he said. Then he handed the microphone back to the representative of the Socialist Party, who read his speech to a silent crowd that had just received, and learned, a small lesson in democracy. The demonstration leader was a leading activist in the democracy movement who objected to just about everything the socialist representative had to say. Yet he made sure that the representative *had* his say. In that small act, the leader modeled precisely the kind of democratic ideals that he and his colleagues were advocating. That kind of modeling provides coaching that surely exceeds in power and consequence even the most competently conceived and perfectly timed coaching intervention that any of us could devise.

PART III

OPPORTUNITIES

7

Imperatives for Leaders

W hen we think about a great team, the image we conjure up almost always includes a great leader. A surgical team flawlessly executes a risky and demanding procedure. The lead surgeon emerges from the operating room to receive the gratitude of the patient's family. An industrial team regularly sets new plant production records. The team leader receives an award and soon thereafter is promoted. An airplane encounters serious problems, but the crew finds a way to work around them and lands safely. All applaud the captain. The final chords of Mahler's Resurrection Symphony reverberate in the concert hall. The conductor, exhausted but beaming, turns to accept the applause of the audience.

Our tendency to assign to the leader credit or blame for successes or failures that actually are team outcomes is so strong and pervasive that I'm tempted to call it the "leader attribution error." It occurs for unfavorable as well as favorable outcomes—the standard remedy for an athletic team that experiences a string of losses is to replace the coach, for example, and it is the conductor who is excoriated in newspaper reviews of a poor orchestral performance. Moreover, it is not just outside observers or bosses who make the error. Team members themselves, the people who worked together to generate the collective product, also are vulnerable. Organizational psychologist Richard Corn asked members of a diverse set of teams, ranging from community health groups to a mutual fund company to military units, to identify the "root cause" of their team performance. For teams that were performing well, over 60 percent of the explanations had something to do with someone's personality or behavior—and that someone frequently was the team leader. For teams that were performing poorly, 40 percent of the initial attributions were about personality or behavior.[1]

Even *inaction* by a leader is often viewed as causing what transpires in a team. For example, members of self-analytic groups (i.e., groups whose purpose is to help members learn from analysis of their own group experiences) generally hold their leader responsible for the rocky start that they invariably experience. In most such groups, the leader remains silent for the first few moments to ensure that all behaviors that occur are spontaneously generated by—and therefore owned by—group members themselves. The leader attribution error is so strong that the leader's silence itself often is viewed by members as the main cause of what transpires. Only gradually do they come to accept and explore their own responsibility for the behaviors they have generated.

Highly trained and experienced professionals, people who perform demanding team tasks as part of their daily work, are as vulnerable to the leader attribution error as anyone else. A player in a top symphony orchestra, describing to me an extraordinary performance by the orchestra, reported that the conductor had "pulled out of us a performance I didn't know we had in us." A player in a different orchestra, explaining an unsatisfactory concert, complained that the conductor "just couldn't get us to play beyond the notes on the page." Only when there is significant ambiguity about whether a team's performance was a success or a failure is the leader attribution error muted.[2]

Sometimes, of course, a team leader's actions really *do* spell the difference between team success and failure. That fact, reinforced by the leader attribution error, has fueled a steady flow of tests, surveys, and educational programs intended to help organizations select and train great group leaders. That flow persists despite the rather poor track record, discussed next, of team leader selection tools and training programs.

LEADER TRAITS AND STYLES

Clearly, some people are better than others as leaders of teams. It is quite reasonable, therefore, to try to identify the traits that distinguish naturally good leaders from those who consistently fail to get the best out of the people with whom they work. Literally hundreds of research studies have attempted to do exactly that, measuring a panoply of leader traits (e.g., intelligence, sociability, self-confidence, and dozens more) to see which ones predict leadership effectiveness. As long ago as the 1950s, it had become clear that research would not succeed in identifying any set of universal traits that could reliably distinguish good from poor leaders.[3] Many different attributes of individuals were found to be modestly associated with rated leader effectiveness and (especially) with who would be chosen to occupy leadership positions. But the practical usefulness of those lists was limited, both because they were so long (a dozen desirable attributes provide less clear guidance for action than does a handful) and because the size of the empirical relationships obtained was usually so small.

Contemporary research has not been much more successful in identifying the traits of superb team leaders than that done decades ago.[4] Neither hope nor the leader attribution error dies easily, however, and the common-sense belief that a leader's personal traits somehow determine his or her effectiveness in leading teams continues to guide both research and practice. The power of such thinking is perhaps best exemplified by the readiness of many members of the management community, as well as the general public, to accept the claim that a leader's "emotional intelligence" is the key determinant of team and organizational effectiveness. The irony is that many of the skills that are grouped under the emotional intelligence label are learnable. But use of the word *intelligence* as part of the label implies that whatever it is that emotionally intelligent leaders possess is at least an enduring personal attribute and perhaps even innate. It is bad enough that analytic intelligence, the kind of thing often referred to as "IQ," is so widely viewed as wired in at birth; it is even more troublesome that learnable leadership and interpersonal skills are labeled in a way to suggest that they are as well. Next, I suppose, someone will suggest that it is one's genetic endowment that determines how effective he or she can be as a team leader.[5]

There is a potentially optimistic implication of the rather pessimistic conclusions just drawn. If traits are not controlling, then perhaps *anyone* can be a good team leader as long as he or she learns the right ways to behave. If it could be established that certain leadership styles are better than others for leading teams, then leaders could be trained to exhibit those styles no matter what their personalities or demographic attributes happen to be. This was the approach taken in a training course for airline flight crews that I once observed. Each pilot-student took a paper-and-pencil test that, when scored, revealed his or her characteristic style of operating in teams. Instructors then suggested that certain styles were better than others for promoting crew effectiveness. Students were taught, for example, that captains should foster task accomplishment and interpersonal harmony simultaneously, and that they should avoid both autocratic and relentlessly democratic leadership styles. And they learned that first officers and flight engineers should be assertive with their captains (but not excessively or unpleasantly so) when they notice something that concerns them. The hope was that the styles taught in the classroom would be used to good effect when the pilot-students returned to their regular flying duties.

Although the pilots, like others who take tests measuring leadership style, found them interesting and informative, I have a number of concerns about such devices.[6] For one thing, research has shown that there is no one leadership style that works well across all situations.[7] A style that may be just what is needed when working with competent, trusted colleagues to develop a team work plan may fail badly when a newly formed team encounters an emergency situation that requires a rapid, decisive collective response. For this reason, research on leader styles has evolved from a search for the one best style to contingency models that specify which styles should be used in different circumstances. Such models identify those attributes of the situation and of the group being led that determine what leader behaviors are likely to work best, and they provide research-based guidance about how leaders ought to behave in various circumstances.[8] Contingency models necessarily become quite complex as research identifies more and more contingencies that moderate the relationship between leader behavior and team outcomes. In that inevitability lies the rub: The more complete and complex a contingency model, the more it requires of leaders a level of online cognitive processing that can exceed human capabilities.[9]

A second problem with leadership styles derives from our everyday assumption that leader behavior is the *cause* of member behavior and team dynamics. In fact, a leader's style may in many circumstances be as much a consequence of members' behaviors as it is a cause of that behavior.[10] If, for example, a leader is charged with managing a team of subordinates who are both competent and cooperative, the leader is likely to use a considerate, participative leadership style. But if team members are obviously not competent in carrying out the work and, moreover, exhibit hostility in their interactions with the leader, a much more structuring, directive, and autocratic style is likely to be exhibited. A team leader's style is not fixed. Just as a parent's style of interacting with a child often is more an effect of how that child is acting at the moment (tougher when the child is behaving poorly, democratic when the child sweetly suggests an after-dinner family conference to reconsider bedtime conventions) than a consistent expression of one's preferred style of parenting, a leader's behavior often is driven as much by how team members are acting as by the leader's espoused or preferred style.

Finally, there is the problem of getting newly learned styles transferred from the training setting back to the workplace. Leaders almost always like, and feel helped by, well-run training programs that seek to improve their styles. Moreover, training settings are explicitly designed to encourage participants to experiment with new behavioral styles, and to reinforce improvements in their existing styles. The problem comes when a participant leaves the supportive training environment and returns to his or her regular workplace where colleagues may have become quite expert in dealing with the "old" style of the leader—and therefore may be quite unreceptive to the new style the boss developed while away at training. In a contest between a fresh and still somewhat fragile style learned in school and the demands and expectations of the trainee's regular work setting, the new style almost always comes out the loser.

Indeed, those times when a newly learned style might be most valuable (e.g., when there is extremely important work to be accomplished under considerable stress or time pressure) are precisely the times when that style is *least* likely to appear. When a person becomes highly aroused (as typically happens under stress), he or she reverts to well-learned behaviors, exhibiting whatever response is dominant for that person in that situation.[11] Dominant responses rarely are displaced by what is taught and learned in a leadership training course; they are too deeply ingrained for that. To return to our pilot-trainees, even the best students in the seminar are likely to revert to their old, tried-and-true behaviors when a highly stressful situation such as an engine fire or the loss of all generators is encountered in line flying. A story told by Captain Reuben Black of Delta Airlines illustrates. Some years ago, an instructor was attempting to get his students to memorize the thirteen steps that were to be taken in the event of a heater fire on a certain aircraft. The students were having trouble committing the list to memory, but the instructor persisted. Finally one veteran captain captured the essence of the problem when he exploded, "How the hell do you expect me to remember all this shit when I'm *scared?*" How, indeed?

So what is going on here? On the one hand, we all tend to overattribute responsibility for collective outcomes to the team leader. Although that tendency is often exaggerated to some extent—the leader attribution error— there is no doubt that what a team leader does (and doesn't do) is highly consequential for team effectiveness. On the other hand, researchers have been unable to generate usable knowledge about either the traits that characterize great leaders or their characteristic behavioral styles.

Is it just that we need to try harder to identify and measure the right personal attributes and behavioral styles of team leaders to be able to select and train them well? Management scholar Chris Argyris, who I believe shares my pessimism about the efficacy of existing leader selection and training technologies, proposes that any substantial improvement in leader effectiveness requires a fundamental recasting of leaders' "theories in use," which are the perceptual templates and behavioral programs that people rely on in planning and executing their actions.[12] If one seeks to create enduring improvements in leaders' behavioral styles, Argyris's strategy of essentially reprogramming their personal cognitive models may well be warranted. But is there another approach to the development of competent team leadership, one that does not require such fundamental change in leaders' personal styles of acting and interacting?

I believe there is. That alternative, which is explored in the rest of this chapter, involves a change of focus, from *who* the leader should be (leader traits) and *how* the leader should behave (leader behavioral style) to *what* the leader does and *when* in the life of a team it is done.

WHAT EFFECTIVE LEADERS DO

Effective leaders attend first to the basic conditions that foster team effectiveness—the features of the team and the organizational context that have been discussed in this book. First of all, they make sure that they have created a real work team that will have some stability over time (chapter 2). They provide the team with a compelling direction (chapter 3). They fine-tune the structure of the team so it fosters rather than impedes teamwork (chapter 4). They tweak the organizational structures and systems so they provide teams with ample support and resources (chapter 5). And they arrange for, or themselves provide, expert coaching to help teams take full advantage of their favorable performance situation (chapter 6). Effective leaders do these things in their own way, using the idiosyncratic behavioral styles and strategies that they have found to work best for them. And they attend carefully to timing, moving quickly and decisively when opportunities for action open, but never trying to force an intervention when the time for it is not right.

Stacking the Deck

Great team leaders do not rely on any single strategy for promoting work team effectiveness. Instead, they stack the deck by getting all of the conditions we have been discussing aligned and pulling in the same direction, thereby reinforcing the impact of their own hands-on coaching. We saw in the previous chapter that good coaching helps a team in three ways. First, by building the level of *effort* that members apply to the work. Second, by increasing the task appropriateness of their *performance strategies*. And third, by helping members use well their pool of *knowledge and skill*. As figure 7-1 shows, each of these three performance processes also is strengthened by a compelling direction, an enabling structure, and a supportive context.

A compelling direction carries a team a long way. It energizes team members, promoting collective effort. It orients members' attention and action, which provides the basis for making good choices among alternative performance strategies—or for inventing an entirely new strategy that is uniquely attuned to task requirements and opportunities. And it engages members' full complement of talents as they pursue collective aspirations that are of great consequence for the team or those the team serves.

Even good direction is insufficient, however, if the team is not well structured—if it has a poorly designed task, if norms of conduct are absent or dysfunctional, or if the team itself is poorly composed. Each of the three components of a good structure has an important role in enabling a team to take advantage of good direction. A well-designed task promotes member

FIGURE 7 - 1

How Team Design Shapes Team Performance Processes

Compelling direction		Enabling team structure		Supportive organizational context		Team performance processes
Energizes	+	Team Task Design	+	Reward System	→	Effort
Orients Attention	+	Norms of Conduct	+	Information System	→	Performance Strategy
Engages Talents	+	Team Composition	+	Educational System	→	Knowledge and Skill

motivation and effort. Norms of conduct that explicitly promote active environmental scanning and strategy planning increase the chances that the team will develop and implement a performance strategy fully appropriate for the task being performed. A well-composed team is small enough, and diverse enough, to facilitate the development and efficient use of member talents.

Finally, a supportive organizational context smoothes the path to team excellence. When a team has ample resources and support, members are able to keep moving toward their collective objectives without having to divert time and energy to surmount organizational impediments or circumvent bureaucratic roadblocks. A reward system that recognizes and reinforces excellent group performance fosters high and sustained team effort. An information system that keeps the members up to date about environmental demands and opportunities increases the chance that the team will develop and deploy performance strategies that are both efficient and appropriate. And an educational system that provides timely training and technical consultation increases the likelihood that the team will bring to the task the maximum possible level of task-relevant talent.

If a work team were in a boat on a river, having a compelling direction, an enabling structure, and a supportive organizational context would metaphorically allow members to row with the river's flow—simultaneously lessening the labor they must expend and hastening their arrival at the team's destination. If one or more of these conditions were *not* present, however, teamwork might well feel like rowing upstream against a strong, unpredictable current. The team might eventually get to its destination, but it would involve a lot more work and be a lot less certain than if the basic performance conditions were favorable.

Getting the Order Right

A *New Yorker* cartoon some years ago, as I recall it, depicted a bleary-eyed man sitting on the side of his bed, looking at a sign he had posted on the bedroom wall. The sign read: "First slacks, *then* shoes." Direction, structure, and context are the slacks. Coaching is the shoes. Unfortunately, coaches sometimes are called on by their organizations to do the shoes first, to try to salvage a team that operates in a performance situation that is fundamentally flawed. Even first-rate coaching can make little constructive difference in such circumstances—and may even do more harm than good by distracting members' attention from more fundamental aspects of their design or context that they ought to be addressing.[13]

For example, consider a team working on a mechanized assembly line where inputs are machine paced, assembly procedures are completely programmed, and performance operations are simple and predictable. How could a coach help that team? Not by encouraging members to work harder or more efficiently, because the amount of work processed is under control of the engineers who pace the line, not the team. Not by helping them develop more task-appropriate performance strategies, because the way the work is to be done is completely prespecified. And not by helping them develop or better use members' knowledge and skill, because the required operations are so easy that an increase in team talent would merely mean that an even smaller proportion of the team's total pool of talent would be used. In this situation, team performance processes are so severely constrained and controlled that the team has almost no leverage to improve them. For the same reason, there is little that even a great coach can do in working with the team to better its performance. Through no fault of the members, the team is essentially uncoachable.

Two questions come to the fore when one encounters an uncoachable team. First, can the performance situation be fundamentally restructured so the team *can* have a meaningful level of control over its own performance processes? And, if that is not possible, should the team exist at all? There are some kinds of work for which teams are a wholly inappropriate design choice, and some organizational settings in which teams can never succeed. It is never a good idea to "force" a team in such circumstances.

Even when a performance situation is not as team-unfriendly as the one just described, the quality of a team's design strongly conditions the impact of leaders' coaching interventions, as was documented by Ruth Wageman in a study of self-managing field service teams.[14] For each team studied, Wageman obtained independent assessments of the team's design, the coaching behaviors of its leader, the team's level of self-management, and its objective performance. She predicted that a team's design features would make a larger difference in both level of team self-management and team performance outcomes than would the leader's coaching behaviors, and she was right. Design was four times as powerful as coaching in affecting a team's level of self-management, and almost forty times as powerful in affecting team performance.[15] Clearly, design features do have causal priority over leader coaching in shaping team performance processes and outcomes.

Perhaps the most fascinating finding of the Wageman study turned up when she compared the effects on team self-management of "good" coaching (e.g., helping a team develop a task-appropriate performance strategy) with those of "bad" coaching (e.g., identifying a team's problems and telling members exactly what they should do to fix them). Figure 7-2 shows these effects for good coaching (the left panel of the figure) and bad coaching (the right panel). Good coaching significantly helped well-designed teams exploit their favorable circumstances, but made almost no difference for poorly designed teams. Bad coaching, on the other hand, significantly compromised poorly designed teams' ability to manage themselves, worsening an already difficult situation, but did not much affect the self-management of teams that had an enabling team structure and a supportive organizational context.

We seem to have here yet another instance in which the rich get richer (well-designed teams are helped most by good coaching) and the poor get poorer (teams with flawed designs are hurt most by bad coaching). Great coaching can be enormously valuable to a team in exploiting the potential of a fundamentally sound performance situation, but cannot reverse the impact of poor direction, a flawed team structure, and an unsupportive organizational context. The key to effective team leadership, then, is first to ensure that the team's performance situation is sound and then to help team members take the greatest possible advantage of their favorable circumstances.

HOW EFFECTIVE LEADERS DO IT

Question: How do great leaders create the conditions that promote team effectiveness?

Answer: Any way they can.

Hidden within that brief, unhelpful question-and-answer dialogue are a number of imperatives that can guide leaders in improving the effectiveness of almost any organizational work team. So let us take the question and answer apart, phrase by phrase, and explore what lies inside.

FIGURE 7 - 2

How Team Design and Leader Coaching Jointly Affect Team Self-Management

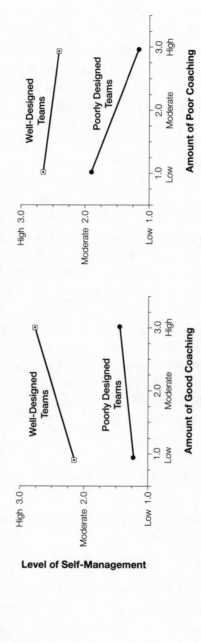

Source: Reprinted by permission, R. Wageman, How leaders foster self-managing team effectiveness: Design choices versus hands-on coaching, *Organization Science*, volume 12. Copyright 2001, The Institute for Operations Research and the Management Sciences, 901 Elkridge Landing Road, Suite 400, Linthicum, Maryland 21090-2909 USA.

. . . *great leaders*

As you read the words "great leaders," what came to mind? Did the leader attribution error do its work, prompting an image of an individual person who occupies a formal leadership role? My choice of the plural form in the section title was deliberate, to signal that team leadership can be— and, at its best, often is—a *shared* activity. Anyone and everyone who clarifies a team's direction, or improves its structure, or secures organizational supports for it, or provides coaching that improves its performance processes is providing team leadership. An external manager may be well positioned to do some of these things, such as setting a direction for the team that is well linked to broader organizational purposes, or securing organizational resources and supports. Other things are better done by leaders who work more closely with team members, such as tailoring a team's direction to its particular circumstances, fine-tuning the team's structure, and helping members learn how to use well the organizational supports the team enjoys. And it is the regular, rank-and-file members of the team who may be best able to provide the kind of peer coaching that can focus and refine team performance processes, thereby helping teammates work together in ways that minimize process losses and generate synergistic process gains. The question, then, is not so much who provides team leadership but rather how much the team is getting. So long as the focus of leadership activities is on creating conditions that enhance team performance, the more leadership the better.

. . . *create the conditions*

When we plan an action intended to make a difference in some part of our world, we almost always think in cause-effect terms. Hit the nail with the hammer and it goes into the wood. Compliment a colleague and that person will be pleased and maybe even like you better. Flash your headlights thrice just after someone has passed you at high speed and the other driver is almost certain to slow down (and, as a bonus, may experience that special sinking feeling that comes with realizing that one may have just sped by an unmarked police car).

Cause-effect thinking is so pervasive and useful that it sometimes can mislead us into behaving in inappropriate or self-limiting ways. We saw a few pages ago that leader style, which commonly is viewed as one of the main causes of subordinate behavior, is itself shaped by how competently and cooperatively those subordinates are behaving. In such cases, the usual direction of the causal arrow between leader and subordinate is reversed, from subordinate behavior to leader style rather than vice versa. That is useful information to have, but it raises a more fundamental question: If not the leader's style, what *does* determine how subordinates act? And what are the implications of that for the behavior of those who provide leadership to a team?

One of the main aims of this book has been to offer readers an alternative to traditional cause-effect models of team leadership by showing that team behavior is shaped, often in unseen and nonobvious ways, by the task and organizational conditions that characterize the performance setting. Leaders often are most helpful to teams, therefore, when they back off a bit from direct interventions intended to keep a team on a good course minute by minute and focus instead on creating and maintaining perfomance-enhancing organizational conditions. Even hands-on coaching, which would seem to be an instance when the leader's style has direct and immediate effects on team behavior, actually serves a larger and more general purpose—namely, to gradually build the team's capability to manage itself well.

Leaders always behave in accord with some model, even if implicit and even if incorrect, that specifies what actions are likely to yield what results. To replace a cause-effect model with one that focuses on the creation of enabling performance conditions is a significant change of orientation, and one that has implications for leader behavior at all stages of a team's life. Whether one is launching a new team, assisting a team that has encountered performance problems, or helping an already well-performing team do even better, the same diagnostic questions apply. Is the team a *real* team, bounded and stable over time, that requires members to work interdependently to achieve some common purpose? Is the team's direction clear, consequential, and challenging? Does the team's structure—its task, composition, and norms—facilitate good performance processes? Does the organizational context—the reward, information, and educational systems—provide the team with the supports that the work requires? And is there expert coaching available to the team to help members minimize the inefficiencies in their performance processes and instead harvest the potential synergies of teamwork?

Leaders, whether those who have formal responsibility for a team or others (including team members themselves) who seek informally to help the team do well, can refer to this simple checklist repeatedly during the life of a team. Almost always the answer to one or more of the diagnostic questions will point to some structural or contextual problem, or to an unexploited opportunity for strengthening the team's performance circumstances.

There is no way to "make" a team perform well. Teams create their own realities and control their own destinies to a far greater extent, and far sooner in their lives, than we generally recognize. After a team has launched itself on a particular track, its own actions create additional new realities which then guide members' subsequent behavior, which can set in motion either a cycle of ever-increasing competence and commitment or a downward spiral that ends in collective failure. Once members have established their shared view of the world and settled into a set of behavioral routines, there is not a great deal that leaders can do to change the team's basic direction or momentum.[16] What leaders *can* do (and a big job it is) is make sure the team is set up right in the first place, that it is well supported organizationally, and that members have ready access to the kind of coaching that can help them exploit the team's potential to the fullest extent possible. To ask a leader to do more than that is to ask too much— and, in the bargain, to impede the team's own development into a truly self-managing performing unit.

. . . *that promote team effectiveness*

Throughout this book, we have relied upon a three-dimensional conception of team effectiveness (see chapter 1). Effective teams, in this view, generate products, services, or decisions that are fully acceptable to those who receive or use them. *And* they become more capable as performing units over time. *And* their members find in the work of the team more learning and fulfillment than frustration and disillusionment. A team that is significantly and consistently subpar on any of these three criteria would not be viewed as effective.

Unfortunately, teams sometimes slip into a pattern of behavior that focuses too intently on one or two of the three criteria to the detriment of the others. In the course of my research, I have seen instances in which each of the three has become so dominant that a team's long-term effectiveness has been compromised. Most common, of course, is when meeting customer or client requirements captures virtually all of the team's attention and energy. Members focus intently and relentlessly on getting the work out, and if they even notice that the well-being of the team and its members is being overlooked, they defer such matters until "later, when we have a little breathing room." But later may not arrive until, perhaps, the team and its members have become so depleted that an operational breakdown occurs. At that point, the team may be unable to recover precisely because the resources that were being expended were never replenished. This phenomenon, surely, contributed to the collapse of some dot-com startups whose members enacted the "24/7" ethic with a vengeance and, in the process, depleted their collective resources to the point that they eventually had none left to deal with one more crisis, not even a relatively small one.

Organizational psychologist Edy Greenblatt observed a similar phenomenon in a setting where one might least expect to see it—namely, a vacation resort where the work done by organizational staff involved doing things that we usually define as play.[17] All day, every day, teams of staff members led guests in recreational activities ranging from dancing to diving, from singing to sailing. The level of emotional labor involved in presenting a relentlessly happy collective face to guests was extraordinary, but that was what needed to be done—and that was what the staff did, day after day, week after week. Burnout in this happy vacation setting was much higher than one might have predicted, especially among those who kept their attention so intently focused on guests' pleasure that they neglected to find ways of restoring, let alone enriching, their stores of personal and collective resources.

Sometimes the imbalance is in the opposite direction. Leaders can become so focused on training and team building that they lose sight of a team's purposes and customers. I once visited the startup of a plant whose managers were extraordinarily proud of their programs to train new employees intensively in state-of-the-art production technologies and to build robust self-managing teams to operate those technologies. The training and team-building programs were indeed impressive and showed real promise of providing a model that eventually could be diffused throughout the parent corporation's existing, more traditionally managed plants. Unfortunately, plant managers and employees became so captivated by their innovative human resource strategy that they lost their focus on the plant's reason for being—namely, to produce high-quality products at the lowest possible cost for the company's customers. In part because of the high and continuing investments made in the plant's people and teams, labor costs were higher than budgeted and production targets remained just beyond reach. About a year after startup, an economic downturn hit the parent corporation particularly hard and the new plant was closed. Because plant managers had focused so intently on the second and third components of effectiveness, we will never know whether the heavy investment they had made in developing the plant's people and teams eventually would have paid off for its customers and shareholders.

Actively managing trade-offs among the three components of effectiveness spawns many benefits for work teams. The team is less likely to fall victim to the hidden costs that almost always accompany an exclusive focus on any single aspect of overall effectiveness. Members are likely to be more attentive and thoughtful in planning what the team will do, thereby lessening the risk that they will reactively respond only to the most salient or immediate demands that press upon them. The team's purposes will remain at the center of members' attention, reducing the risk that the team will experience the dysfunctions that can surface when members focus more on their procedures than their goals.[18] Over time, the team surely will become a more flexible and effective self-managing performing unit than otherwise would be the case.

Team leaders are uniquely well positioned to help teams manage these trade-offs, for several reasons. The team leader often is in closer touch than team members with a team's broader context, including its links with other organizational units and with customers or clients, and therefore is in a good position to alert members if they start to overlook the interests of any one of the team's constituencies. Ideally, he or she will be less wrapped up in the hurly-burly of dealing with the demands and pressures that a team encounters in its daily work, and therefore more likely to notice if a team begins to slip toward an overemphasis on one or another of the components of effectiveness. And, finally, the team leader role usually carries some special legitimacy for raising questions about the focus of a team's work activities, thereby providing an opportunity for constructive interventions of a kind that come from members themselves only in the most mature self-managing teams.

Even so, helping a work team recognize that its long-term well-being involves active management of trade-offs among the three components of effectiveness can be quite challenging, since team members may not always welcome or see the wisdom of interventions that appear to raise questions about how they are allocating their attention and energies. The challenge is worth taking on, however, because when well and sensitively met it can significantly strengthen the self-management capabilities of almost any organizational work team.

. . . *any way*

A while back, I needed to get from Boston to New York for a research meeting. There were multiple ways I could have accomplished that—by airplane, by train, by bus, even by driving my own car five hours to the meeting site. Each mode of transportation had distinctive advantages and disadvantages in terms of cost, convenience, vulnerability to weather delays, and the possibility of working while traveling. Still, each and every one of them would eventually have gotten me to New York. That fact exemplifies for individual choice what systems theorists call *equifinality.*[19] According to the principle of equifinality, there are many different ways that an open system such as a person, team, or organization can behave and still achieve the same outcome—in this case, to get to New York.

I drove. Driving was a little cheaper than the other options, but it took more time and offered zero possibility of getting work done en route. A colleague, surprised at my choice, used the phrase "really dumb" to characterize it. But I *like* to drive. Even more, I like having the flexibility of leaving the instant I am ready to go, and having choice about the route I will take. So I picked a way to get to New York that suited me just fine. My colleague would have made a different choice—but also would have gotten to New York. That is what is meant by equifinality.

As I write this, I am starting to think about the first meeting of a new research group that I will convene next month. How should I handle the first few minutes of that meeting? Should I begin by telling members the main objectives of the research project? Or should I ease into the purposes of the project gradually, perhaps starting out by inviting each member to talk briefly about his or her own research interests? Or should I prepare a read-ahead handout describing the project and open the meeting by asking members for their reactions and questions? Should I strike a formal, task-oriented tone, or be more casual and interpersonally oriented?

Once again, there is no right answer to those questions, no one best way for me to act as I launch my team. What *is* important is that somehow I get conditions established that help the group get off to a good start. As we have seen in previous chapters, this involves three activities: helping the team come to terms with its immediate task and ensuring that all understand how it is linked to the team's broader purposes; bounding the group as a performing unit so all members understand and accept that we, collectively, are the people responsible for the project; and establishing the basic norms of conduct that will guide member behavior in the initial phase of the group's life. Those are the things I must accomplish in that first meeting. But I have enormous latitude in *how* I accomplish them.

In fact, my actual behavior at the first meeting will be significantly shaped by the circumstances of the moment: Is everybody present when the meeting is supposed to start? Do all members already know one another? How much enthusiasm do they seem to have for the project? My behavior also will depend on my own preferred style of operating: Am I more comfortable taking an active, assertive leadership role, or do I prefer to solicit input from others and then summarize and integrate their ideas? Do I generally lead using a matter-of-fact style, or do I like to liven things up with humor? Am I someone who can describe a project in a way that engenders shared excitement in a group, or am I better at helping each member identify the particular aspects of the work that he or she personally finds most engaging? These and other considerations too numerous to mention—and certainly too complex to preprogram even with the most complicated decision tree—together will shape the actual behaviors I exhibit at the research group meeting. There are many different ways that I can create the conditions for a good team launch, and no particular style of leading is necessarily better than others for getting those conditions in place.

The principle of equifinality applies even in settings where much of what a leader must do is technologically determined or dictated by required procedures. The airline flight deck is one such setting. Because small deviations from proper procedures by a cockpit crew can spawn highly adverse consequences, much of the behavior of the crew leader, the captain, is highly standardized. Members can count on each new captain conducting some kind of briefing before the first flight begins, for example, because that is required by most airlines. What captains actually *do* in those briefings, however, is mostly up to them—and we saw in chapter 6 that the way a captain handles the briefing establishes a pattern of interaction that persists throughout a crew's life. But do captains who are viewed by their peers as excellent team leaders behave differently in their initial crew briefings than do those who are seen as only so-so team leaders?

To find out, researcher Robert Ginnett asked flight standards staff, who regularly fly with the airline's pilots to ensure that the highest standards of professionalism are maintained, to identify captains who all were fine pilots but who they considered to be either excellent or marginal team leaders. He then selected a number of captains in each of these two groups and, without knowing whether the nominators had placed a given captain in the excellent or marginal category, observed that captain's briefings of two different crews on two different occasions. Ginnett captured everything that happened from the moment pilots and flight attendants began to arrive in the briefing area—where they sat or stood, the content and style of the leader's remarks, how much other crew members participated, how long the briefing lasted, and more.

His first pass through the data revealed enormous variation among captains in both groups in the length, style, and content of their briefings. Closer inspection, however, showed that all of the captains who had been nominated as excellent team leaders accomplished, in their own idiosyncratic way, three things. First, they established the *legitimacy of their authority* as crew leader. They exhibited neither a laissez-faire nor fully democratic approach in conducting the briefing. They communicated their own authority and competence by unapologetically specifying what they sought and expected from the crew—but they also identified without embarrassment or apology the matters about which they needed information or assistance from others. Second, they established the *boundaries* of the crew, taking special care to ensure that all members, pilots and cabin crew alike, recognized that they shared responsibility for the flight and for the flying experience of their passengers. And third, they affirmed the *norms of conduct* that would guide crew behavior, that is, their expectations about how members would act and interact, particularly regarding how they would communicate and coordinate with one another.[20]

It is noteworthy that the captains gave less attention in their briefings to the *task* that the crew would perform than has been observed for excellent leaders of other types of work teams.[21] In airline operations, individual and collective tasks are defined and engineered in such detail that there is little need for the captain to clarify or reinforce what the crew is there to accomplish. Even so, the excellent captains often did give special reinforcement to the importance of keeping safety in the forefront of everyone's attention—and, once again, did so in their own idiosyncratic ways.

The great diversity of styles used by team leaders in launching their crews is seen not just when a team first comes together, but also in how leaders establish and maintain the other conditions that foster team effectiveness—clarifying a team's direction, getting its structure right, arranging for contextual supports, and ensuring that the team receives competent coaching at the appropriate times. Recall how Hank, the manager of the semiconductor manufacturing teams, worked with senior managers of human resources, maintenance, and engineering to obtain contextual supports for his teams. Hank did not have the authority to commandeer the support his teams needed from other plant departments. What Hank did have, however, was political acumen, great credibility as a leader who got results, and widely shared respect for his skills as a back-country hunter. As we saw in previous chapters, Hank drew on these personal resources in a highly idiosyncratic way, one that surely would raise the eyebrows of most management theorists, to obtain for his production teams the organizational supports they needed.

The leader of a university computer support team I once observed used an entirely different strategy. This leader, who we will call Frieda, had solid credibility with senior university officials. Perhaps because her formal supervisors also were clients of her team, as well as being the people who occasionally had to field complaints from faculty who wanted their malfunctioning e-mail immediately fixed, they were highly motivated to do anything they could to help Frieda's team succeed. When she needed additional resources or support from the central university administration, Frieda would prepare a careful analysis of her team's present situation and of the future demands it was likely to face. Then she would calmly present the results of these analyses, along with her recommendations for action, to appropriate university officials—who almost always would accept her proposals. What Frieda wanted for her teams, Frieda usually got.

Hank and Frieda could hardly have been more different from one another in their backgrounds, roles, and influence strategies. Yet both of them obtained from their organizations most of what their teams needed to perform well. Both tailored their influence attempts to the particularities of their roles and organizational circumstances, and both used the leadership styles and strategies that suited them best. There is no one right way to provide leadership to a work team.

Let me hasten to add, however, that there also are many *wrong* ways to go about creating the conditions for team effectiveness—strategies or styles that backfire or whose short-term benefits are negated by long-term liabilities. One way to get it wrong is to mislead or lie to those who are in a position to provide teams with the structures, resources, or supports they need in their work. Beyond the moral problems of lying, disingenuous strategies destroy the credibility of those who use them when, as inevitably happens, others discover that what is claimed cannot be trusted.

Another way to get it wrong is to ape someone else's style, or to follow prescriptions from a textbook or training course that specify how good leaders are supposed to act. It always is embarrassing to observe someone trying to enact a leadership style that is not the person's own—such as the junior manager who admiringly adopts the style of the charismatic chief executive but succeeds only in calling attention to the enormity of their difference in competence. The junior manager would be better advised to cease practicing in front of a mirror and instead to spend that time and effort identifying and honing his or her *own* best style of leading.[22] It can be just as embarrassing to observe someone who has learned from a textbook or management training course how good leaders behave, and who then attempts to act that way back at work. "What happened to Charlotte at that training course?" team members ask one another. "Well, let's just wait it out; she'll probably be back to normal soon." And indeed she will.

The third way to get it wrong is to relentlessly enact one's preferred manner of leading even in the face of data that it is not working very well, to keep on keeping on with a style that is indeed one's own and with which one may be quite comfortable but that consistently yields unanticipated and unfavorable results.[23] Some leaders, for example, are most comfortable with what can be called a "command and control" style of leadership. They issue orders about what is to be done—not just by the team they are leading but also by their peers and even bosses. Sometimes command and control is fully appropriate—for example, among airline captains when a potentially catastrophic event such as an engine fire requires immediate and decisive action. On those occasions, the leader will be reinforced for using that style: "Immediate action was required, I issued the orders, team members did what I told them, and it worked out fine." But other times, such as in launching a team or exploring the implications for the team's performance strategy of a changing external environment, that style may be inimical to what needs to be accomplished. The leadership problem becomes severe when the leader does not recognize that his or her actions are not having the intended effects—or, worse, when the leader sees that things have not gone well but blames either the situation ("Nobody could have turned that around—it was wired for failure") or team members ("They just wouldn't do what I told them—they need to shape up real soon"). In such cases, there is no opportunity for the leader to self-correct because he or she is not open to data that might suggest that the leader's own actions contributed to the poor outcome.

Ginnett observed this inability (or unwillingness) to self-correct among those captains in his study who had been nominated by their peers as marginal team leaders. Although there was as much variation in briefing style among the marginal captains as among those who were viewed as excellent team leaders, there were two major differences between the two groups. First, no matter what style they used in conducting their crew briefings, the marginal captains failed to establish the conditions needed for a good team launch. Second, all of them, again in their own ways, exhibited significant problems with *control* that made it nearly impossible for them to use their experiences to become more effective. Some of these captains were persistently overcontrolling, not asking for input from other team members and ignoring or diverting any suggestions that members did manage to make. Others were persistently undercontrolling, so democratic or laissez-faire in conducting their briefings that crew members were left uncertain about how the team was supposed to operate. Worst of all were captains who vacillated between overcontrolling and undercontrolling in ways and at times that could not be anticipated, which in some cases nearly incapacitated team members in carrying out their own parts of the work. Ginnett's observations documented that even though these captains' briefings did not go well, they either did not recognize the dysfunctional effects of their style or they were unable (or unwilling) to alter it. How they led was how they led, no matter what consequences ensued.

Excellent team leaders, by contrast, are aware of their natural styles—
they know what they like to do, what they can do easily and well, and what
they can accomplish only with difficulty if at all. They learn over time how
to exploit their special strengths and preferences, and how to contain or
circumvent their weaknesses. They attend carefully to the circumstances
of the moment, and vary their behavior in real time to exploit unanticipated leadership opportunities and circumvent obstacles that risk blunt-
ing their initiatives. They may never have heard of the principle of equifinality, but they behave in accord with it. And, most important of all, they
are continuously alert for signs that their actions may not be having their
intended effects. For great leaders, expanding and strengthening their
repertoire of leadership behaviors is a lifelong learning project.

. . . *they can.*

Some organizations provide team leaders with so little latitude for tailoring their leadership to the circumstances of the moment that to say, as I
have said, that "great leaders create the conditions that promote team
effectiveness any way they can" has no practical significance. Just as
there is little point to having a work team if all performance processes are
dictated by technology or prespecified operating procedures, so too there
is little point to having someone occupy the role of team leader if he or
she has no room to maneuver.[24] It is the difference between a jazz musician and a section player in a symphony orchestra: The former has lots of
room to improvise, whereas the latter must follow exactly a detailed
score—and do so under the direct and constant supervision of a conductor. Team leaders should be more like jazz musicians.

Not everyone can do it, not even when they have lots of latitude and
support. Although I am chastened by the modest findings from researchers'
decades-long search for leadership effectiveness traits, it nonetheless seems
to me, based on my and my colleagues' studies of teams, that there are a
handful of personal qualities that do distinguish excellent team leaders
from those for whom team leadership is a struggle. Specifically, I suggest
that effective team leaders have the following four qualities: (1) they *know*
some things, (2) they know how to *do* some things, (3) they have *emotional maturity* sufficient for the demands of the leadership role, and (4)
they have a good measure of personal *courage*.[25]

Know Some Things.   The first attribute listed—knowledge about conditions that foster team effectiveness and the skill to create those conditions—is something that people who are "naturals" as team leaders know implicitly. Hank, who so successfully created and supported production teams at his semiconductor plant, never had a course in management or organizational behavior. Yet he somehow sensed what had to be in place for his teams to succeed, and he did what he needed to do to create those conditions.

Fortunately for those of us who do not have Hank's impressive intuition, knowledge about the conditions that foster team effectiveness can be taught. This book seeks to do just that, and it also can be done in university courses and in management training seminars. A training course could, for example, help team leaders understand the importance for team effectiveness of having a clear, engaging, and consequential direction by using case analyses of effective and ineffective teams, or could teach them about the importance of timing in coaching interventions by analysis of videotapes of team coaches in action. Similar pedagogical devices could be used to teach team leaders about the other conditions discussed in this book. If a team leader does not already know what it takes to promote team effectiveness, he or she can readily learn it.

Know How to Do Some Things.   It is not sufficient for those who lead work teams merely to know about the conditions for effectiveness; they also need to know how to create and maintain those conditions—in a word, they need to be *skilled* in leading teams. Two kinds of skills are critical to team leadership: skill in diagnosis, and skill in execution.

Effective team leaders carefully target their interventions, aiming them at those aspects of a team's interactions, its structure, or its context where the contemplated action is both feasible and likely to make a substantial and constructive difference. To choose intervention targets wisely requires *diagnostic skills*. Effective leaders are able to extract from the complexity of the performance situation those themes that are diagnostically significant (as opposed to those that are merely transient noise or that are of little consequence for team behavior). These themes, which summarize what *is* happening in the group or its context, are then compared with what the leader believes *should be* happening to identify interaction patterns or organizational features that are not what they could be. Only then is the leader in a position to craft interventions that have a reasonable chance of narrowing the gap between the real and the ideal. Natural team leaders do all of this intuitively and seemingly without effort. The rest of us may have to go through the diagnostic process step by step until, eventually, it becomes natural for us as well.

Beyond their excellence in diagnosing work situations and team dynamics, effective team leaders also are skilled in executing actions that narrow the gap between a team's present reality and what could be. Leaders who have a rich and diverse portfolio of *execution skills* are better able to do this than leaders who have but a few things they can do well. Richard Walton and I attempted to identify the execution skills that are most critical to team leader effectiveness; what we came up with is reproduced in table 7-1. Even though moderately long, the list necessarily is incomplete. There always are new skills to be acquired by those who lead teams. Leaders who keep on with that learning continuously expand the options they have available for helping the teams they lead.

Once again, some individuals are naturally talented in doing the right thing at the right time and in the right way to help their teams succeed, but others require training to develop their skills in taking action. Much is known about training procedures that can help people develop new skills or hone existing ones, and one of the things that is known is that skills cannot be mastered by reading books, listening to lectures, or doing case analyses.[26] Instead, skill training involves observation of positive models (i.e., people whose behavior illustrates highly competent execution of that which is being taught) coupled with repeated practice and feedback. Training in execution skills is necessarily personalized and for that reason is expensive and time consuming. But it is a critical ingredient in the mix that makes for a great team leader.[27]

Even with extensive training, not everyone is able to master the execution skills that can spell the difference between excellent and poor team leadership. Much is implicitly revealed about an organization by noting how senior managers deal with that fact. In Hank's semiconductor manufacturing organization, for example, team leaders were selected quite thoughtfully and deliberately; only people who managers felt were almost certain to be effective leaders were invited to participate in the leadership training course that was required of all candidates for team leader positions. Even so, the classroom performance of some individuals showed, for

TABLE 7 - 1

Execution Skills of Team Leaders

Envisioning Skill

The ability to envision desired end states and to articulate and communicate them to others.

Inventive Skill

The ability to think of numerous nonobvious ways of getting something done.

Negotiation Skill

The ability to work persistently and constructively with peers and superiors to secure resources or assistance that is needed to support one's team.

Decision-Making Skill

The ability to choose among various courses of action under uncertainty, using all perspectives and data that can be efficiently obtained to inform the decision.

Teaching Skill

The ability to help team members learn both experientially and didactically.

Interpersonal Skill

The ability to communicate, listen, confront, persuade, and generally to work constructively with others, particularly in situations where people's anxieties may be high.

Implementation Skill

The ability to get things done. At the simplest level, knowing how to make lists, attend to mundane details, check and recheck for omitted items or people, and follow plans through to completion. At a more sophisticated level, the ability to constructively and assertively manage power, political relationships, and symbols to get things accomplished in social systems.

Source: From Hackman and Walton (1986). Leading groups in organizations. In P. S. Goodman (Ed.), *Designing effective work groups* (pp. 72–119). San Francisco: Jossey-Bass. This material is used by permission of John Wiley & Sons, Inc.

whatever reason, an inability to master the leadership skills being taught. It was a sign of the organization's commitment to leadership excellence that those individuals were not appointed to team leader roles.

By contrast, consider the training of pilots who fly commercial aircraft. The technical training of pilots, whether in a civilian flight school or in the military, is demanding and stringent. Those who cannot master the skills of safely flying an aircraft wash out and do not become pilots. The decision rule is more forgiving, however, once a pilot has logged enough years of service to be upgraded to captain, to move from being a team member to a team leader. Although captain upgrade courses in most commercial airlines do include leadership training, I am aware of no otherwise qualified pilot who was refused promotion to captain because of an inability to demonstrate mastery of leadership skills. This was advantageous for Bob Ginnett, whose research design required him to observe a number of captains who, although well qualified technically, were shaky as leaders of their teams. But the failure of airlines to insist that captains be superb leaders as well as superb pilots is surely less advantageous for the younger pilots they lead and, perhaps, for those who fly on the aircraft they command.

Emotional Maturity.   The inability of some people to master leadership skills may have less to do with their cognitive capabilities than with their emotional make-up. Leading a team is an emotionally demanding undertaking, especially in dealing with anxieties—both one's own and those of others. Leaders who are emotionally mature are willing and able to move toward anxiety-arousing states of affairs in the interest of learning about them rather than moving away to get anxieties reduced as quickly as possible.

Competent team leadership often involves inhibiting impulses to act (e.g., to correct an emerging problem or to exploit a suddenly appearing opportunity) until more data have become available or until the time is right to make an intervention. Sometimes it even is necessary for leaders to take actions that temporarily *raise* anxieties, including their own, to lay the groundwork for subsequent interventions that seek to foster team learning or change.

Imagine that you have formed a task force that has one month to come up with an important new organizational policy. A full week has passed, and there is little apparent progress. Various policy proposals have been offered and debated, but members' views are not coalescing and you are concerned that no momentum is developing. Two task force members come to you individually and privately to express their concern about how things are going and to suggest that you "do something" to get the task force moving. To do what the members ask would reduce their and your anxieties, but could undermine the development of the task force as a self-managing team. Moreover, it may be too early to intervene—the task force is still logging experience, and it might be better to let the tensions continue to build in hopes of a creative release at the group's midpoint. How do you respond to the members' pleas? The temptation to act is strong, but there also are good arguments for holding off for the moment, letting anxieties continue to build a while longer. To make a wise decision in this case requires not just knowledge of the life-cycle dynamics of time-bounded work teams but also the ability to manage one's own anxieties and emotions.

Another example. You lead a team in a municipal agency that manages the assessments of residential properties and provides data to those who prepare homeowners' tax bills. Your team relies heavily on a large database in carrying out its work, as do workers in several other municipal departments. This morning you received a memo from the senior manager of information technology announcing that the city had contracted with a vendor to convert its database of housing stock to a new system that will provide greater centralized control of the data and therefore reduce errors. The senior manager's memo states that the database will be unavailable for five days beginning the first of the next month while the vendor accomplishes the changeover, and thereafter all data changes will be submitted to staff in his department rather than be handled directly by end users. When you finish reading, you are furious. You were not consulted about either the new system or how the changeover will be handled. The first of each month, when the database will be temporarily unavailable, is exactly the time when your team most needs it. And, most infuriating of all, the new requirement to submit change requests to information technology staff will significantly compromise your team's ability to manage its work in its own way and on its own schedule. How do you respond to the memo? My own impulse, stronger than I wish it were, would be to craft a scorching reply to the information technology manager, with copies to the city manager and the mayor. That would be emotionally satisfying, to be sure. But would it be the most likely to ensure that my team would continue to have the information technology tools and support it needs in its work?

The impulse to get things taken care of sooner rather than later, or to strike back when one feels threatened or abused by others' actions, can be almost irresistible. It takes a good measure of emotional maturity for a leader to resist such impulses, to find ways to deal with one's anxieties and emotions that neither deny their reality and legitimacy nor allow them to dominate one's behavior.

Courage. The king of Asteroid 325 in Antoine de Saint-Exupéry's *Little Prince* found an excellent way to be a successful leader—he discerned what his subjects wished to do and then decreed that they do precisely that. Political candidates, these days, seem to have taken their cue from that king: Pollsters tell them what the people want, and the candidates promise to provide it. Such strategies may help one get elected, remain in favor with one's subordinates, or even hold onto one's job, but they are not *leadership* strategies.

Leadership involves moving a system from where it is now to some other, better place. It means that one often is at the margins of what people presently like and want, working close to the edge of what is acceptable rather than at the center of the collective consensus. To help a team address and modify dysfunctional group dynamics, for example, a leader may need to challenge existing group norms and disrupt established routines—and most likely will incur some anger from group members in doing so. To improve a team's contextual supports or to increase the resources available to it, a leader may need to rock the organizational boat—and may risk a loss of esteem with his or her peers and superiors in doing so. To redirect a group from its traditional purposes to new ones that better reflect a changed external reality or revised organizational values, a leader may engender resistance so intense that it places his or her own job at risk. Such behaviors require courage.[28]

Leaders differ in how prepared they are to step up to these challenges, as is seen in the behavior of two executive team leaders described to me by Jim Burruss, a senior consultant at Hay McBer who works extensively with such teams. One of the leaders joined an organization that needed both trimming and redirection. The trimming would unfortunately involve a reduction in staff, but the redirection offered the prospect of an attractive new beginning. The manager informed his executive team that he planned to move simultaneously and immediately on both fronts by informing a significant number of staff that their present jobs no longer existed but that they were free to apply for new positions in the reconfigured organization. Executive team members were worried that their leader might be attempting too much too quickly. The manager heard them out but decided to proceed anyway—the worst that could have happened, he later said, was that he could have failed and lost his job.

The second leader regularly needed to have his backbone stiffened by his executive team. "You just *have* to take a stand on that issue," members would tell him. And, after hearing their arguments, he would agree to do so. But whenever one or another of his team members would speak to him later about the possible downside of the action he had agreed to take, he would back off to give the matter "additional thought." The strong actions that the organization actually needed, Jim reports, never happened.

In these examples, the leader who behaved courageously kept his job and prospered, and the one who could not muster his courage did not. It often is the other way around. Leaders who behave courageously are indeed more likely than those who do not to make significant and constructive differences in their teams and organizations—but they often wind up paying a substantial personal toll.[29]

What Can Be Learned. The four qualities just discussed are differentially amenable to training—and in the order listed. It is relatively straightforward to help team leaders expand what they *know* about the conditions that foster team effectiveness. It is more challenging, but with sufficient time and effort entirely feasible, to help them hone their *skills* in diagnosis and execution. To foster team leaders' *emotional maturity* is harder still, and is perhaps better viewed more as a developmental task for one's life than as something that can be taught.[30] *Courage* may be the most trait-like of the four attributes. Although there indisputably are differences in courage across individuals, it is beyond me to imagine how one might help leaders become more willing than they already are to take courageous actions with their teams, peers, and bosses to increase the chances that their teams will excel.

Because of the paucity of proven educational strategies for developing the emotional maturity and courage of would-be team leaders, the best present strategy for assuring they have these resources may be to carefully select for leadership roles those persons who have already exhibited them. Simply electing someone from the group as "team leader" or choosing as leader the member who has demonstrated the greatest *task* competence, for example, often will result in the wrong person occupying what can be a critical role for a work team. Leader selection processes, in this way of thinking, would rely more on direct evidence of behavioral competencies than on either standard personality measures or off-the-shelf tests of verbal and analytic ability.[31]

The personal attributes I have suggested here as key to team leader effectiveness may seem strange to those who are accustomed to thinking of leadership qualities mainly in terms of personality traits or behavioral styles, and I have offered my views in a speculative spirit. But it is nonetheless true that the superb team leaders I have observed over the years have most, if not all, of these very qualities. It may be worthwhile to give new thought to old questions about how team leaders might be selected, assessed, and trained on these difficult-to-measure but potentially significant attributes.

GETTING IT DONE

There are nontrivial implications for organizational practice in the question with which the previous section began ("How do great leaders create the conditions that promote team effectiveness?") and in its answer ("Any way they can"). The main work of team leaders is to do whatever needs to be done to ensure that the handful of conditions that foster team effectiveness are in place—and stay there. Is the work team a *real* team, or just a collection of individuals who go by that name? Does it have a clear, engaging, and consequential direction? Does the team's structure enable rather than impede competent teamwork? Does the team's organizational context provide the supports and resources that the team needs in its work? And does the team have available ample and expert coaching to help members get over rough spots and take advantage of emerging opportunities?

As we have seen, some of these conditions are best created before the team even meets for the first time, others at its launch meeting, others around the midpoint of its work, and still others when a significant piece of work has been completed. Serendipity and history play important roles in determining when the enabling conditions can be created or strengthened, how that might best be accomplished, and how hard it will be to do so. Sometimes most of the conditions will already be in place when a team is formed, and fine-tuning them will not pose much of a leadership challenge; other times, such as in an established organization that has been tuned over the years to support and control *individual* work, it can take enormous effort and ingenuity to establish even the basic conditions required for competent teamwork.

We also have seen that there is no one best strategy or style for accomplishing this kind of leadership work, nor any one person who is mainly responsible for getting it done. Instead, team leadership involves inventing and competently executing whatever actions are most likely to create and sustain the enabling conditions. Anyone who helps do that, including both external managers and team members who hold no formal leadership role, is exercising team leadership. What is important is that the key leadership *functions* get fulfilled, not who fulfills them and certainly not how they go about doing it.[32]

The richer the set of leadership skills held by team members and organizational managers, the greater the number of options available for getting the enabling conditions in place. It is like the difference between driving and taking the train. I pointed out earlier that when driving there are always alternative routes to the destination if one road is blocked. A train, however, has but one set of tracks. If there is an obstruction on the tracks, the train cannot proceed until the obstruction is removed. Relying on any single person to provide leadership is the equivalent of taking the train. By contrast, having multiple individuals with diverse skills pitching in to help create and sustain the enabling conditions gives a team lots of room to maneuver. If one strategy for moving forward is blocked, perhaps by a recalcitrant manager or by technological constraints that would be enormously expensive to change, there are other strategies that also could work.

The more members who are contributing to the real work of leadership (that is, helping to create, fine-tune, and exploit the benefits of the enabling conditions), the better. Still, it usually is a good idea to have one person identified as the "leader" of even a self-managing work team to facilitate communication and coordination among members. Who that person is can rotate from time to time and even can be selected by members themselves, as was the practice of the domestic airline flight attendants described in chapter 1. But making sure that things do not fall between the cracks and that information finds its way to the people who need it are activities usually handled most efficiently by a single individual who has an overview of the entire work process.

One of the main objectives of this chapter has been to offer for consideration a nontraditional model of how leaders can help their teams and organizations do well, a model that focuses more on the functions that leaders fulfill than on anything about their personalities or styles. This approach to team leadership differs from commonsense notions, which posit that influence flows dominantly from the person identified as "leader" to the team rather than in all directions—upward to bosses and laterally to peers as well as downward from formal leaders to regular members. It differs as well from leadership theories that focus mainly on the personal characteristics of good leaders, or that specify the best leadership styles, or that lay out in detail all the major contingencies that researchers have documented among traits, styles, and situational properties.

There can be no useful theory of leadership without an accompanying theory that specifies what is required for systems to achieve their main purposes. I have tried to provide here a way of thinking about team leadership that integrates what we know about the conditions that foster work team effectiveness with what has been learned over the last several decades of research about leadership. This approach is more complex than any list of "principles of good management" or "one-minute" prescriptions. Yet it also is simpler (there are just a few key conditions) and more usable (create and sustain those conditions any way you can) than either contingency models of leadership or those that require fundamental reprogramming of leaders' personal models of intervention.

The present approach also is more optimistic than some others—for example, those that claim that leaders make no substantial difference, that they are but pawns in a larger drama driven by external forces,[33] or others that posit that high-status leaders should keep their distance from the group that is performing the work so they do not unduly influence members' deliberations.[34] Instead, I have attempted to lay out a way of thinking about leadership that empowers both formal and informal leaders so that, through their behavior, they have a reasonable chance of helping a team evolve into a performing unit that meets the legitimate expectations of its clients, becomes stronger over time, and contributes positively to the personal learning and well-being of its members.

8

Thinking Differently about Teams

Work teams were among the most popular workplace innovations of the last decade, as shown in a careful survey of 694
manufacturing organizations by MIT economist Paul Osterman. He found that more than half the companies surveyed were using
teams to accomplish work—and that 40 percent of the companies surveyed
had the majority of their employees working in teams.[1] Findings from a
1998 survey of nearly 100 leading-edge companies by the Work in America
Institute reinforce Osterman's findings. When asked to identify the research
topics that would have the greatest value to their organizations, 95 percent of the respondents gave highest priority to "teamwork: creating and
sustaining team-based organizations." That was, the Institute reported,
the strongest response ever obtained on one of its surveys.[2]

But how well do organizational work teams actually perform? To
judge from all the books and articles written about them, the answer is
clear: Teams markedly outperform individuals, and self-managing (or self-
regulating, self-directed, or empowered) teams do best of all. Here are

some reports from the field, cited by Jack Osburn and his colleagues in *Self-Directed Work Teams: The New American Challenge*. At Xerox, the authors report,

> [P]lants using work teams are 30 percent more productive than conventionally organized plants. Procter & Gamble gets 30 to 40 percent higher productivity at its eighteen team-based plants. . . . Tektronix Inc. reports that one self-directed work team now turns out as many products in three days as it once took an entire assembly line to produce in fourteen days. . . . Federal Express cut service glitches, such as incorrect bills and lost packages, by 13 percent in 1989. . . . Shenandoah Life processes 50 percent more applications and customer service requests using work teams, with 10 percent fewer people.[3]

Heady stuff, that, and it is reinforced by back-cover blurbs for the book. Tom Peters: "Self-directed work teams are the cornerstone of improved competitiveness." Bob Waterman: "*Self-Directed Work Teams* seems too good to be true: dramatic improvement in productivity and a happier, more committed, more flexible work force. Yet . . . they do just what they promise for the likes of P&G, GE, and Ford."

Might the claims be a bit exaggerated? If so, it does not much concern me. Claims for management practices that have come into vogue are always exaggerated as enthusiasm grows and people seek to catch the wave—to sell books, to build consulting practices, to market training programs, to become gurus. What does bother me is the pervasive view, found in book after book, that it is easy to make a great team. Just *do* it and the benefits will start to flow. In the foreword to *Self-Directed Work Teams*, David Hanna, then manager of organization development at Procter & Gamble, identifies skepticism as the largest single roadblock to success: "Beware of skepticism!" he warns. "Self-directed teams really do work."[4]

Well, I want to violate my friend Dave Hanna's admonition and be just a little bit skeptical. I trust the accuracy of the numbers that are reported about productivity and service gains, but I am not entirely sure whether those numbers mean what they seem to mean. There are two reason why. One has to do with the attributions that are made about the causes of the obtained gains, the other with their likely staying power.

- *Causes.* After self-managing work teams are implemented in an organizational unit, the unit's performance typically is compared with that of a traditional unit (or, perhaps, with the same one before teams were installed). Such comparisons are fraught with interpretive ambiguities because there invariably are many differences between the units compared—such as in technologies, labor markets, senior managers, and so on. It almost never is the case that the *only* change is that work otherwise done by individuals or manager-led teams is now performed by self-managing teams. Was it the teams that generated the improvements, or was it one of the other differences? It is not possible to know for sure.[5]

- *Staying power.* When a new management program is implemented in an organization, be it self-managing teams or anything else, the unit where the changes are to be made invariably is scrutinized very intently. Taking a close look at any work unit that has been operating for a while almost always surfaces some inefficiencies and poor work procedures. As part of the change process, these incidental problems also are corrected—it would be foolish not to. But in doing so, an interpretive ambiguity is introduced. Was it the team design that resulted in the improvements found, or was it that a shoddy work system was cleaned up? I believe that virtually any intervention that is not itself destructive has a better-than-even chance of generating short-term improvements, simply because of the value of taking a close look at a work system.[6] The question is whether those short-term improvements are sustained over time as the newness wears off and inefficiencies begin to creep back into the work system. Again, it is not possible to know for sure—at least not without longitudinal data and an appropriate research design.

My skepticism is reinforced when I reflect on the research literature about the performance of task-performing teams.[7] Some time ago, social psychologist Ivan Steiner developed a simple model of team performance:

$$AP = PP - PL$$

In words, the model says that the *actual* productivity of a team equals its *potential* productivity (i.e., what the team is theoretically capable of, given the resources brought by members) minus process losses of the kind discussed in detail in chapter 6.[8] When I first studied Steiner's model, I was surprised to find that it did not have a term for process *gains,* the synergistic benefits that come from people working together interdependently. The model, I thought, should really read as follows:

$$AP = PP - PL + PG$$

Ivan encouraged me to go to the library and find evidence to support my additional term—which I did, but without success. When interacting teams are compared with what are called *nominal* groups (i.e., groups that never meet, whose output is constructed by combining the separate contributions of those who would have been members), nominal groups usually win. And when Steiner's model fails to predict empirical findings about team performance, it invariably is because the model is too optimistic—groups do not do even as well as his conservative predictions. So what is going on here? How can we reconcile the amazing reports from the field about the benefits of work teams with the gloomy picture that emerges from scholarly research on group performance? Do teams generate the benefits for their organizations that are claimed for them, or do they not?

My observations of work teams suggest that they frequently are found at *both* ends of the effectiveness continuum. That is, teams that are poorly designed and poorly led are easily outperformed by smoothly functioning traditional units. On the other hand, self-managing teams that function well can indeed achieve a level of synergy and agility that never could be preprogrammed by organization planners or enforced by external managers. Members of such teams do respond to their clients and to each other quickly and creatively, which can result both in superb task performance and ever-increasing personal and collective capability. Work teams, then, are somewhat akin to audio amplifiers: Whatever passes through the device—be it signal or noise—comes out louder.

To ask whether organizational performance improves when teams are used to accomplish work is to ask a question that has no general answer. Work teams can, and sometimes do, perform much better than traditionally designed units. But they also can, and sometimes do, perform much worse. Moreover, even if there were a clear answer to this question, which there is not, it probably would not make much of a difference in managerial choices about how performing units are designed and led. As we will see in this chapter, such choices are driven far more powerfully by managerial preferences and ideologies than by empirical research findings. Systems designers are not nearly so rational or data-oriented in assessing the costs and benefits of various organizational designs as some management theorists would have us believe.

OBSTACLES TO TEAM EFFECTIVENESS

Consider a team that meets all of the conditions that have been discussed in this book. It is a real work team, well bounded and reasonably stable over time. It has a compelling direction that energizes, orients, and engages the talents of team members. Its structural features—task design, core norms of conduct, and composition—promote rather than impede competent teamwork. It has an organizational context that actively supports and reinforces excellence through systems, policies, and managerial practices that are specifically tuned to the team's needs. And ample, expert coaching is available to the team at the times members most need it and are ready to receive it.

All of the evidence that my colleagues and I have been able to collect over the years suggests that a team that has these conditions in place would be likely to perform very well.[9] There is, however, no guarantee of good performance. The conditions we have explored in this book merely increase the *probability* that a team will be effective. There are always exogenous factors that can sink even a wonderfully designed team (the hurricane just swept the entire inventory out to sea) or rescue one whose design was so bad that failure seemed assured (the firm that was competing for the contract just went belly-up). Moreover, teams create their own realities. Sometimes, for reasons that cannot be discerned by an observer, a team creates a reality that is unexpectedly supportive of, or inimical to, productive teamwork. Because that is the way social systems work, all that leaders can do is apply their best efforts and skills to tilt the probabilities in a favorable direction. Not even the best team leader on the planet can make a team be effective.

Still, it is much easier to create the conditions that foster effectiveness for some types of teams, and in some kinds of organizations, than in others. Creating favorable conditions may be relatively straightforward for, say, a product development team in an entrepreneurial organization. The product development process lends itself to teamwork because it requires coordinated contributions from several different specialties. Product development teams generally have a clear and engaging direction, and perform whole pieces of work for which they are relatively autonomous and about which they receive direct feedback (i.e., the product is created and works, or it isn't and doesn't). There are no built-in obstacles to composing the team well or to establishing task-appropriate norms of conduct. Such teams typically have access to the information and technical assistance they need for their work, and substantial rewards and recognition commonly are bestowed upon successful product development teams. With ample material resources and a little coaching to help in navigating the rough spots, there is no reason why most product development teams cannot be primed for good performance.

Startup organizations, such as new plants or offices, also provide favorable settings for establishing the conditions that support team effectiveness. So long as those who design the new organizational unit are relatively free of structural or policy constraints imposed by a parent organization, they should be able to design a team-based unit in which the conditions for team effectiveness are in place. For this reason, many of the most successful team-based organizational startups have been located far from corporate headquarters. A remote location provides a measure of freedom from potentially constraining corporate systems and policies that is not enjoyed by units within sight of corporate offices. (Indeed, a number of highly successful team-based startups have gotten into trouble when corporate managers eventually discovered that the startup organization was ignoring or violating corporate policy in the interest of creating a favorable environment for teamwork.)

Yet there are many circumstances, perhaps the majority, when creating the conditions that foster team effectiveness is more like pedaling up a steep hill than coasting down a gradual one. Why should this be so? The conditions themselves are not subtle, complex, or difficult to understand. Indeed, they are just the kinds of things that an alert manager surely could learn from experience. Are there more fundamental obstacles on the road to successfully structuring, supporting, and leading teams? I have observed two such obstacles, one more commonly found in organizations that aspire to cooperative or democratic ideals, the other more characteristic of teams in established business corporations and public agencies.

The Co-op Obstacle

It has always bothered me that we in the United States, who cherish the principles of political democracy, so infrequently apply those principles to the workplace. Some years ago, therefore, I took a close look at worker cooperatives, organizations whose charters explicitly embrace democracy and where all important matters are decided by membership vote. Some of the co-ops I examined were so small that the whole organization operated as a single work team; others were larger enterprises that had many teams within them.

I found a number of successful work teams in cooperative organizations, but also a surprisingly large number of failures. The reasons for the failures are instructive. Too often, co-op members debated endlessly about their values, purposes, and collective directions—while competitors who had a more focused business strategy took their customers away. Collaboration and teamwork were so highly valued that virtually all tasks were done by teams, even those that would have been better performed by individuals. Egalitarianism and participation were such dominant values that members found it difficult to delegate real authority to any of their number. To maximize the choices of member-owners, team composition often was based solely on personal preference rather than on an analysis of the mix of skills that the work actually required. And, finally, I found members of many co-ops quite reluctant to establish and enforce the use of organizational structures and systems that could have supported teams in their work. The democratic ideals of co-ops are wholly consistent with the use of self-managing teams to perform work. It is ironic, therefore, that in cooperative organizations those ideals frequently get in the way of creating the very conditions that promote team effectiveness.

The difficulties sometimes encountered by cooperative organizations also occasionally are seen in other organizations, including businesses and public agencies, where ideological considerations come to dominate decision making about organizational structures and practices. Of all the organizations that have been discussed in this book, one of the most intriguing is People Express Airlines, which was founded in the 1980s by Don Burr and his colleagues and had a highly instructive five-year life. That company turned out to experience some of the same kinds of issues in structuring and supporting its many self-managing teams as do worker cooperatives, and for some of the same reasons.

Part of Burr's vision for People Express was to create a nonbureau-cratic organization in which the inherent power of individuals and teams, locked up or suppressed in traditionally structured firms, could be un-leashed in the service of customers, colleagues, and shareholders. To accom-plish this, Burr and his senior management colleagues formulated a set of precepts that served as the guiding vision for the enterprise, they created self-managing teams throughout the company, and they made sure that every organization member was supported by leaders who had been well trained in the People Express precepts (see chapter 1).

In its early years, when organization size was fewer than 1,000 people, People Express was a remarkable success—one of the fastest growing firms in the history of American business. Coordination among individu-als and teams happened naturally in real time in the halls of the company offices at Newark Airport, on airfield ramps, and in airplanes. Customers queued up to get seats on People Express, the company was the darling of Wall Street, and social scientists (including this one) wrote articles that described the company's innovative organizational form and probed the reasons for its success.[10]

As People Express grew, it became increasingly difficult for members to coordinate in halls and airplanes, and operational problems became fre-quent and severe enough that many backers of the organization suggested that the time had come to beef up the organization, to install structures and systems to support its self-managing workforce. To do so, however, would have been a retreat from the values on which People Express had been founded—namely, the transcending power of vision and leadership to unleash and direct the energies of organization members.

Values prevailed. Rather than installing the structures and systems that his backers advocated, Burr and his colleagues redoubled their efforts to ensure that all members of the organization deeply understood the com-pany's vision, and added even more trained leaders to coach and teach organization members. In a time of trouble, the founders reaffirmed the principles that had been responsible for their early success and behaved more vigorously than ever in accord with them.[11]

It did not work. As People Express continued to grow and as other airlines developed strategies for competing with it in the marketplace, financial and operational results deteriorated further. Eventually, disillusionment set in for some organization members, and, finally, the operation itself cratered. At that point, it was only a matter of time until the company was acquired by a competitor and People Express ceased to exist.

In both the worker cooperatives and People Express Airlines, ideological currents ran strong and deep. And in both cases, perversely, those strong collective values made it nearly impossible for leaders to install the structural and contextual features that are among the key conditions for team effectiveness. These organizations, and many like them, attest to the fact that visionary direction and abundant coaching, by themselves, are insufficient to ensure the success of work teams in organizations.[12]

The Corporate Obstacle

The organizational structures, systems, and policies of many existing businesses and public agencies have been tuned over the years to control and support work performed by *individual* employees. Managers are understandably reluctant to overturn well-established organizational features just to see whether or not work teams actually generate the benefits claimed for them. Veteran managers, after all, have weathered quite a number of organizational innovations that had their origins in the behavioral sciences—management by objectives, job enrichment, T-groups, zero defects, quality of worklife, gain sharing, TQM, and a multitude of others. And, no doubt, there will be more to come after self-managing work teams have had their time in the spotlight and moved to the rear to join all the other interventions that once were stars but are no more.[13]

Managers who seek to implement work teams without upsetting the corporate apple cart can use either of two quite different strategies. One is to try to capture the benefits of teamwork by relying mainly on rhetoric and training. Members are told that they are now in teams, team leaders are appointed, and everyone is sent off to get training in good team processes. It is easy to implement teams this way—neither organizational structures nor managers' own behaviors need change. But, as we saw in chapter 2, such teams are more ephemeral than real. Mere changes in appearances rarely yield measurable improvements in organizational outcomes.

The second strategy is to form real teams—intact performing units whose members share responsibility for some product or service—but to lay them atop existing organizational structures and systems. The rationale, as one manager told me, is to see how well they perform before making other organizational changes that could be hard to reverse. With this strategy, one typically sees encouraging results early in the lives of the new teams, followed by a gradual diminution of both team performance and member commitment as the teams encounter obstacles rooted in long-standing and team-unfriendly organizational arrangements. That pattern is inevitable, I believe, when one seeks to obtain the benefits of work teams on the cheap, without providing the organizational supports that teams need to prosper over the long term. And these supports turn out to be harder to arrange in established corporations and public agencies than is usually acknowledged either by managers who form teams or social scientists who study them.

It is ironic that top-management teams frequently stumble over the corporate obstacle. Senior managers, after all, are the very people who create the organizational structures and policies that serve as the context for teams throughout their organizations. Yet when it comes to their *own* context, executive teams often come up short. In research being conducted collaboratively with Hay McBer, a consulting firm that works extensively with such teams, we are finding that executive teams often are significantly impaired by insufficiencies of information, educational assistance, and even basic material resources. These teams, it appears, give less attention to providing a supportive context for themselves than for front-line production and service-delivery teams in their own organizations.[14]

An often-heard observation these days is that leading a large organization has become so demanding that it is unrealistic to expect any one person to do it alone. If that observation is correct (and I have my doubts), an executive team would seem to be a natural and appropriate device for handling the senior leadership of an enterprise. But if such teams are to be worth the executive time they consume, they must be well designed, supported, and led. Top-management teams require clarity of direction, a good structure, an enabling context, and competent coaching every bit as much as do other work teams.

Roots of the Obstacles

The co-op obstacle and the corporate obstacle are two sides of essentially the same coin. In both cases, there is an unwillingness or inability to establish the set of conditions that enable teams to perform well. For co-ops, the reluctance stems from an ideologically based preference for collective vision and leadership over hierarchy, structure, and bureaucracy. For corporations, it stems from the unfriendliness to teams of those organizational structures and systems that already exist and with which managers are reluctant to meddle.

Both of these obstacles are hard to circumvent because they preserve existing collective answers to four fundamental questions about how an enterprise operates. These questions are central to the identity of any organization and therefore are quite resistant to change.

1. *Who decides?* Who has the right to make decisions about how the work is carried out, and to determine how problems that develop are resolved?

2. *Who is responsible?* Where do responsibility and accountability for performance outcomes ultimately reside?

3. *Who gains?* How are monetary rewards allocated among the individuals and groups who help generate them?

4. *Who learns?* How are opportunities for learning, growth, and career advancement distributed among organization members?

Creating the conditions that promote effective teamwork almost always involves changing the answers to some or all of these four questions, and therefore is certain to threaten the turf, prerogatives, or preferences of currently advantaged organizational actors. Those individuals are likely to respond by coming up with lots of good reasons why it would be ill advised or excessively risky to alter standard ways of operating just to accommodate team working. The meetings that ensue to discuss such concerns can persist so long into the future that nothing significant ever happens.

Moreover, the answers to the four questions are, in established enterprises, supported by deeply rooted organizational structures: the authority structure ("Who decides?"), the work structure ("Who is responsible?"), the reward structure ("Who gains?"), and the opportunity structure ("Who learns?"). The influence of these structures generally is not obvious to casual observers. They operate in the background as part of the fabric that invisibly shapes how things are done in an organization, and they foster predictability and continuity.[15] Predictability and continuity are much to be valued during times of business as usual. But when circumstances change and innovations such as work teams are called for, an organization's deep structures can be among the strongest impediments to getting teams in place and working well.

WHAT IT TAKES . . .

The conditions that foster team effectiveness are simple and seemingly straightforward to put in place. Yet, as we have seen, creating these simple conditions can be a daunting undertaking in many work organizations, something that cannot be accomplished either as an "add on" (as managers in some corporations appear to wish) or as a one-step transition to utopia (as members of some cooperative enterprises appear to wish).

Implementing self-managing work teams in a stable organization that has been fine-tuned to support and control individual work behavior is in some ways like introducing a foreign substance into a healthy biological system: The antibodies come out and take care of the intruder. There may be a bit of fever and discomfort along the way, but eventually things return to normal. The same is true for social systems. Small difficulties are dealt with routinely, without entertaining the possibility that they may be signaling a larger organizational malady. Only when things get so bad that a system's very survival is threatened do leaders (sometimes) take the actions that might fundamentally change how that system operates.[16]

At risk of inviting incredulity on the part of colleagues who actually do research on organizational change processes (and who have developed thoughtful and practical guides for planned change), let me offer here my very own change model. Intended specifically for use when implementing work teams in organizations, my model has but two steps: (1) Be prepared. (2) Lie in wait.

Being Prepared.   When a usually closed door opens, one must be ready to walk through it without delay. Organizational doors *do* open on occasion, but they may not stay that way very long. This means that those who wish to introduce fundamental changes in how work is accomplished in an organization (and I hope I've already convinced you that creating and supporting work teams usually does involve fundamental change) must be prepared so that when the time is right, they can initiate action swiftly and competently.

Preparation is real work. It involves study, to be sure—thinking, reading, visiting other organizations where teams are used, attending management seminars and conferences, and doing whatever else one can do to expand and deepen one's knowledge of the best ways to create, support, and lead work teams. But it also involves imaginative work—envisioning what might be created, what the teams would do, how they would be set up and led, and all the other matters we have explored in this book. And, finally, it involves political action—sharing with others one's vision of how teams would work and what they could accomplish, building a coalition of organization members who are prepared to support that vision, and taking initiatives to align the interests of powerful and potentially skeptical others whose cooperation will be necessary to launch and sustain work teams.[17]

It is hard to take advantage of an emergent opportunity if one has not already thought through what one seeks to accomplish, developed an image of the desired end state that can be readily apprehended and appreciated by others, and lined up the key individuals and groups who can help make the vision a reality. When preparation has been done well, the network of individuals who will make the change happen is in place and ready. Then, when the time is right, the network can be activated and change processes can begin in earnest. One does not set out on a planned sailing trip when the weather is bad. Instead, one makes sure that the boat is ready, the crew is ready, and the intended course and destination are understood by all. And then, when the weather breaks, one can say, "OK, we can go now" and be off the dock within the hour.

Lying in Wait. Sigmund Freud once said, "He who knows how to wait need make no concessions."[18] To make compromise after compromise so that one can proceed immediately to initiate change can erode one's aspiration almost beyond recognition. That is why work teams sometimes turn out to be teams in name only—getting them implemented requires making so many concessions that one winds up with work units that are *called* teams but that actually do not much differ from what already exists. To wait until the time is right, on the other hand, offers at least the possibility of a fundamental alteration in how work is construed and accomplished.

One of the great features of work organizations for those who aspire to change them is that it is rarely a long wait for *something* to happen that destabilizes the system and thereby offers an opening for change. Perhaps a senior manager leaves. Or an organizational unit enters a period of rapid growth or belt-tightening. Or one organizational unit is merged with another. Or the entire organization acquires, or is acquired by, another. Or financial disaster seems about to descend upon the enterprise. Or a new technology is introduced that requires abandonment of standard ways of operating. All of these, and more, offer opportunities for change: The balls go up in the air, and the prepared leader brings them back down in another, better configuration.[19]

All systems regularly move back and forth between periods of relative stability and periods of turbulence, and it is during the turbulent times that change occurs. Learning and change almost never occur gradually and continuously, with each small step followed by yet another small forward step. Instead, an extended period when nothing much seems to be happening is followed by a period of rapid and multidimensional change, and then by yet another period during which no visible changes are occurring. This pattern is called *punctuated equilibrium,* and it characterizes the evolution of the species, human development, adult learning—and organizational change.[20] Wise leaders, recognizing that change initiatives during periods of equilibrium have little chance of making much of a difference, watch and wait for the times of punctuation. They know that during turbulent times major interventions have a greater chance of success and that even small changes may yield disproportionately large effects.

Like preparation, waiting is work. One feels as if nothing is happening and, worse, that no one is doing anything constructive to stem further organizational deterioration. Anxious leaders cannot bear the wait, initiate change too soon, and fail to achieve their aspirations. Change-savvy leaders wait.

Forcing the Issue.   Sometimes leaders decide that the wait for turbulence is taking too long and toss a few balls into the air themselves, personally manufacturing a bit of chaos in hopes of creating just enough instability to give change a chance. Theater director Anne Bogart occasionally does that when stymied by an artistic problem during rehearsal:

> Right there, in that moment, in that rehearsal, I have to say, "I know!" and start walking toward the stage. During the crisis of the walk, something *must* happen: some insight, some idea. The sensation of this walk to the stage, to the actors, feels like falling into a treacherous abyss. The walk creates a crisis in which innovation must happen, invention must transpire. I create the crisis in rehearsal to get out of my own way. I create despite myself and my limitations and my hesitancy. In unbalance and falling lie the potential of creation. When things start to fall apart in rehearsal, the possibility of creation exists.[21]

It is tempting to exhort organizational managers to follow Bogart's courageous lead and take action that hastens the arrival of turbulence, thereby allowing change to occur sooner rather than later. Political revolutionaries regularly do this to accelerate the fall of a regime that is viewed as undesirable. Organizational leaders would never condone subversion, inciting public disobedience, or promoting violence to bring their enterprises to a state of readiness for change, of course. But they do the organizational equivalent of those political acts when they take actions that cannot be ignored and that make it literally impossible for the system to continue on its present path.

Examples abound. The executive team leader described in chapter 7 eliminated a significant number of jobs and then allowed incumbents to apply for newly defined roles in a reconfigured organization. Other leaders may choose to impose a significant across-the-board budget cut. Although purportedly done to achieve cost savings, the more important function of large budget cuts may be to force everyone to rethink how they do their business. That is what the management team of Sealed Air Corporation did when it deliberately increased the company's debt burden, using the proceeds to pay a substantial dividend to shareholders. According to economist Karen Wruck, that action, taken when the firm's financial performance was fully satisfactory, forced managers to find ways to improve internal control mechanisms that they almost certainly would not otherwise have considered.[22] Downsizing can serve the same function. So can preemptive abandonment of a technology, a product line, or even a geo-graphical location that has long been part of the organization's identity. Boeing not headquartered in Seattle? Never could happen. Except that it did, and one has to wonder if the decision to move to Chicago was at least partly driven by a hope that the move would jar the organizational balls into the air and allow, if not invite, fresh thinking about how Boeing does its business.

Draconian strategies that make it literally impossible for a system to continue operating in its traditional ways always introduce plenty of tur-bulence and therefore always offer the opportunity for constructive change. But, as many political and organizational revolutionaries have learned the hard way, such strategies by no means guarantee that the changes that are initiated will turn out to be good for the organization, for its people, for those it serves, or even for the leaders who fomented the revolution. People get hurt in revolutions, even those who lead them, and even when they are successful.[23]

. . . AND WHAT IT CAN COST

We have seen that, in many organizational circumstances, creating the conditions that actively support work teams must be more a revolutionary than an evolutionary undertaking. That is what it eventually turned out to be for Hank, the semiconductor plant production manager discussed in previous chapters. Recall that Hank was remarkably successful in convinc-ing managers much senior to himself to alter compensation, maintenance, and engineering policies or practices so they would better support the work of his production teams. The teams continued to perform well, but eventu-ally their rate of improvement slowed considerably. And Hank still kept them on a relatively short leash, retaining unto himself decision-making authority about those matters he considered most important.

David Abramis and I finished up our research at the plant, which showed that although there was much to admire in what Hank had created, the teams were not really self-managing.[24] And then, taking advantage of the turbulence that accompanied an economic downturn in the semicon-ductor industry, Hank finally decided to go all the way. The production teams, he declared, would now be called "asset management teams" and they would be given authority to manage all of their resources in pursuing collective objectives.

The transition to asset management teams was difficult, as transitions always are when decision-making authority and accountability for outcomes are altered. No matter how many times it was explained to them in team meetings, some team members seemed unable to understand that they now really were running their own part of the business. Others understood all too well and didn't want any part of it—life was much more comfortable when the buck stopped with Hank rather than with themselves. These responses are not uncommon when people have to come to terms with the fact that they are now the ones who call the shots and who will have to take the heat if things do not go well.

Eventually the changes "took," teams accepted and began to use their new authority, and performance measures for Hank's fab reached new highs. Indeed, his unit was more profitable than any comparable unit not just in the plant but in the entire corporation. Hank began receiving visitors from headquarters, from managers at other high-tech manufacturing firms, and even from academics and journalists who wanted to learn more about what he had accomplished—and how he had pulled it off. By all measures, Hank had a great success on his hands.

Not long thereafter, I received one of my occasional telephone calls from him. "Probably you ought to come out for another visit," he said. "This time to say good-bye. They've decided that some changes need to be made in my area, and the main change is going to be me." It turned out that the human resources department recently had completed its annual employee attitude survey, and the job satisfaction of people in Hank's area had dropped somewhat from its previously high level. That was the reason Hank was given for his termination. In my many years of organizational research I have often seen managers whose units had extraordinarily high employee satisfaction get sacked because their productivity was subpar. This was the first time I had ever heard of someone whose production numbers were off the top of the scale being fired purportedly because of a dip in scores on an attitude survey.

Hank actually was let go because he had gone too far. Drawing both on his intuitive understanding of what it takes to make a great team and on his considerable political skill, he had succeeded in putting in place almost all of the conditions that are needed to foster work team effectiveness. His work was revolutionary, and it was more than his organization could tolerate.

People get hurt in revolutions. Especially those who lead them. Even when they are successful.[25]

THINKING DIFFERENTLY ABOUT TEAMS

Scholars and organizational actors construe influences on work team performance differently. We scholars want to know specifically what causes a team's level of performance. To find out, we take the performance situation apart piece by piece. First we think through what might be the ingredients that are most critical for team effectiveness, and then we collect data to test our ideas empirically. Sometimes we conduct controlled experiments to isolate suspected causal factors and assess their effects. Other times we collect survey or archival data and use multivariate statistics to identify the main causes of performance. Whatever strategy we use, we seek to rule out as many alternative explanations as we can. We want to pin down the *true* causal agent.

Organizational actors, on the other hand, are not much interested in teasing out the relative influence of various possible causes of performance. Instead, they are prepared to draw on all resources at their disposal to overdetermine outcomes in the direction they prefer. They welcome rather than shun both the confounding of variables (which scientists detest because they cannot disentangle the separate causal effects of different factors) and redundant causation (which is a sure sign in scientific work that concepts have not yet been specified clearly or cleanly enough).

Although the preferences of scientists and practitioners differ, they are not mutually exclusive. There is no a priori reason why one cannot generate models of social system phenomena that are, at the same time, conceptually sound, capable of guiding constructive action, *and* amenable to empirical assessment and correction. The model of team performance that has been laid out in this book was generated in that spirit. Rather than specify the main causes of group productivity (or provide a long list of all possible causes), I have proposed a small set of conditions that, when present, increase the chances—but by no means guarantee—that a group will develop into an effective performing unit.

Conditions Rather Than Causes

To think about the conditions within which groups chart their own courses is very different from conventional scholarly models (in which the attempt is to link external causes tightly to group effects) as well as from action strategies that derive from those models (in which practitioners attempt to manage team processes more or less continuously in real time).

The difference between creating favorable conditions and actively managing causal factors in real time is evident in the two different strategies that can be used by a pilot in landing an aircraft. One strategy is to actively fly the airplane down, continuously adjusting heading, sink rate, and airspeed with the objective of arriving at the runway threshold just above stall speed, ready to flare the aircraft and touch down smoothly. The alternative strategy is to get the aircraft stabilized on approach while still far from the field, making small corrections as needed to heading, power, or aircraft configuration to keep the plane "in the groove." It is well known among pilots that the safer strategy is the second one; indeed, when a pilot finds that he or she is in the first situation the prudent action is to go around and try the approach again.[26]

To be stabilized on approach is to have the basic conditions established such that the natural course of events leads to the desired outcome—in this case, a good landing. The same way of thinking applies in many other domains of human endeavor. Consider, for example, constantly tinkering with a nation's interest rates, money supply, and tax policies versus getting fundamentally sound economic conditions in place and letting the economy run itself. Or micromanaging the development of a child versus creating a good family context that promotes healthy autonomous development by the family's youngest member. Or managing a physical injury such as a moderately serious burn with surgery and multiple drugs versus fostering the general health of the patient and letting the body heal itself. Or trying to foster creativity by telling someone to "be creative" and giving the person lots of creativity exercises versus providing a relaxing and resource-rich setting and letting the creative response appear when it will.

In all of these instances the better strategy is to devote the first and greater portion of one's energies to establishing conditions that lead naturally to the desired outcomes, and the lesser portion to on-line process management. The same considerations apply to the design and management of social systems, as well as to research that seeks to generate trustworthy findings that inform both social science theory and leadership practice.[27]

Both scholars and practitioners compromise their own espoused objectives when they hold constant the very conditions that may be among the most substantial influences on their phenomena of interest. Yet we regularly do this. Experimental researchers routinely control team authority, structure, and context, for example, because not to do so would be to allow powerful, uncontrolled forces to muddy the interpretive waters. Practitioners do it as well, to avoid the daunting task of having to negotiate changes in organizational structures, policies, and practices that lie in the province of powerful others. To think about conditions rather than causes is to think differently about teams. And, as I have attempted to show throughout this book, that simple change in how we construe work teams has significant implications both for the behavior of practitioners who create and lead work teams and for social scientists who study them.[28]

Making Magic

Michelle Walter, former executive director of the Richmond Symphony, tells of that orchestra's performance of Beethoven's Fifth Symphony for an audience of local youngsters and their parents, many of whom were making their first foray into the concert hall. Although neither Michelle nor the musicians could explain afterward why it happened, the orchestra that day gave a transcendent performance of a symphony that is surely one of the most-played pieces in the repertoire. As the reverberations of the final chords echoed and faded, complete silence held for four or five seconds, a sure sign that something special had just happened. Then the hall, filled with people who knew not the first thing about classical music, simply erupted.

The Richmond orchestra, that day, had a magical moment. We all have experienced such moments, times when a team somehow comes together in a way that produces an extraordinary outcome—a great performance, a brilliant insight, an amazing come-from-behind win. It would be wonderful if we could create magic at will, if we could somehow engineer it, but we cannot. As the cellist protagonist in Mark Salzman's novel *The Soloist* gradually comes to realize, "You cannot make great music happen; you can only *prepare* yourself for it to happen. To a degree, your preparation determines what will happen, but once it starts happening you have to surrender yourself to it."[29]

There are two certain ways to make sure that team magic does *not* occur, both of which are seen far too often in work organizations. One way to go wrong, to stay in the realm of music for another moment, is to act like a maestro on the podium, body and limbs in constant motion in an effort to pull greatness from an orchestra. It is as if the orchestra were the maestro's personal instrument, being played for all it is worth. Team leaders in maestro tradition would prefer to do the work all by themselves, without having to engender and coordinate the efforts of others. But since that is not possible, they do the next best thing and personally manage every aspect of the work process, keeping a close eye on all that is transpiring and issuing to team members an unending stream of instructions and corrections. Magic is not commonly observed in teams whose leaders act like maestros.

The other way to get it wrong is to do nothing much at all, on the assumption that the magic of teamwork comes automatically and therefore the best thing a leader can do is stay out of the way. A guest conductor who was rehearsing a symphony orchestra for an upcoming pops concert took exactly this strategy. "You people know this music better than I do," he said, "so just go ahead and play it. I'll wave my arms around a lot at the concert to please the audience, but don't pay much attention to what I'm doing." I am not making this up. It was the purest, most beautiful example of leader abdication I have had the pleasure to observe.

So what *should* a leader do to increase the likelihood that a team will have a magical moment every now and then? Split the difference between the maestro and the abdicator, being half controlling or being controlling half the time? Of course not. What is required, as I have argued throughout this book, is a different way of thinking about the leadership of teams. A leader cannot make a team be great, but a leader can create conditions that increase the chances that moments of greatness will occur—and, moreover, can provide a little boost or nudge now and then to help members take the fullest possible advantage of those favorable conditions.

This model, too, is sometimes (although not all that often) seen on the podium in concert halls. Some years ago, I had the opportunity to watch Russian conductor Yuri Temirkanov conduct a major U.S. orchestra in a performance of a Mahler symphony—the kind of piece that can invite the grandest arm-waving, body-swaying pyrotechnics. But not from Temirkanov. He cued the musicians to begin, and then his hands went to his sides. The orchestra played, and he *listened*. When some adjustment or assistance was needed, he provided it—signaling players with his eyes or body, or guiding a transition with his arms and hands. But that was about the extent of it. He had prepared the orchestra well during rehearsals, and all the right conditions were in place. Now, at the performance, when it counted the most, he was managing at the margin. And the orchestra responded by creating a little magic for itself and its audience.

LEADING TEAMS

The main message of this book for leaders and members of work teams is, I hope, clear by now. Their first priority should be to get in place the basic conditions that foster team effectiveness. Once those conditions are established, then leaders and members can make small adjustments and corrections as needed to smooth a group's progress toward its objectives. We have seen that dealing with emergent team problems and opportunities is manyfold easier—and far more likely to be successful—if conditions favorable to team performance are already in place. Moreover, under favorable conditions, there always is the possibility that some team magic may actually occur.

We also have seen that it is much easier to describe the conditions that foster team effectiveness than it is to create and sustain them in work organizations. It is true that skilled leaders can find or invent ways to create well-designed work teams in most organizational circumstances. Yet constraining work technologies or team-unfriendly organizational values occasionally can make it nearly impossible to form stable work teams that have a compelling direction, an enabling structure, and a supportive organizational context.[30] When that is the case, even highly skilled coaching cannot make much difference in work team performance.

Leaders who are considering creating work teams, therefore, are well advised to pause and analyze their organizational circumstances before charging ahead. Given the work to be accomplished, any technological or organizational constraints, and existing collective values, will it be possible to create teams that stand high on the key conditions that foster work team effectiveness? If not, then should teams be used at all? Or might it be better to manage well what now exists, and defer introducing teams until organizational circumstances make it possible to design and support them well?

The wise way to proceed is not always obvious. Some leaders will choose to move ahead, counting on changing times and their own political skills to arrange later whatever is needed to support teams in their work. My own impulse is more conservative, in that I would rather not use teams at all than risk inviting the kinds of problems that so often develop when one forces the formation of teams in circumstances where they cannot be designed or supported well.

Even when circumstances are basically favorable, creating, supporting, and leading teams well requires no small measure of knowledge, skill, and political savvy. At least at this point in the evolution of work cultures in the United States, creating and sustaining the conditions that foster work team effectiveness can be something of an uphill battle even for well-intentioned and well-motivated leaders. As I have argued throughout this book, to win that battle will require a fundamental change in how team leaders and members think about work teams and the factors that shape team behavior and performance.

A decade ago, my colleagues and I put together a book that summarized what we had learned from an intensive study of some thirty-three different work groups of various kinds—athletic teams, industrial production workers, top-management teams, prison guards, airline crews, musical ensembles, and more.[31] I proposed that our book be titled *Groups That Work*, a catchy phrase with what I thought to be a clever pun.

Bill Hicks, our editor at Jossey-Bass, sat me down and told me that he would be happy to publish the book—but not with that title. There were just too many groups in our study that barely worked at all. I went back to the manuscript and found that he was right. Probably four of our thirty-three groups were actually effective teams. The rest had problems so severe that our analysis was mainly about what had gone wrong with them. So the book eventually was published with a parenthetical phrase after my clever title: *Groups That Work (And Those That Don't)*. Until both scholars and practitioners accept the risks of revolution and break out of our traditional ways of construing and leading social systems, we all would be well advised to keep our parentheses handy.

Notes

Chapter 1

1. Research on the international airline was conducted jointly with Susan Vinni-combe, now at the Cranfield Institute of Technology. Certain identifying details about the airline have been altered in this account.

2. The research reported in this section was conducted at People Express Airlines during its highly successful early years. The founder and chairman of the company, Donald Burr, made self-managing teams a key feature of the firm's organizational design. For a detailed account of how cabin service teams were structured and led at People Express, see Cohen and Denison (1990).

3. For other approaches to conceptualizing and measuring group effectiveness, see Brodbeck (1996), Pritchard and Watson (1992), and Sundstrom, McIntyre, Halfhill, and Richards (2000).

4. For an overview of the research setting and analyses of the strengths and weaknesses of two particular teams in this organization, see Davis-Sacks (1990a, 1990b).

5. For an overview of the findings from this research, see Allmendinger, Hackman, and Lehman (1996).

6. A discussion of the mechanisms by which groups influence their members, and the consequences of those effects for people, groups, and organizations, is provided by Hackman (1992).

7. For details, including an analysis of the strengths and limitations of this approach to the development of team members' skills, see Eisenstat (1984).

Chapter 2

1. An unusual reversal of this tendency is seen in the *New York Times* report (21 April 1986, p. C1) of the defeat of the Chicago Bulls by the Boston Celtics in a 1986 NBA playoff game. The headline reads: "Jordan Scores 63 in Loss." One has to examine the small-print box of game statistics to learn that six Celtics players scored ten or more points in the game, whereas only one Bulls player other than Michael Jordan had more than ten points. Although one would not know it from the newspaper account, this clearly was a case in which a talented *team* defeated an individual star.

2. There is considerable research and clinical literature on how groups affect the roles and behaviors of individual members (Hackman, 1992; Smith, 1983) and on the reasons why individual behaviors in groups often are best understood as expressing collective sentiments rather than the dispositions of the persons who act (Bion, 1961; Smith & Berg, 1987).

3. *New York Times Magazine*, 1 July 2001, p. 25.

4. The degree to which people tilt toward individualistic versus collective explanations for such events is strongly shaped by cultural context, as is seen in the account by Smith and Berg (1987, pp. 153–155) of how a group of five managers drafted a memo to their vice president taking collective responsibility for an accident involving the automobile in which they carpooled. Smith and Berg suggest that this act, which took place in Japan, would be quite unlikely in a Western country. For a conceptual framework that explores how the meaning of teams and teamwork varies across national and organizational cultures, see Gibson and Zellmer-Bruhn (2001).

5. See Helmreich and Foushee (1993) and Helmreich and Merritt (1998, chap. 1).

6. For alternative views of the essential properties of groups, see Alderfer (1977) and McGrath (1984).

7. Although some authors, such as Katzenbach and Smith (1993), take great care to distinguish between the terms *team* and *group,* I do not. I use the terms interchangeably and make no distinction whatever between them.

8. Sometimes managers seek to induce teamwork by making members interdependent for rewards even though the work is performed entirely by individuals. Although rewards that are contingent on the performance of larger organizational units can reinforce the benefits of good team work design (see chapters 4 and 5), there is a serious risk of confusion when the work design and the reward system pull performers in different directions. For an analysis of the nature and varieties of teams, including the different team dynamics induced by task and outcome interdependence, see Wageman (2000).

9. Some details of this example have been altered for simplicity and clarity.

10. Alderfer (1980, p. 269). For a detailed analysis of the implications of boundary permeability for system vitality, also see Alderfer (1976).

11. For analysis of the types of cross-boundary exchanges that are especially critical to effectiveness, see Alderfer (1980) and Ancona and Caldwell (1992).

12. What the chief executive really wanted, it turned out, was for his top-management group to become what I call a *learning team*—that is, a group whose primary task is to promote members' individual and collective learning about managerial and organizational issues. Learning teams are an important, pervasive, and very special kind of group. They are found not only in executive suites but also in classrooms and training seminars. Indeed, much of what we know about group processes and group development has been generated from the experiences of learning teams (see, for example, Gibbard, Hartman, & Mann, 1974; Gillette & McCollom, 1990). A substantial portion of the material in this book has implications for the design, support, and leadership of learning teams. But groups whose main purpose is to help their members learn are not our primary concern. Our focus, instead, is on organizational teams that are charged with generating products, services, or decisions for use by clients or customers who are not themselves members of the team that created them.

13. See Zaleznik (1997) for a discussion of the importance of focusing on real managerial work rather than the processes and politics that too often come to preoccupy executives.

14. For details, see Haas (2002).

15. For more detail about the social and emotional dynamics that are set in motion when authority is exercised in team and organizational leadership, see Heifetz (1994), Kahn and Kram (1994), and Smith and Berg (1987).

16. Although the figure is presented as if the columns represent four distinct types of performing units, that is merely for convenience. In fact, the horizontal axis of the figure is a continuum reflecting increasing amounts of authority held by unit members relative to managers, and teams often fall on the column boundaries.

17. For examples of self-managing teams, see Goodman, Devadas, and Hughson (1988), Lawler (1978), Manz and Sims (1993), and Walton (1985).

18. For details, see Gersick (1990).

19. For documentation of the dysfunctions of overdesigning and overcontrolling work, as is sometimes done for manager-led teams, see Blauner (1964), Hackman and Oldham (1980, Pt. 1), or O'Toole (1977).

20. Governance systems provide the means by which members of social systems, including self-governing teams, make choices about collective purposes. The design of governance systems is a complex and important topic in its own right but is beyond the scope of this book. For an overview of corporate governance, see Clark (1986); for analysis of the governance of small worker cooperatives, see Saglio and Hackman (1982).

21. National Transportation Safety Board (1994, pp. 40–41). Similar findings were obtained in an internal study of on-time performance conducted by the flight operations staff of Delta Air Lines (Rand, 1998). The researchers collected data on over 12,000 departures from Delta's Atlanta hub to determine if pilots and flight attendants who remained together and on the same aircraft had better on-time performance than crews whose membership or aircraft changed during their duty period. They did.

22. For details of the NASA study, see Foushee, Lauber, Baetge, and Acomb (1986).

23. Here are pointers to a sampling of the research literature on which the assertions in this paragraph are based. Familiarity with one another, the work, and the setting: Goodman and Leyden (1991) and Goodman and Shah (1992). Shared mental models and collective mind: Cannon-Bowers, Salas, and Converse (1993), Gruenfeld and Hollingshead (1993), Mathieu, Heffner, Goodwin, Salas, and Cannon-Bowers (2000), and Weick and Roberts (1993). Shared knowledge and transactive memory: Carley (1991), Hutchins (1991), Liang, Moreland, and Argote (1995), and Wegner (1987). Skill in using shared knowledge: Watson, Michaelsen, and Sharp (1991) and Argote, Insko, Yovetich, and Romero (1995). Dealing with deviant or less competent members and building team commitment: Hackman (1992). For an overarching theoretical framework that addresses patterns of membership continuity and change in organizational work groups, see Arrow and McGrath (1995).

24. See, for example, Moreland, Argote, and Krishnan (1998). The advantages of training teams as units will not be fully realized, of course, unless team composition is stable enough for members to reap the benefits of that training in their subsequent work together. It would be hard to justify the additional expense involved in training teams as units if members were assigned to work with different teammates after completing training.

25. See Katz (1982), Katz and Allen (1982), and Wells and Pelz (1976). However, Allen, Katz, Grady, and Slavin (1988) did not replicate the curvilinear relationship between tenure and performance for a sample of 181 diverse research and development teams, which raises questions about the robustness of the earlier findings.

26. For a fascinating account of the history and dynamics of this superb quartet, see Steinhardt (1998). The conditions that foster team effectiveness discussed in this book are almost always present for professional string quartets, which is why most of them get better and better over time. By contrast, a team that is badly structured and supported is likely to start off poorly and, unless something happens to alter its structure or context, exhibit ever-increasing process and performance problems the longer members stay together and keep trying to work together (see chapter 6). That may not be for very long, however, because most of us have a strong impulse to escape from a failing group whenever we can.

27. Hapgood (1994, p. 38).

28. For further analysis of these issues, see Hackman (1993).

Chapter 3

1. As we will see in subsequent chapters, direction also is a prerequisite for good managerial decision making about how a team should be structured. Unless the main purposes of a team are clear and well understood by those who have managerial responsibility for it, managers risk making consequential errors in designing, launching, and supporting the team.

2. Campbell (1990).

3. The availability of such a tool does not mean that all teams will use it or that those who do will use it well. Despite the insistent collective focus on the precepts at People Express, for example, some individuals and teams still dismissed them as "just a bunch of nice words" and went their own ways. Direction is not in itself sufficient to ensure good team decision making about work strategies. As will be seen in chapter 6, expert coaching often is needed to help teams learn how to exploit the advantages even of direction that is both compelling and well communicated.

4. For analyses of the dynamics of various types of athletic teams, see Kahn (1990) and Wood (1990); for an assessment of the value and limitations of sports teams as a metaphor for other kinds of task-performing groups, see Katz (2001).

5. A video of Orpheus in action, along with a written case study about the orchestra, is available from the Kennedy School of Government at Harvard University (Lehman & Hackman, 2001).

6. For details and evidence, see Hackman (1990) and Woolley (2001). Lotte Bailyn (1985) makes a related distinction, between "strategic" and "operational" autonomy, in her studies of research and development professionals. Strategic autonomy is the freedom to determine research objectives, whereas operational autonomy is the freedom to use means of one's own choosing in pursuing those objectives. Consistent with the present position, Bailyn (personal communication) reports that research productivity usually is highest when operational autonomy is high but strategic autonomy low.

7. See, for example, the direction that management set for the self-managing paint production teams at the Sherwin-Williams plant studied by Poza and Marcus (1980).

8. For detailed analyses of the multiple processes by which goals shape group dynamics and performance outcomes, see Weingart and Weldon (1991), Weldon and Weingart (1993), and Zander (1971).

9. For analyses of teams whose work requires high reliability, see Snook (2000) and Weick and Roberts (1993). For a discussion and examples of how having clear ends but unspecified means can spur innovation by teams and organizations, see Gladwell (1997).

10. For a description of TQM principles, see Deming (1986) or Juran (1974). For an analysis of the strengths and weaknesses of TQM teams, including how they are directed, structured, and supported, see Hackman and Wageman (1995).

11. These problems are endemic to any work system in which central planners specify in detail what those on the front line should do (Hayek, 1988), as Jutta Allmendinger and I observed in our research on symphony orchestras in the former East Germany (Allmendinger & Hackman, 1996). The policy of the East German concert and theater agency under state socialism was that orchestras would emphasize in their programs music by contemporary composers from socialist countries. Although most people we interviewed assured us that this policy had been implemented, concert programs said otherwise. We selected one program for each orchestra in our sample and recorded the birth dates of the composers whose works were played.

Only 8 percent of the works performed by East German orchestras were by composers born in the twentieth century, compared with 20 percent for West Germany, 24 percent for the United Kingdom, and 32 percent for the United States. These orchestras, apparently, asserted their control over their own work by doing the *opposite* of what they had been instructed to do by central planners. This phenomenon is a collective manifestation of the state of psychological "reactance" that is induced when an individual's choices are constrained by someone in authority (Brehm, 1966).

12. For discussion of this issue, see Klein (1994).

13. Human factors psychologist Earl Wiener has speculated lightheartedly about the next generation of aircraft. There will be a crew of two, he predicts: a person and a dog. The job of the person will be to feed the dog. And the job of the dog will be to bite the person if he or she touches anything.

14. For details about the concept of perverse effects, see Hirschman (1989). For a discussion of how adding protective devices and systems intended to prevent incidents in chemical plants can actually increase their likelihood, see Dowell and Hendershot (1996).

15. For details, see Torbert and Hackman (1969).

16. The risk of falling into the upper-left quadrant of the matrix in figure 3-1 is especially high for self-governing teams whose members have the authority and responsibility for specifying their own purposes (see chapter 2). Self-governing teams cannot turn to a manager for direction because no external manager has the authority to specify their purposes. It can be daunting for members of such teams to decide about their main purposes and processes, because decisions about direction always involve choosing *not* to do some other things that members also deem worthy or desirable. As hard as decisions about direction can be for self-governing teams, they still must be made because coordinated forward motion cannot happen without a collective focus.

17. From the film *Work Redesign,* produced by Neal Wolff and distributed by the University of Mid-America.

18. For a discussion of these dynamics, see Bion (1961) and the collection of papers edited by Gillette and McCollom (1990).

19. For an account of one organization's struggle to bring its grand, abstract vision down to a level that members could use in carrying out their work, see Langeler (1992).

20. See, for example, Bennis and Nanus (1985), Berlew (1979), and House (1977). For a general discussion of the value of strategic ambiguity in organizational communications, see Eisenberg (1984).

21. For details about sense-making processes in organizational settings, see Maitlis (2001) and Weick (1993).

22. For details, see Locke and Latham (1990) and Locke, Soari, Shaw, and Latham (1981).

23. This example was provided by Ruth Wageman. For details of her studies of field service teams at Xerox, see Wageman (1995, 2001).

24. Note, however, that contingent rewards also can reinforce the performance-enhancing effects of challenging team objectives, as demonstrated by Knight, Durham,

and Locke (2001). Ethical issues presumably appear only when the contingent rewards are so large as to be of enormous personal consequence for performers.

25. Dunningan and Nofi (1999, pp. 75–76).

26. The role that language plays in the dynamics of work teams is explored in depth by Donnellon (1996).

27. For an analysis of the role of goal imagery in motivated performance, see Schultheiss and Brunstein (1999). Anita Woolley has pointed out to me, however, that the beneficial effects of goal imagery greatly depend on *what* end states are envisioned. Woolley suggests that encouraging team members to envision, for example, the exultation they would experience upon learning that they had won an important contest would not help members perform well (because the focus of collective attention would be on celebration rather than on the realities to be faced in doing the work itself). By contrast, eliciting images of the actual performance outcome (i.e., the properties of a product that would have a chance of winning the contest) should strengthen the team's focus on what must be done to actually generate that outcome. Although providing rich and engaging imagery about what is to be achieved is always a good idea in setting direction for teams, leaders also should make certain that the end states imagined are about the work itself rather than about the rewards that good work eventually can bring.

28. Managing trade-offs among multiple desirable outcomes is an unalterable fact of group and organizational life (Boettger & Greer, 1994). As Margolis (2001) notes, values always collide in organizations and they almost never can be assessed and compared on any single scale. To pretend otherwise (e.g., by providing a team with a rank ordering of desirable outcomes) is to introduce an artificiality that will serve poorly both the team and those who receive and use its work. (But for a well-reasoned alternative view—that to have multiple objectives is to have no objective at all—see Jensen, 2000.)

29. The dart-throwing example is adapted from a ring-toss task developed by John Atkinson and his colleagues in their research on achievement motivation (e.g., Atkinson & Litwin, 1960). For an analysis of the reasons why motivation peaks when chances for success are about fifty-fifty, see Atkinson (1958); for a discussion of the rationale for establishing "stretch aspirations" for teams in high-commitment organizations, see Walton (1985).

30. These accounts have been condensed and edited.

31. For accounts of this extensively analyzed team performance, see Allison (1971) and Janis (1982). For an analysis that uses the conceptual framework of the present book, see Hackman and Walton (1986).

Chapter 4

1. Freeman (1973).

2. Sociotechnical systems theorists call this design strategy "minimum critical specification" (Trist, 1981, p. 53).

3. A major proponent of this view in architecture was Horatio Greenough

(1958), who relied on organic forms found in nature as the source of the main principles of construction. These principles were to be adapted to particular circumstances without dictating design: "[L]et us learn principles and not copy shapes; let us imitate them like men, and not ape them like monkeys" (p. 65).

4. For an overview of this work, see Hackman and Oldham (1980) and the earlier analyses by Lawler (1969) and Hackman and Lawler (1971) on which it is based.

5. Bandura (2000) has pointed out that a sense of personal efficacy, the belief that one can produce desired effects and forestall undesired effects through one's actions, also exists at the group level when interdependent actors share a belief in their power to produce effects by collective action. Teams whose work fosters collective internal motivation are likely, over time, to develop a sense of collective efficacy.

6. This account is based on *Work Redesign*, a film produced by Neal Wolff and distributed by the University of Mid-America, and from an account in the *World of Work Report* (November, 1977), published by the Work in America Institute.

7. For an analysis of the dynamics of group multitasking, see Waller (1996).

8. For details about the motivation decrement (as well as performance decrements that arise for slippage in coordination among members), see Steiner (1972). For a discussion of social loafing, see Latane, Williams, and Harkins (1979), and for an economic analysis of free riding in groups, see Williamson (1975, chap. 3).

9. Cooper (1976, pp. 128–129).

10. In addition to enhancing learning, group feedback directly enhances productivity by providing members the knowledge of results they need to monitor and manage their ongoing performance activities (Pritchard, Jones, Roth, Stuebing, & Ekeberg, 1988).

11. For an exploration of the key role that a shared sense of psychological safety plays in team learning, see Edmondson (1999).

12. Continuous improvement, of course, is one of the main aspirations of the Total Quality Management (TQM) movement; that is why the analysis of data about production processes is so central to TQM philosophy and plays such an important role in quality programs (Hackman & Wageman, 1995).

13. There are many different views about the best way to construe and measure group norms. In this book, I rely on the conceptualization offered by Jackson (1965). For additional exploration of the relationship between group norms and work performance, see Hackman (1992).

14. For example, a manufacturing team might decide to divide itself into three subgroups, each of which would produce one subassembly, with the final product to be assembled later. Or a basketball team might decide to use a modified zone defense, with one player assigned to guard the opposing team's best shooter. Or a team of financial analysts might devise a system for checking and rechecking for errors in reports that go to clients. All of these are choices about task performance strategy. For details about the concept of a performance strategy, see Hackman and Morris (1975) or Hackman (1987); for empirical documentation of the importance of tailoring performance strategies to specific task demands, especially as they change over time, see Tschan, Semmer, Naegele, and Gurtner (2000).

15. The ways in which habitual routines shape behavior in work teams are explored in greater detail in chapter 6.

16. These are powerful psychological forces. Indeed, Anthony Giddens (1984) suggests that the human impulse to control diffuse anxiety is "the most generalized motivational origin of human conduct" (p. 54). Team leaders and members who overlook or minimize the role of anxiety management in guiding behavior in groups do so at their peril.

17. For analysis and empirical evidence about how the importation of norms happens, see Bettenhausen and Murnighan (1985).

18. See, for example, Argyris (1976), Gergen (1972), Giacalone and Rosenfeld (1989), Goffman (1967), and Jones and Pittman (1982).

19. For an analysis of how the behavior of "deviant" members can help a group affirm its identity as a social system, see Dentler and Erikson (1959).

20. See Nemeth and Staw (1989) for an analysis of how behaviors that push the outer limits of what is acceptable in a group can prompt innovation and creativity.

21. An academic dean once said to me in frustration, "Hackman, you wear your marginality on your sleeve!" I took it as a compliment.

22. For an analysis of the knowledge, skill, and ability requirements for teamwork, see Stevens and Campion (1994). For analyses of group composition more generally, see Gruenfeld (1998) and Moreland and Levine (1992).

23. For further discussion of the dynamics and dysfunctions of large groups, see Levine and Moreland (1998, pp. 419–422).

24. Brooks (1995, p. 25).

25. Steiner (1972).

26. My guess is that the number of process problems experienced by a task-performing team tracks not the number of members, but the number of *links* among members—that is, the total number of pairwise relations. The number of links is given by the formula $[n \times (n-1)] / 2$, where n is the group size. That quantity grows at an accelerating rate as size increases, consistent with Steiner's curves and Brooks's observation. A dyad has but a single link, a triad has 2, a quartet has 6, and a quintet has 10. A twelve-person group has 66 links among members—a sufficiently large number of relations that we can forgive groups of this size for usually not managing them very well. And we won't even talk about process losses in a twenty-four-person board of directors (552 links).

27. Hackman and Vidmar (1970).

28. Behavioral ecologists refer to social settings that have more, or fewer, participants than are required for optimum functioning as *overmanned* and *undermanned*, respectively (Wicker, 1979). My reading of this literature suggests that overmanning is a greater risk for team performance than is undermanning.

29. Myers and Norris (1968).

30. The advantages of small size are just as substantial for organizations, such as an industrial plant or a headquarters office, as they are for work teams. Mitch Kapor, who founded Lotus Development Corporation, says he knew it was time for him to leave when the organization became too large for everyone to eat lunch in the same room at

the same time. A rule of thumb used by others is that no more than 150 people should work at any one organizational site, that being roughly the number of people who all can know one another. Mondragon, the highly successful complex of worker cooperatives in the Basque region of Spain, also limits the size of each cooperative. In the wake of a traumatic strike at its 3,500-member Ulgor cooperative in 1974, it was decreed that no co-op in the system should exceed 500 members (Morrison, 1991). When a co-op's success brings too much growth, it executes the organizational version of cell division, converting one large facility into two reasonably sized ones (Whyte & Whyte, 1988). Mondragon is more liberal about the maximum allowable size of its constituent units than would be dictated by the 150-person rule of thumb. Still, the lesson co-op members learned from their difficulties with very large units affirms the argument of economist E. F. Schumacher (1973) that "small is beautiful."

31. One tongue-in-cheek possibility was offered by a *New Yorker* cartoonist (4 February 1985, p. 37). An executive is speaking to his associates: "The big committee hasn't been able to do anything with this problem, the middle-sized committee hasn't been able to do anything with it, and the small committee hasn't been able to do anything with it, either. Following protocol, I suggest that we now forward it to the teentsy-weentsy committee." (c) *The New Yorker* Collection 1985 David Pascal from Cartoonbank.com.

32. Lipton and Lorsch (1992) reach the same conclusion for corporate boards, suggesting that seven or eight directors is about the right size.

33. For details, see Cusumano (1997).

34. For details, see Seifter and Economy (2001).

35. For overviews of research on team diversity, see Jackson (1996) and Levine and Moreland (1998, pp. 422–424).

36. When composing project groups in my undergraduate course, I like to provide students a great deal of choice about what they will work on and whom they will work with. But I also deliberately constrain their choices to make sure that each group is at least moderately well composed. As previously mentioned, I impose a constraint on team size. I also do not allow a group to form unless the *mix* of members meets a preannounced set of criteria. These criteria include academic major, gender, year in school, and previous training and experience. It would not be possible, for example, for a project group to consist entirely of senior male psychology majors with no work experience.

37. For details about how this process unfolds, see Hackman (1992).

38. This team-level analysis closely parallels the "attraction-selection-attrition" (ASA) paradigm developed by Schneider (1987) to explain how entire organizations come to have a unique culture that in many ways reflects the characteristics of the people who are attracted to, selected by, and remain in an enterprise. For a review of evidence regarding the ASA framework, see Schneider, Goldstein, and Smith (1995).

39. See Allmendinger and Hackman (1995), Alexander, Lichtenstein, and D'Aunno (1996), and Chatman and Flynn (2001).

40. For a review of research findings about the effects of team homogeneity, see Bowers, Pharmer, and Salas (2000). One type of homogeneity merits special note.

Homogeneity of *ability*, when team members have uniformly high or low capabilities, appears to amplify the main effects of individuals' abilities. Tziner and Eden (1985) found in a study of military crews that uniformly high-ability crews far exceeded the level of performance that would have been expected of them based on the abilities of individual members, and that uniformly low-ability crews fell substantially below their expected performance level.

41. See, for example, Amason (1996), Hoffman (1965), Jehn (1995), Jehn, Northcraft, and Neale (1999), Schweiger and Sandberg (1989), Simons and Peterson (2000), and Smith, Johnson, and Johnson (1981).

42. For an analysis of the dynamics and consequences of interpersonal (as opposed to task) conflict, including the relative efficacy of different ways of dealing with it, see De Dreu and Van Vianen (2001). For exploration of the organizational conditions under which cultural diversity enhances or detracts from team effectiveness, see Ely and Thomas (2001).

43. See McLeod, Lobel, and Cox (1996) and Watson, Kumar, and Michaelsen (1993); for an alternative perspective, see O'Reilly, Williams, and Barsade (1998).

44. Note that the Butler teams were composed to be moderately heterogeneous on task skills, not member personality. Although it is intuitively plausible that the fit among members' personalities and personal styles also would affect team dynamics, research has not yet generated findings about the matter robust enough for use in composing work teams in organizations. As Moreland and Levine (1992, pp. 262–265) note, most research on the impact of team member personalities assumes an additive model in which the average level of some personality trait influences group dynamics or performance. It is perhaps more likely that it is the *configuration* of personalities that affects how team members interact, as originally suggested many years ago by Schutz (1958) and more recently by Belbin (1981; but also see Furnham, Steele, & Pendleton, 1993). For a sampling of contemporary findings about the impact of member personalities on group functioning, see Barrick, Stewart, Neubert, and Mount (1998), Neuman and Wright (1999), and Paletz and Maslach (2000).

45. For a case analysis, with commentary, of strategies for dealing with team destroyers, see Wetlaufer (1994).

46. For a discussion of the circumstances in which intergroup explanations of individual behaviors may be called for, see Smith (1983).

47. For additional discussion of splitting and related phenomena, see Smith and Berg (1987, chap. 4).

48. Melville (1846/1993, p. 22).

49. See Ginnett (1990, 1993) and Hackman (1986).

50. This state of affairs is not uncommon. Distal and often invisible features of the environment can powerfully shape each of the three structural features discussed in this chapter: the team task, team norms of conduct, and team composition. Tasks are shaped and constrained by the nature of available technology, norms by broad cultural values, and composition by labor markets. In each case, professional groups within organizations mediate between the organizational environment and team structures:

Industrial and system engineering groups draw on available technology to create tasks, human resource groups express shared values in how they design and deliver training and socialization practices, and personnel groups respond to labor market forces in developing and implementing recruitment and selection policies. Ironically, the greater the professionalism of these groups, the more influence they have on how teams are structured—and the less the influence of line managers on the structural features of the teams they create.

51. For rather breathless accounts of the Gore organization, see Rhodes (1982) ("No ranks, no titles, nothing but profits. W. L. Gore & Associates has an unusual approach to management structure—none at all") or Shipper and Manz (1992). For a description of network organizations, including the conditions that give rise to them, see Powell (1990). For a basic introduction to complexity theory, see Gleick (1987); for its application to leadership and organization, see Drazin and Sandelands (1992) or Wheatley (1999).

52. For a typology of virtual teams, see Bell and Kozlowski (in press).

53. See, for example, Cummings (2001).

54. See, for example, Buckley (2001), Gibson and Cohen (in press), and Klein and Kleinhanns (2001).

Chapter 5

1. Almost all work teams must manage relations with individuals or groups in the larger social systems within which they operate. Usually this social system is the team's parent organization, and this chapter focuses on the kinds of supports from the parent organization that facilitate team effectiveness. Sometimes, however, people or groups located outside the organization are more salient—for example, the opposing team and spectators for an athletic team, customers for an industrial work group, or clients for a financial services team. How well teams manage their relationships with such external entities also can be highly consequential for their performance. For an analysis of teams' cross-boundary exchanges, see Ancona and Caldwell (1992), and for an exposition of the multiple functions that contexts serve for groups in organizations, see Hackman (1999).

2. To stretch the metaphor to (and perhaps beyond) its breaking point, one also could view the watering of the seedling early in its life as akin to the team-building activities of the team leader, discussed in the next chapter.

3. See, for example, Sundstrom (1999), Wageman (1999), Walton (1980), and Yeatts and Hyten (1998, Pt. IV).

4. See Druskat and Kayes (1999), Glaser and Klaus (1966), Lawler (2000), and Spreitzer, Noble, Mishra, and Cooke (1999).

5. For a description and analysis of work teams at this plant in the early stages of their development, see Abramis (1990).

6. Lawler (2000). For an examination of the factors that determine the "incentive intensity" of different kinds of team rewards in various organizational circumstances, see Zenger and Marshall (2000).

7. Wageman (1995); see chapter 6 for additional details about how leaders can expand their opportunities to administer spontaneous rewards.

8. This is an especially prevalent problem in public sector and nonprofit organizations. Because team managers in these organizations share the general tendency to think mainly in terms of money when they think "reward," they sometimes erroneously conclude that there is nothing they can do to tangibly reward excellent team performance. It is true that teams cannot be offered a share of the profits in an organization where there are none. But that very fact can spur public and nonprofit managers to think creatively about other kinds of rewards and recognition that may be uniquely available within, or uniquely appropriate to, their special kinds of organizations.

9. Lepper, Greene, and Nisbett (1973).

10. See Deci (1975) and Lepper and Greene (1978).

11. See Amabile (1993) for further evidence that the supposed trade-off between intrinsic and extrinsic motivation is neither as straightforward nor as general as sometimes has been claimed.

12. For details about how this was done for service teams at Xerox, see Hackman, Wageman, Ruddy, and Ray (2000) and Wageman (1995).

13. Williams (1986).

14. Wood (1990).

15. To try to capture the benefits of both teamwork and individual achievement, managers sometimes adopt a mixed model in which some parts of the work and the reward system are structured for individual performance, whereas other parts require teamwork and provide team-based rewards. Such models rarely work well because they send contradictory signals to members, engender confusion about who is accountable for what portions of the work, and generally create units that underperform both individuals and real teams (Wageman, 1995).

16. For an exploration of special reward system challenges and opportunities for teams in high-commitment work systems, see Walton (1980); for an analysis of special reward system issues for different types of work teams, see Lawler (1999); and for a discussion of reward system design for virtual teams, see Lawler (in press).

17. See Hargadon (1999) and Spreitzer, Noble, Mishra, and Cooke (1999).

18. Note that the present focus is on the actual *information* that is available to a work team—the data and projections that members can use in forging a task performance strategy appropriate to the team's particular circumstances. There also exists a considerable body of knowledge about ways information technology can facilitate communication among team members, especially when they are not geographically co-located (for overviews, see Benbasat & Lim, 1993; Cummings, 2001; Mankin, Cohen, & Bikson, 1996; McGrath & Hollingshead, 1994; and Sundstrom, 1999, Pt. Three). Examples include the provision of online chat rooms for real-time computer-mediated interaction, collaborative editing software, and virtual environments that allow members to feel as if they are working together in the same room when they actually are not. Many of these devices and programs can be helpful in easing, and even in enriching, interaction among dispersed team members, but their efficacy depends heavily on the degree to which the fundamental design of the work team is

sound. As MIT management professor Wanda Orlikowski notes, groupware technologies "are designed to support groups, but I find that these technologies are used ineffectively or not at all, because the organizational context does not support group work and the teams themselves have no norms or structures to facilitate their work" (personal communication, March 28, 1994). Groupware and other advances in information technology also have fostered the development of dispersed "communities of practice" (Brown & Duguid, 2000). Members of such communities archive, retrieve, and exchange their knowledge and expertise, but they are not task-performing teams of the kind being discussed in this book (see chapter 2).

19. As sometimes was true at People Express, the airline minimized the risk of going too far in one direction (in this case, toward secrecy) by swinging too far in the other. When one thinly disguised representative of U.S. Air was discovered sitting in the gate area of the Newark Airport counting the number of people boarding People Express planes during the airline's first week of operations, a CSM introduced him to a general manager who simply handed him the numbers he had been sent to obtain covertly. "There was no need for him to waste his whole day counting," the manager later explained, "when I already had the numbers he'd been told to get."

20. See, for example, Hansen and Haas (2001). Information overload is not driven solely, or even mainly, by recent advances in data processing and storage capabilities; over two decades ago, Feldman and March (1981) explored the reasons why organizations systematically gather far more information than they either need or could possibly use.

21. A number of details about the emergency response center have been altered in this account.

22. See Haas (2002).

23. How much information a team actually *needs* also depends in part on its latitude to manage its own affairs. Those teams that have the authority to invent their own strategies and manage their own performance processes require relatively complete data about both the parameters of the performance situation and the likely consequences of alternative ways of proceeding. Manager-led teams that do not have such responsibilities generally have less need for such data.

24. For details, see Emerson (1962).

25. But not always. Sometimes those who design work systems go too far the other way, leaving the manager almost completely dependent on the team, with no countervailing dependence of the team on the manager. This can be just as dysfunctional for system effectiveness as the more typical system in which the power equation is tilted too far in the manager's direction.

26. For details, see Eisenstat (1990).

27. This example is adapted from Hackman and Oldham (1980, p. 197).

28. For an overview of research and theory on the training of intact teams, see Moreland (2000) and Moreland, Argote, and Krishnan (1998).

29. See, for example, Wiener, Kanki, and Helmreich (1993).

30. The impact of such supports, as well as that of team-focused crew resource

management training, is substantially greater when crews have stable membership than when they are continuously forming and reforming. Educational and technical assistance helps stable teams continuously expand and deepen members' *collective* knowledge and expertise over time (see chapter 2).

31. For a discussion of issues and challenges in devising and delivering training for intact teams, see Ilgen (1999, pp. 133–134).

32. The extent of the problem was captured by Steve McIntosh, who directed a highly professional training and development group at PPG Industries, in an interview with management professor Jay Liebowitz: "The biggest obstacle to self-managed teams [at PPG] is the Human Resources Department. The problem is that Human Resources is so system bound. Some of the things standing in the way of self-managing teams are the rigid seniority system, the overtime rules, and traditional pay practices. These systems are not flexible enough to address the team workers' needs" (Liebowitz, 1993, p. 3).

33. For an analysis of the issues and challenges faced by professional teams in organizations whose main responsibility is the support of other units, see Davis-Sacks, Denison, and Eisenstat (1990).

34. For a model of how effective external leaders move back and forth across boundaries to support their teams, see Druskat and Wheeler (2001).

Chapter 6

1. Even though thoughtfully crafted, such interventions often are based on flawed assumptions about the dynamics of human behavior and therefore yield unexpected outcomes that may be the opposite of what is intended. Argyris and Schon (1996) describe the reasons this happens and offer an alternative way of thinking about intervention into human systems that, their research suggests, is less likely to yield unanticipated dysfunctional consequences.

2. For analyses of how mindless habitual routines operate to shape human behavior, and what can be done to counter their dysfunctional consequences, see Langer (1989), Louis and Sutton (1991), and Weiss and Ilgen (1985); for a discussion of the role of routines in group life, see Cohen and Bacdayan (1994) and Gersick and Hackman (1990).

3. For details, see Hackman and Morris (1975) and Hackman and Wageman (2001).

4. A detailed description of the work performed by these teams and how they typically operate is provided by Wageman (1995).

5. For an account of how this was accomplished at Xerox, including a discussion of the obstacles that managers encountered in getting these conditions established in their organization, see Hackman, Wageman, Ruddy, and Ray (2000).

6. For additional details about the origins, dynamics, and consequences of process losses in groups, see Steiner (1972).

7. By contrast, social loafing is rare in small teams with well-designed tasks,

which reinforces the importance of keeping team size small and designing team tasks that foster collective motivation (see chapter 4).

8. Still, team spirit is not without risk. Under some circumstances (for example, when there are strong incentives for performing well), team spirit can evolve into group ethnocentrism and spawn dysfunctional competition and conflict *between* groups.

9. A full report of the investigation of this accident is available from the National Transportation Safety Board (1982). The analysis that follows is adapted from Gersick and Hackman (1990, pp. 65–67).

10. National Transportation Safety Board (1982), Gersick and Hackman (1990, pp. 65–67).

11. Ibid.

12. For details, see Argyris (1985) and Smith and Berg (1987).

13. The practice of breaking up a high-performing team and spreading the talent around to strengthen other teams is not without risk. This actually was tried at Xerox, but the practice turned out to weaken the high-performing team almost as much as it strengthened the target teams (Hackman, Wageman, Ruddy, & Ray, 2000).

14. See Tuckman (1965). For a more recent review of stage models of group development, see Moreland and Levine (1988).

15. See, for example, Ancona and Chong (1999), Argote and McGrath (1993), Gersick (1988), Ginnett (1993), Mann (2001), McGrath and Kelly (1986), and McGrath and O'Connor (1996).

16. Since groups' projects in the original study (Gersick, 1988) were of varying duration, these periods varied from several days to several weeks. A subsequent experimental study (Gersick, 1989), in which all groups had the same amount of time to complete their task, found the same life-cycle dynamics as did the original field study.

17. For details, including discussion of conditions under which time-inappropriate motivational, educational, and consultative coaching interventions may nonetheless succeed, see Hackman and Wageman (2001). Timing issues in coaching teams are also explored in a teaching case and video; see Wageman and Hackman (1999), *The overhead reduction task force* [Case No. 9-400-026], [Videocassette No. 9-400-501], [Teaching Note No. 5-400-027]. Boston: Harvard Business School Publishing.

18. It is a characteristic of all social systems, from small groups to large organizations, that decisions made early in a system's life have consequences over its entire life span (David, 1986; Scott, 1991, pp. 178–179).

19. For details, see Ginnett (1990, 1993). Consistent with these findings, an experimental study by Smith, Salas, and Brannick (1994) showed that the kind of briefing pilots received (teamwork-oriented versus leader-dominant) significantly affected their subsequent attitudes and behavior as flight crew members.

20. These days, almost all airlines provide captains with training in how to conduct team-building briefings, and briefings have become standard practice in commercial aviation. Flying is safer because of it.

21. Although I am aware of no systematic research on the process by which work teams revise and redefine their assigned tasks, the task redefinition process has been examined for individual performers (see Hackman, 1969, and Staw & Boettger, 1990).

22. For details, see Hackman, Brousseau, and Weiss (1976).

23. For details, see Woolley (1998).

24. For an analysis of TQM as an intervention for improving team work processes, see Hackman and Wageman (1995).

25. Edmondson (1999) provides an informative conceptual and empirical analysis of the conditions that foster team learning, with special emphasis on the role of psychological safety in making collective learning possible.

26. For details, see Corn (2000).

27. See, for example, Komaki (2000) and Komaki, Desselles, and Bowman (1989).

28. For details, see Wageman (1995).

29. For details, see Walton (1980) and Walton and Schlesinger (1979).

30. See, for example, Kozlowski, Gully, Salas, and Cannon-Bowers (1996), Schein (1988), and Schwarz (1994).

31. I am grateful to Doug Marty, a varsity player at Stanford University who subsequently became a professional player and coach, for sharing with me his insights and observations about basketball coaching.

32. Different sports do invite different coaching styles. In a review of books about great coaches, Malcom Gladwell points out the striking differences in how soccer and football coaches behave:

> In soccer, the coach is a distant figure on the sideline. He may shout occasionally to his players, but the field is generally too large and the crowd too loud for him to be heard. His ability to call plays, or send in substitutions, is severely limited. A soccer coach is not the director of the action, he is more like the producer—a man to handle broad strategy and logistics. The American football coach is, by contrast, a micromanager. . . . The movements of every player on a football field are, with few exceptions, rehearsed and choreographed by the coaching staff, and the coach issues explicit instructions to his team before every play through a direct wireless connection between his headset and the helmet of his quarterback. (Gladwell, 2000, p. 30)

In terms of the framework discussed in chapter 2, soccer teams are self-managing, whereas football teams are manager-led. Differences in coaches' behaviors, in their relative value to their teams, and in their personal accountability for team outcomes all follow from this fundamental difference in how authority is partitioned between coach and team.

33. When observing a youth league coach behaving this way, one wants to yell "Just let the kids *play!*" For some reason unknown to me, we seem to be more accepting of college and professional coaches who pace relentlessly up and down the sidelines yelling and complaining without pause than we are of youth league coaches.

34. For details, see Staw (1975).

35. See Kaplan (1979). For other reviews that reach highly similar conclusions, see Salas, Rozell, Mullen, and Driskell (1999) and Woodman and Sherwood (1980).

36. See Delbecq, Van de Ven, and Gustafson (1975).

37. Two findings are of special interest in the present context. Jehn (1995) found

that task conflict could facilitate group performance for engaging tasks, but that it impaired group functioning for tasks that were highly routine. This finding further affirms the interdependence between team structure (here, the design of its task) and group interaction processes. Coaching interventions that help team members identify and address differences in their views about how the task ought to be performed can be helpful if the team task is motivationally well designed—but can backfire if the task is routine and repetitive. Research by Jehn and Mannix (2001) highlights the role of timing in understanding and addressing conflict among members. Among other findings, these researchers observed that well-performing teams exhibited moderate levels of task conflict at the midpoint of the group interaction. And, as we have seen, the midpoint is exactly the time when teams are most open to coaching interventions intended to help members bring their task performance strategies into better alignment with task and situational demands.

38. For details, see Lehman and Hackman (2001), Seifter and Economy (2001), and Traub (1996).

39. The idea of shared leadership is generally more attractive in theory than it is in practice. Not to have some single individual who is responsible for making sure things stay on track is to invite coordination problems ("Who *was* supposed to do that?") and unnecessary interpersonal conflict as those who are supposedly sharing leadership arrange themselves into a hierarchy. Ideas such as "Co-CEOs" and the "Office of the President" sound better than they actually work.

40. It also is possible, of course, for a coach to be *oppressively* present. If the coach takes over and handles personally all the problems he or she believes to be really serious, then members will be unlikely to ever develop their collective capabilities as a self-managing team.

Chapter 7

1. For details, see Corn (2000).

2. See Meindl, Erlich, and Dukerich (1985); for a discussion of the mechanisms that drive leader attributions, see Meindl (1990).

3. Influential and pessimistic early reviews of research findings on leader traits were published by Stodgill (1948) and by Mann (1959), the latter focusing on the personality traits of *group* leaders. For reviews of more contemporary research on leadership traits and assessments of the present state of leadership research more generally, see Hogan, Curphy, and Hogan (1994), Hollander (1985), and the integrative books by Bass (1990), Chemers (1997), and Yukl (2002).

4. Among the most promising contemporary research streams on leader personality and collective performance identified by Hogan, Curphy, and Hogan (1994) are the studies of "charismatic" leaders by Robert House and his colleagues (e.g., House, 1977; House, Spangler, & Woycke, 1991) and research by Robert Helmreich and his colleagues on the role of airline captains' personalities in shaping crew dynamics and flight safety (e.g., Chidester, Helmreich, Gregorich, & Geis, 1991).

5. This possibility has been at least hinted at recently by one commentator (Nicholson, 2001).

6. My credibility on this topic may be lessened somewhat by what happened when I participated as a guest in one airline's training program. I took the test that was offered and, upon plotting my scores, discovered that my characteristic behavioral style was most similar to that of "housewife." This category was not viewed by other participants as among the most desirable. Although they acknowledged that a university professor might well fall into it, a real *pilot* surely would not. We laughed about the episode, but I could not help wondering about the feelings of those pilot participants who shared the category with me.

7. See, for example, Bass (1990) and Fleishman (1973).

8. For a review of contingency models of leadership, see Yukl (2002, chap. 8); for an example of a contingency model that focuses on leaders' cognitive resources, see Fiedler and Garcia (1987); for one that provides carefully drawn implications for leader behavior, see Vroom and Jago (1988).

9. Humans are quite limited in their ability to process multiple contingencies in making decisions about their behavior (Gigerenzer, 1999; Simon, 1990). Recognizing this, one distinguished contingency theorist had an electronic device constructed to guide leaders' decisions about their behavior. The leader sets various switches in accord with the characteristics of the decision situation, pushes a button, and has electronically revealed the course of action that, according to this scholar's contingency theory, should be followed. The device has not been marketed (indeed, its construction was something of a lighthearted enterprise), but it nicely symbolizes the difficulty of using complex contingency theories as guides for leader behavior.

10. See, for example, Farris and Lim (1969) and Lowin and Craig (1968).

11. Zajonc (1965). See Fiedler and Garcia (1987) for additional evidence about how a leader's ability to use his or her cognitive resources is compromised in stressful circumstances.

12. See, for example, Argyris (1993).

13. For further discussion of how the impact of coaching is conditioned by a team's direction, structure, and context, see Hackman and Wageman (2001).

14. For details of this study, see Wageman (2001). Design factors are likely to moderate the impact of almost any process-focused intervention, not just leader coaching. For example, consider the effects of "brainstorming" interventions on group creativity. As noted by Hargadon (1999), research evidence provides little support for brainstorming as a means for enhancing creativity. Would that conclusion hold if the groups researched had been superbly designed? Hargadon's own findings suggest that if brainstorming groups have both an information-rich context and a set of collective norms that actively support use of that information, the intervention may indeed promote creativity.

15. In statistical language, design features controlled 40 percent of the variation in team self-management, compared with 10 percent for leader coaching. For performance outcomes, design features controlled 37 percent of the variation, compared with less than 1 percent for leader coaching.

16. For discussion of the factors that make it difficult for a team to change course once members have established a standard mode of operating, see Gersick and Hackman (1990).

17. For details, see Greenblatt (2001).

18. For evidence about the risks of an overemphasis on procedures, see Woolley (2001).

19. See Katz and Kahn (1978, chap. 2).

20. For a detailed report of these findings, see Ginnett (1987, 1993).

21. See Hackman and Walton (1986) for a discussion of the special issues that arise for different types of teamwork.

22. The temptation to mimic the style of the master is a significant risk of the "apprenticeship" model of professional education. The risk is encountered in numerous domains. In schools of education, students may be so intent on mimicking the style of master teachers with whom they are working that they shortchange the development of their own unique talents as educators. In conservatories, talented young players may defer the development of their own musical voices in favor of learning to play in the style of the master with whom they are studying. Even in research training, apprentices may learn well how to design and conduct studies in the fashion of the senior scientist with whom they are working—but depart their training a pale copy of that scientist: "He's quite good," the letter of recommendation says, "but not as good as his professor." There is much to be learned from masters, but the best learning occurs when what the master has to offer is incorporated into the novice's evolving personal style of teaching, performing, researching—or leading.

23. The recovery community has an only slightly tongue-in-cheek aphorism that captures this phenomenon: "Insanity is doing the same thing over and over again, and expecting different results."

24. One airline that participated in our research went to great lengths to impress upon captains that their behavior was critical in helping the airline weather the difficult economic and operational times it had encountered. "If there is a delay before pushback," captains were told, "get out of the cockpit and see if you can help resolve the problem. You may be the one person who can really do something about it." It is ironic that these same captains, exhorted to exercise their authority to deal with problems formally beyond the bounds of their own job, found their latitude in doing their *real* work ever more limited.

25. These attributes closely parallel those previously identified in joint work with Richard Walton (Hackman & Walton, 1986).

26. See, for example, Campbell (1988), Goldstein (1991), and Goldstein and Sorcher (1974).

27. Schools of management generally are excellent in helping their students develop diagnostic and analytic skills, but most of them provide little or no training in the execution skills that would help management students *use* to good effect what they have learned. This state of affairs may reflect the fact that it is much more labor intensive to help students develop leadership skills than it is to teach them concepts

and analytic techniques. Or it may be that educators assume that leadership skills are best developed informally on the job. In either case, not to provide management students the opportunity to practice the skills they will need to enact team leadership roles is to significantly shortchange them. I am reminded of a cartoon depicting the first day of work of a freshly minted M.B.A. He has been given a tour of the facilities by his boss, and finally has arrived at his new office. "That was all very interesting," he says. "But now it's time to get to work. Where's the case?"

28. For an exploration of managerial courage, including strategies for keeping one's job while exhibiting it, see Hornstein (1986).

29. If courage is required of those who hold formal leadership roles, that quality is needed even more by regular members of teams who have no special obligation to lead but who nonetheless elect to take leadership initiatives. Official team leaders generally have some resources that regular members do not. They have at least modestly more formal power and more ready access to information, resources, and managerial colleagues. And they usually have a positive balance of what Hollander (1958) has termed "idiosyncrasy credits," the latitude to deviate from established group norms without incurring the corrections or sanctions that would be applied to other team members. Without these role-conferred advantages, it can be quite risky for a team member to courageously take an action or raise a question about matters that others have come to accept as "the way things are done here."

30. Organizations do, however, differ enormously in the degree to which they provide a context that supports the emotional development of their members. In some, reflection on and thoughtful exploration of emotional issues is an accepted and valued part of organizational life. Other organizations are more like emotional playrooms for perpetual adolescents.

31. The case for focusing on competence rather than "intelligence" in selecting among candidates is persuasively made by David McClelland (1973). Based on McClelland's work, the Hay McBer consulting firm has developed competence-based models for identifying leaders and composing senior management teams. Research now being conducted by Ruth Wageman of Tuck School at Dartmouth College and Mary Fontaine of Hay McBer is seeking to identify those team leadership competencies that are helpful to a team so long as they are held by any team member, regardless of role, versus those that are helpful only if they are held by the formal team leader.

32. For further exploration of the functional approach to leadership, see Hackman and Walton (1986) and McGrath (1962). For an application of a functional approach to group decision-making processes, see Hirokawa (1985).

33. The debate about how much difference leaders actually make has addressed mainly the impact of CEOs on corporate performance. This literature is reviewed by Wasserman, Nohria, and Anand (2001), who conclude that the question "Does leadership matter?" is unlikely ever to be satisfactorily answered. A more tractable and useful question, they suggest, is "*When* does leadership matter?"

34. The proposal that leaders should keep their distance is among the recommendations offered by Janis (1982) to minimize the chances of "groupthink."

Chapter 8

1. For details, see Osterman (1994). Devine, Clayton, Philips, Dunford, and Melner (1999) obtained very similar findings from a survey of a random sample of U.S. organizations conducted in 1997.

2. News release from Work in America Institute, July 15, 1998. Not everyone is sanguine about the increasing use of teams in work organizations, however. Leadership researcher Abraham Zaleznik, in an interview with Thomas Kiely published in the October 15, 1993, issue of *CIO*, worries that the trend toward teams and collaboration is eroding both leadership and accountability in contemporary organizations; and Sinclair (1992) suggests that team ideology can tyrannize individual members "by camouflaging coercion and conflict with the appearance of consultation and cohesion" (p. 611).

3. Osburn, Moran, Musselwhite, and Zenger (1990, pp. 5–6).

4. Osburn, Moran, Musselwhite, and Zenger (1990, vii).

5. The proper way to determine what is responsible for the differences is to conduct an experiment in which some units are randomly chosen to receive a treatment (in this case, work teams) and others are control units. The value of experimental research is that it allows unambiguous inferences to be drawn about what caused any treatment effects obtained. Unfortunately, experiments rarely are a viable option for assessing interventions such as the introduction of work teams in organizations. For one thing, the level of experimenter control required in such studies (i.e., to randomly assign people to units and units to conditions) would not be tolerated by most managers who have work to get done. Moreover, if an organization were found in which managers *would* relinquish such control to experimenters, there would be serious questions about the generalizability of findings obtained in such an unusual place (Hackman, 1985).

6. Additionally, positive effects may be observed simply because of the well-known "Hawthorne effect" (Roethlisberger & Dickson, 1939).

7. For reviews, see Kozlowski and Bell (in press) and McGrath (1984).

8. Steiner (1972).

9. There is an already large and growing research literature on the performance effectiveness of work teams. Here is a starter set of illustrative and informative pieces: Cohen and Bailey (1997), Cohen and Ledford (1994), Cordery, Mueller, and Smith (1991), Jackson, Mullarkey, and Parker (1994), Poza and Marcus (1980), and Wall, Kemp, Jackson, and Clegg (1986). For empirical analyses and reviews of the potency of design factors in shaping team effectiveness, see Campion, Medsker, and Higgs (1993), Cohen (1994), Scott, Bishop, and Casino (1997), Wageman (2001), and Yeatts and Hyten (1998).

10. See Hackman (1984).

11. People often become increasingly rigid when they come under threat, which can result in heightened commitment to established ways of doing things—even though what may really be needed in such circumstances is innovative thinking (Staw, Sandelands, & Dutton, 1981).

12. Even value-driven enterprises that successfully circumvent the cooperative obstacle are not out of the woods, as Katherine Newman (1980) found in her research on workers' collectives: "Some of the collectives included in this study *were* able to create and sustain the ideal organization they had hoped for. However, most of them moved toward hierarchical structures of authority, thus metamorphosing into the opposite of what they had intended to be" (p. 145). It is a continuing challenge for self-governing organizations to avoid the unwanted encroachment of hierarchy as they seek to balance between the rights of owners and the proper prerogatives of those responsible for the day-to-day management of the enterprise (National Center for Employee Ownership, 1991).

13. For a description of how fashionable organizational practices ebb and flow over time, see Pascale (1990, chap. 1); for an analysis of how biases in access to information about the performance of other organizations can create never-ending cycles of innovation adoption and abandonment, see Strang and Macy (in press).

14. One possible reason for this state of affairs is that the core purposes of senior executive teams often are unclear (see chapter 2). If members have differing views about what their executive team exists to accomplish, it is unlikely that they will agree about the kinds of resources and support they most need to carry out their work.

15. Forces that foster similarities across organizations and the persistence of organizational features over time are referred to by sociologists as "institutional" forces (Zucker, 1977). Paul DiMaggio and Walter Powell (1983) have identified three processes that can foster similarities across organizations and the persistence of organizational features over time. Imitative processes involve organizations turning to others of the same general type, especially those that are viewed as successful, as guides for how their own enterprise should be structured. Normative processes involve the cross-organization diffusion of socially defined "correct" ways of operating. It is not so much a question of how things actually *are* done in other enterprises, but what collective values and the expectations of the broader community specify about how they *should* be done. Coercive processes involve agents with legitimate authority, such as government representatives, specifying how certain things *must* be done. Institutional forces provide a prepackaged set of right answers for organizational design and management, and they are notoriously difficult to redirect—even in the face of resolute managerial action or significant environmental shocks.

16. For a discussion of the power of momentum in organizational life, see Miller and Friesen (1980). For examples of the lengths to which corporations sometimes go to avoid making fundamental change even when senior leaders have ample data that it is called for, see Jensen (1993).

17. Consistent with the findings of Yorks and Whitsett (1989) about what it takes for work redesign interventions to diffuse throughout an organization, the strategy advocated here has more in common with the practice of international political diplomacy than with organizational change programs of the flip chart and to-do list variety.

18. Freud (1922/1959, p. 23). In the passage quoted, Freud was discussing how to avoid making "concessions to faintheartedness" by talking circumspectly about sex.

19. Under conditions of *extreme* turbulence, however, change processes become qualitatively different and less amenable to management even by well-prepared leaders. For an analysis of how organizations react to conditions of hyperturbulence, see Meyer, Goes, and Brooks (1993).

20. For an overview of punctuated equilibrium models, see Gersick (1991). For examples of how these models can inform the process of organizational transformation, see Romanelli and Tushman (1994) and Tyre and Orlikowski (1993).

21. Dixon and Smith (1995, p. 10).

22. Wruck (1994).

23. For example, see Heifetz (1994, chap. 10).

24. Abramis (1990).

25. Hank spent several months in a corporate outplacement center looking for work, and eventually accepted a position as production manager at a box manufacturing plant in Mexico. Some months later he moved back to the United States and shortly thereafter suffered a fatal heart attack.

26. Because I wanted to make sure that the technical details of this example were correct, I asked Jack Maher, a Delta Airlines captain, to review it. His response amplifies the point of the example:

> The first strategy is typical of pilots who are new to an airplane. They tend to overcontrol because they are behind the airplane, see change too late, and make aggressive control inputs that usually are excessive. They cognitively tunnel on the control instruments and have a very limited ability to sense and process environmental cues. New pilots also tend to be procedure bound, which for them is safer. But if a pilot flies like that all the time, we know immediately he or she is weak, flying is a struggle, and the pilot is not having fun. The second strategy is where we like to be. In sports psychology it is called optimum flow, such as in basketball when you become one with the game. Although I joke about it with other pilots, I hum to myself during approach and landing to facilitate the state of flow. The nice result is that in this state I can see more of the environment and expand my cognitive ability to plan adaptive responses to future events. For example, in bad weather I envision the picture I expect to see when we break out of the clouds, I can see where a missed approach would take me, and if I lose an engine I know how I can modify the miss to get more performance out of the airplane and avoid terrain and obstacles.

27. Among possible leads for further developing this way of thinking is the principle of equifinality set forth by systems theorists such as Daniel Katz and Robert Kahn (1978, p. 30) and discussed in chapter 7 of this book, and the theory of multiple possibilities proposed by psychologist Leona Tyler (1983). Equifinality reminds us that the same outcome can occur in response to many different causes, and multiple possibility theory posits that the same cause can generate a variety of different outcomes. Taken together, the two notions offer an intriguing alternative to standard

stimulus-response models in which situational causes are viewed as tightly linked to behavioral effects. Yet another alternative, proposed by Arrow, McGrath, and Berdahl (2000), is to construe work teams as complex, dynamic, adaptive systems. All of these approaches invite the development of research strategies for studying team forma-tion, development, and performance that neither destroy nor caricature systemic phenomena in order to make it possible to study them using conventional cause-effect models and methodologies.

28. For an informative and provocative exploration of the broader implications of thinking about enabling conditions rather than causes, see Cheng and Novick (1991).

29. Salzman (1994, p. 274). Moreover, the protagonist continues, trying to push things can generate the opposite of what you seek: "When, at eighteen, I started try-ing to force great music to happen I ended up making awful music; in fact, it wasn't even music anymore."

30. For a discussion of the ways that work technologies can constrain the cre-ation of conditions that foster team effectiveness, see Hackman and Wageman (2001); for an analysis of how management philosophy and organizational values affect the viability of work teams, see Walton and Hackman (1986); and for an exploration of the differential friendliness of national cultures to teams, see Cole (1985).

31. Hackman (1990).

Bibliography

Abramis, D. J. (1990). Semiconductor manufacturing team. In J. R. Hackman (Ed.), *Groups that work (and those that don't)* (pp. 449–470). San Francisco: Jossey-Bass.

Alderfer, C. P. (1976). Boundary relations and organizational diagnosis. In H. Meltzer & F. R. Wickert (Eds.), *Humanizing organizational behavior* (pp. 109–133). Springfield, IL: Thomas.

Alderfer, C. P. (1977). Group and intergroup relations. In J. R. Hackman & J. L. Suttle (Eds.), *Improving life at work* (pp. 227–296). Santa Monica, CA: Goodyear.

Alderfer, C. P. (1980). Consulting to underbounded systems. In C. P. Alderfer & C. L. Cooper (Eds.), *Advances in experiential social processes* (Vol. 2, pp. 267–295). New York: Wiley.

Alexander, J. A., Lichtenstein, R., & D'Aunno, T. A. (1996). The effects of treatment team diversity and size on assessments of team functioning. *Hospital and Health Services Administration, 41,* 37–53.

Allen, T., Katz, R., Grady, J. J., & Slavin, N. (1988). Project team aging and performance: The roles of project and functional managers. *R&D Management, 18,* 295–308.

Allison, G. T. (1971). *Essence of decision: Explaining the Cuban missile crisis.* Boston: Little, Brown.

Allmendinger, J., & Hackman, J. R. (1995). The more, the better? A four-nation study of the inclusion of women in symphony orchestras. *Social Forces, 74,* 423–460.

Allmendinger, J., & Hackman, J. R. (1996). Organizations in changing environments: The case of East German symphony orchestras. *Administrative Science Quarterly, 41*, 337–369.

Allmendinger, J., Hackman, J. R., & Lehman, E. V. (1996). Life and work in symphony orchestras. *The Musical Quarterly, 80*, 194–219.

Amabile, T. (1993). Motivational synergy: Toward new conceptualizations of intrinsic and extrinsic motivation in the workplace. *Human Resource Management Review, 3*, 185–201.

Amason, A. C. (1996). Distinguishing the effects of functional and dysfunctional conflict on strategic decision making: Resolving a paradox for top management teams. *Academy of Management Journal, 39*, 123–148.

Ancona, D., & Caldwell, D. F. (1992). Bridging the boundary: External activity and performance in organizational teams. *Administrative Science Quarterly, 37*, 634–665.

Ancona, D., & Chong, C. L. (1999). Cycles and synchrony: The temporal role of context in team behavior. In R. Wageman (Ed.), *Groups in context* (pp. 33–48). Stamford, CT: JAI Press.

Argote, L., Insko, C. A., Yovetich, N., & Romero, A. A. (1995). Group learning curves: The effects of turnover and task complexity on group performance. *Journal of Applied Social Psychology, 25*, 512–529.

Argote, L., & McGrath, J. E. (1993). Group processes in organizations: Continuity and change. *International Review of Industrial and Organizational Psychology, 8*, 333–389.

Argyris, C. (1976). *Increasing leadership effectiveness.* New York: Wiley.

Argyris, C. (1985). *Strategy, change and defensive routines.* Boston: Pitman.

Argyris, C. (1993). Education for leading-learning. *Organizational Dynamics, 21* (3), 5–17.

Argyris, C., & Schon, D. A. (1996). *Organizational learning II: Theory, method, and practice.* Reading, MA: Addison-Wesley.

Arrow, H., & McGrath, J. E. (1995). Membership dynamics in groups at work: A theoretical framework. *Research in Organizational Behavior, 17*, 373–411.

Arrow, H., McGrath, J. E., & Berdahl, J. L. (2000). *Small groups as complex systems.* Thousand Oaks, CA: Sage.

Atkinson, J. W. (1958). Motivational determinants of risk-taking behavior. In J. W. Atkinson (Ed.), *Motives in fantasy, action, and society* (pp. 322–339). Princeton, NJ: Van Nostrand.

Atkinson, J. W., & Litwin, G. H. (1960). Achievement motive and test anxiety conceived as motive to approach success and to avoid failure. *Journal of Abnormal and Social Psychology, 60*, 52–63.

Bailyn, L. (1985). Autonomy in the industrial R&D lab. *Human Resources Management, 24*, 129–146.

Bandura, A. (2000). Exercise of human agency through collective efficacy. *Current Directions in Psychological Science, 9*, 75–78.

Barrick, M. R., Stewart, G. L., Neubert, M. J., & Mount, M. K. (1998). Relating member ability and personality to work-team processes and team effectiveness. *Journal of Applied Psychology, 83*, 377–391.

Bass, B. M. (1990). *Bass and Stogdill's handbook of leadership* (3rd ed.). New York: Free Press.

Belbin, R. M. (1981). *Management teams: Why they succeed or fail*. Oxford: Heinemann.

Bell, B. S., & Kozlowski, S. W. J. (in press). A typology of virtual teams: Implications for effective leadership. *Group and Organizational Management*.

Benbasat, I., & Lim, L. (1993). The effects of group, task, context, and technology variables on the usefulness of group support systems: A meta-analysis of experimental studies. *Small Group Research, 24*, 430–462.

Bennis, W., & Nanus, B. (1985). *Leaders: The strategies for taking charge*. New York: Harper-Collins.

Berlew, D. E. (1979). Leadership and organizational excitement. In D. A. Kolb, I. M. Rubin, & J. M. McIntyre (Eds.), *Organizational psychology* (3rd ed., pp. 343–356). Englewood Cliffs, NJ: Prentice-Hall.

Bettenhausen, K., & Murnighan, J. K. (1985). The emergence of norms in competitive decision-making groups. *Administrative Science Quarterly, 30*, 350–372.

Bion, W. R. (1961). *Experiences in groups*. London: Tavistock.

Blauner, R. (1964). *Alienation and freedom*. Chicago: University of Chicago Press.

Boettger, R. D., & Greer, C. R. (1994). On the wisdom of rewarding A while hoping for B. *Organization Science, 5*, 569–582.

Bowers, C. A., Pharmer, J. A., & Salas, E. (2000). When member homogeneity is needed in work teams: A meta-analysis. *Small Group Research, 31*, 305–327.

Brehm, J. W. (1966). *A theory of psychological reactance*. New York: Academic Press.

Brodbeck, F. C. (1996). Criteria for the study of work group functioning. In M. A. West (Ed.), *Handbook of work group psychology* (pp. 285–315). Chichester, England: Wiley.

Brooks, F. P., Jr. (1995). *The mythical man-month* (2nd ed.). Reading, MA: Addison-Wesley.

Brown, J. S., & Duguid, P. (2000). *The social life of information*. Boston: Harvard Business School Press.

Buckley, K. (2001). *Virtual teams: Structure, process, and culture as predictors of effectiveness*. Manuscript submitted for publication.

Campbell, D. (1990). *If you don't know where you're going, you'll probably end up somewhere else*. Allen, TX: Thomas More Publishing.

Campbell, J. P. (1988). Training design for performance improvement. In J. P. Campbell & R. J. Campbell (Eds.), *Productivity in organizations: New perspectives from industrial and organizational psychology* (pp. 177–215). San Francisco: Jossey-Bass.

Campion, M. A., Medsker, G. J., & Higgs, A. C. (1993). Relations between work group characteristics and effectiveness: Implications for designing effective work groups. *Personnel Psychology, 46*, 823–850.

Cannon-Bowers, J. A., Salas, E., & Converse, S. A. (1993). Shared mental models in expert team decision-making. In N. J. Castellan, Jr. (Ed.), *Current issues in individual and group decision-making* (pp. 221–246). Hillsdale, NJ: Lawrence Erlbaum.

Carley, K. (1991). A theory of group stability. *American Sociological Review, 56*, 331–354.

Chatman, J. A., & Flynn, F. J. (2001). The influence of demographic heterogeneity on the emergence and consequences of cooperative norms in work teams. *Academy of Management Journal, 44,* 956–974.

Chemers, M. M. (1997). *An integrative theory of leadership.* Mahwah, NJ: Lawrence Erlbaum.

Cheng, P. W., & Novick, L. R. (1991). Causes versus enabling conditions. *Cognition, 40,* 83–120.

Chidester, T. R., Helmreich, R. L., Gregorich, S. E., & Geis, C. E. (1991). Pilot personality and crew coordination. *International Journal of Aviation Psychology, 1,* 25–44.

Clark, R. C. (1986). *Corporate law.* Boston: Little, Brown.

Cohen, M. D., & Bacdayan, P. (1994). Organizational routines are stored as procedural memory. *Organization Science, 5,* 554–568.

Cohen, S. G. (1994). Designing effective work teams. *Advances in Interdisciplinary Studies of Work Teams, 1,* 67–102.

Cohen, S. G., & Bailey, D. E. (1997). What makes teams work: Group effectiveness research from the shop floor to the executive suite. *Journal of Management, 23,* 239–290.

Cohen, S. G., & Denison, D. R. (1990). Flight attendant teams. In J. R. Hackman (Ed.), *Groups that work (and those that don't)* (pp. 382–397). San Francisco: Jossey-Bass.

Cohen, S. G., & Ledford, G. E., Jr. (1994). The effectiveness of self-managing teams: A quasi-experiment. *Human Relations, 47,* 13–43.

Cole, R. E. (1985). The macropolitics of organizational change: A comparative analysis of the spread of small-group activities. *Administrative Science Quarterly, 30,* 560–585.

Cooper, H. S. F., Jr. (1976). *A house in space.* New York: Holt, Rinehart & Winston.

Cordery, J. L., Mueller, W. S., & Smith, L. M. (1991). Attitudinal and behavioral effects of autonomous group working: A longitudinal field study. *Academy of Management Journal, 34,* 464–476.

Corn, R. (2000). *Why poor teams get poorer: The influence of team effectiveness and design quality on the quality of group diagnostic processes.* Unpublished doctoral dissertation, Harvard University.

Cummings, J. N. (2001). *Work groups and knowledge sharing in global organizations.* Unpublished doctoral dissertation, Carnegie-Mellon University.

Cusumano, M. A. (1997, Fall). How Microsoft makes large teams work like small teams. *Sloan Management Review,* 9–20.

David, P. (1986). Understanding the economics of QWERTY: The necessity of history. In W. Parker (Ed.), *Economic history and the modern historian* (pp. 30–59). London: Blackwell.

Davis-Sacks, M. L. (1990a). Credit analysis team. In J. R. Hackman (Ed.), *Groups that work (and those that don't)* (pp. 126–145). San Francisco: Jossey-Bass.

Davis-Sacks, M. L. (1990b). The tracking team. In J. R. Hackman (Ed.), *Groups that work (and those that don't)* (pp. 157–170). San Francisco: Jossey-Bass.

Davis-Sacks, M. L., Denison, D. R., & Eisenstat, R. A. (1990). Summary: Professional support groups. In J. R. Hackman (Ed.), *Groups that work (and those that don't)* (pp. 195–205). San Francisco: Jossey-Bass.

Deci, E. L. (1975). *Intrinsic motivation.* New York: Plenum.

De Dreu, C. K. W., & Van Vianen, A. E. M. (2001). Managing relationship conflict and the effectiveness of organizational teams. *Journal of Organizational Behavior, 22*, 309–328.

Delbecq, A. E., Van de Ven, A. H., & Gustafson, D. H. (1975). *Group techniques for program planning: A guide to Nominal Group and Delphi processes.* Glenview, IL: Scott, Foresman.

Deming, W. E. (1986). *Out of the crisis.* Cambridge, MA: MIT Center for Advanced Engineering Study.

Dentler, R. A., & Erikson, K. T. (1959). The functions of deviance in groups. *Social Problems, 7*, 98–107.

Devine, D. J., Clayton, L. D., Philips, J. L., Dunford, B. B., & Melner, S. B. (1999). Teams in organizations: Prevalence, characteristics, and effectiveness. *Small Group Research, 30*, 678–711.

DiMaggio, P. J., & Powell, W. W. (1983). The iron cage revisited: Institutional isomorphism and collective rationality in organizational fields. *American Sociological Review, 48*, 147–160.

Dixon, M. B., & Smith, J. A. (1995). *Anne Bogart viewpoints.* Lyme, NH: Smith and Kraus.

Donnellon, A. (1996). *Team talk: The power of language in team dynamics.* Boston: Harvard Business School Press.

Dowell, A. M., & Hendershot, D. C. (1996, November). *No good deed goes unpunished: Case studies of incidents and potential incidents caused by protective systems.* Paper presented at the meeting of the American Institute of Chemical Engineers Loss Prevention Symposium, Houston.

Drazin, R., & Sandelands, L. (1992). Autogenesis: A perspective on the process of organizing. *Organization Science, 3*, 230–249.

Druskat, V. U., & Kayes, D. C. (1999). The antecedents of team competence: Toward a fine-grained model of self-managing team effectiveness. In R. Wageman (Ed.), *Groups in context* (pp. 201–231). Stamford, CT: JAI Press.

Druskat, V. U., & Wheeler, J. V. (2001). *Managing from the boundary: The effective leadership of self-managing work teams.* Manuscript submitted for publication.

Dunnigan, J. F., & Nofi, A. A. (1999). *Dirty little secrets of the Vietnam war.* New York: St. Martin's Press.

Edmondson, A. E. (1999). Psychological safety and learning behavior in work teams. *Administrative Science Quarterly, 44*, 350–383.

Eisenberg, E. M. (1984). Ambiguity as strategy in organizational communication. *Communication Monographs, 51*, 227–242.

Eisenstat, R. A. (1984). *Organizational learning in the creation of an industrial setting.* Unpublished doctoral dissertation, Yale University.

Eisenstat, R. A. (1990). Fairfield systems group. In J. R. Hackman (Ed.), *Groups that work (and those that don't)* (pp. 171–181). San Francisco: Jossey-Bass.

Ely, R. J., & Thomas, D. A. (2001). Cultural diversity at work: The effects of diversity perspectives on work group processes and outcomes. *Administrative Science Quarterly, 46*, 229–273.

Emerson, R. M. (1962). Power-dependence relations. *American Sociological Review,* 27, 31–40.

Farris, G. F., & Lim, F. G., Jr. (1969). Effects of performance on leadership, cohesiveness, influence, satisfaction, and subsequent performance. *Journal of Applied Psychology,* 53, 490–497.

Feldman, M. S., & March, J. G. (1981). Information in organizations as signal and symbol. *Administrative Science Quarterly,* 26, 171–186.

Fiedler, F. E., & Garcia, J. E. (1987). *New approaches to effective leadership: Cognitive resources and organizational performance.* New York: Wiley.

Fleishman, E. A. (1973). Twenty years of consideration and structure. In E. A. Fleishman & J. G. Hunt (Eds.), *Current developments in the study of leadership* (pp. 1–37). Carbondale: Southern Illinois University Press.

Foushee, H. C., Lauber, J. K., Baetge, M. M., & Acomb, D. B. (1986). *Crew factors in flight operations: III. The operational significance of exposure to short-haul air transport operations* (Technical Memorandum No. 88342). Moffett Field, CA: NASA Ames Research Center.

Freeman, J. (1973). The tyranny of structurelessness. In A. Koedt, E. Levine, & A. Rapone (Eds.), *Radical feminism* (pp. 285–299). New York: Quadrangle Books.

Freud, S. (1959). *Group psychology and the analysis of the ego* (J. Strachey, Trans.). New York: Norton. (Original work published 1922)

Furnham, A., Steele, H., & Pendleton, D. (1993). A psychometric assessment of the Belbin Team-Role Self-Perception Inventory. *Journal of Occupational and Organizational Psychology,* 66, 245–257.

Gergen, K. J. (1972, May). Multiple identity. *Psychology Today,* 31–36, 64–66.

Gersick, C. J. G. (1988). Time and transition in work teams: Toward a new model of group development. *Academy of Management Journal,* 31, 9–41.

Gersick, C. J. G. (1989). Marking time: Predictable transitions in task groups. *Academy of Management Journal,* 31, 9–41.

Gersick, C. J. G. (1990). The bankers. In J. R. Hackman (Ed.), *Groups that work (and those that don't)* (pp. 112–125). San Francisco: Jossey-Bass.

Gersick, C. J. G. (1991). Revolutionary change theories: A multilevel exploration of the punctuated equilibrium paradigm. *Academy of Management Review,* 16, 10–36.

Gersick, C. J. G., & Hackman, J. R. (1990). Habitual routines in task-performing teams. *Organizational Behavior and Human Decision Processes,* 47, 65–97.

Giacalone, R. A., & Rosenfeld, P. (Eds.). (1989). *Impression management in the organization.* Hillsdale, NJ: Lawrence Erlbaum.

Gibbard, G. S., Hartman, J. J., & Mann, R. D. (Eds.). (1974). *Analysis of groups.* San Francisco: Jossey-Bass.

Gibson, C. B., & Cohen, S. G. (Eds.). (in press). *Creating conditions for effective virtual teams.* San Francisco: Jossey-Bass.

Gibson, C. B., & Zellmer-Bruhn, M. E. (2001). Metaphors and meaning: An intercultural analysis of the concept of teamwork. *Administrative Science Quarterly,* 46, 274–303.

Giddens, A. (1984). *The constitution of society.* Berkeley: University of California Press.

Gigerenzer, G. (1999). Fast and frugal heuristics: The adaptive toolbox. In G. Gigerenzer & P. M. Todd (Eds.), *Simple heuristics that make us smart* (pp. 3–34). New York: Oxford University Press.

Gillette, J., & McCollom, M. (Eds.). (1990). *Groups in context.* Reading, MA: Addison-Wesley.

Ginnett, R. C. (1987). *First encounters of the close kind: The formation process of airline flight crews.* Unpublished doctoral dissertation, Yale University.

Ginnett, R. C. (1990). Airline cockpit crew. In J. R. Hackman (Ed.), *Groups that work (and those that don't)* (pp. 427–448). San Francisco: Jossey-Bass.

Ginnett, R. C. (1993). Crews as groups: Their formation and their leadership. In E. L. Wiener, B. G. Kanki, & R. L. Helmreich (Eds.), *Cockpit resource management* (pp. 71–98). Orlando, FL: Academic Press.

Gladwell, M. (1997, April). Just ask for it: The real key to technological innovation. *The New Yorker*, 45–49.

Gladwell, M. (2000, February 24). True grit. *The New York Review of Books*, 30–33.

Glaser, R., & Klaus, D. J. (1966). A reinforcement analysis of group performance. *Psychological Monographs, 80* (Whole No. 621), 1–23.

Gleick, J. (1987). *Chaos: Making a new science.* New York: Viking.

Goffman, E. (1967). *Interaction ritual: Essays on face-to-face behavior.* Chicago: Aldine.

Goldstein, A. P., & Sorcher, M. (1974). *Changing supervisor behavior.* New York: Pergamon.

Goldstein, I. L. (Ed.). (1991). *Training and development in organizations.* San Francisco: Jossey-Bass.

Goodman, P. S., Devadas, R., & Hughson, T. L. G. (1988). Groups and productivity: Analyzing the effectiveness of self-managing teams. In J. P. Campbell & R. J. Campbell (Eds.), *Productivity in organizations* (pp. 295–327). San Francisco: Jossey-Bass.

Goodman, P. S., & Leyden, D. P. (1991). Familiarity and group productivity. *Journal of Applied Psychology, 76,* 578–586.

Goodman, P. S., & Shah, S. (1992). Familiarity and work group outcomes. In S. Worchel, W. Wood, & J. Simpson (Eds.), *Group process and productivity* (pp. 276–298). London: Sage.

Greenblatt, E. L. (2001). *A paradox in paradise: Depletion and restoration of personal resources, emotional labor, and burnout in an idyllic total institution.* Unpublished doctoral dissertation, Harvard University.

Greenough, H. (1958). *Form and function: Remarks on art, design, and architecture.* Berkeley: University of California Press.

Gruenfeld, D. H. (Ed.). (1998). *Research on managing groups and teams: Composition.* Stamford, CT: JAI Press.

Gruenfeld, D. H., & Hollingshead, A. B. (1993). Sociocognition in work groups: The evolution of group integrative complexity and its relation to task performance. *Small Group Research, 24,* 383–405.

Haas, M. (2002). *Organizing knowledge work: A study of project teams at an international development agency.* Unpublished doctoral dissertation, Harvard University.

Hackman, J. R. (1969). Toward understanding the role of tasks in behavioral research. *Acta Psychologica, 31,* 97–128.

Hackman, J. R. (1984). The transition that hasn't happened. In J. R. Kimberly & R. E. Quinn (Eds.), *New futures: The challenge of managing corporate cultures* (pp. 29–59). Homewood, IL: Dow Jones-Irwin.

Hackman, J. R. (1985). Doing research that makes a difference. In E. E. Lawler, A. M. Mohrman, S. A. Mohrman, G. E. Ledford, & T. G. Cummings (Eds.), *Doing research that is useful for theory and practice* (pp. 126–149). San Francisco: Jossey-Bass.

Hackman, J. R. (1986). Group level issues in the design and training of cockpit crews. In H. H. Orlady & H. C. Foushee (Eds.), *Proceedings of the NASA/MAC workshop on cockpit resource management* (pp. 23–39). Moffett Field, CA: NASA-Ames Research Center.

Hackman, J. R. (1987). The design of work teams. In J. Lorsch (Ed.), *Handbook of organizational behavior* (pp. 315–342). Englewood Cliffs, NJ: Prentice-Hall.

Hackman, J. R. (1990). *Groups that work (and those that don't).* San Francisco: Jossey-Bass.

Hackman, J. R. (1992). Group influences on individuals in organizations. In M. D. Dunnette & L. M. Hough (Eds.), *Handbook of industrial and organizational psychology* (Vol. 3, pp. 199–267). Palo Alto: Consulting Psychologists Press.

Hackman, J. R. (1993). Teams, leaders, and organizations: New directions for crew-oriented flight training. In E. L. Wiener, B. G. Kanki, & R. L. Helmreich (Eds.), *Cockpit resource management* (pp. 47–69). Orlando, FL: Academic Press.

Hackman, J. R. (1999). Thinking differently about context. In R. Wageman (Ed.), *Groups in context.* Stamford, CT: JAI Press.

Hackman, J. R., Brousseau, K. R., & Weiss, J. A. (1976). The interaction of task design and group performance strategies in determining group effectiveness. *Organizational Behavior and Human Performance, 16,* 350–365.

Hackman, J. R., & Lawler, E. E. (1971). Employee reactions to job characteristics. *Journal of Applied Psychology Monograph, 55,* 259–286.

Hackman, J. R., & Morris, C. G. (1975). Group tasks, group interaction process, and group performance effectiveness: A review and proposed integration. In L. Berkowitz (Ed.), *Advances in experimental social psychology* (Vol. 8, pp. 45–99). New York: Academic Press.

Hackman, J. R., & Oldham, G. R. (1980). *Work redesign.* Reading, MA: Addison-Wesley.

Hackman, J. R., & Vidmar, N. (1970). Effects of size and task type on group performance and member reactions. *Sociometry, 33,* 37–54.

Hackman, J. R., & Wageman, R. (1995). Total Quality Management: Empirical, conceptual, and practical issues. *Administrative Science Quarterly, 40,* 309–342.

Hackman, J. R., & Wageman, R. (2001). *A theory of team coaching.* Manuscript submitted for publication.

Hackman, J. R., Wageman, R., Ruddy, T. M., & Ray, C. R. (2000). Team effectiveness in theory and practice. In C. Cooper & E. A. Locke (Eds.), *Industrial and organizational psychology: Theory and practice* (pp. 109–129). Oxford, England: Blackwell.

Hackman, J. R., & Walton, R. E. (1986). Leading groups in organizations. In P. S. Goodman (Ed.), *Designing effective work groups* (pp. 72–119). San Francisco: Jossey-Bass.

Hansen, M. T., & Haas, M. R. (2001). Competing for attention in knowledge markets: Electronic document dissemination in a management consulting company. *Administrative Science Quarterly, 46,* 1–28.

Hapgood, F. (1994, August). Notes from the underground. *The Atlantic Monthly,* 34–38.

Hargadon, A. B. (1999). Group cognition and creativity in organizations. In R. Wageman (Ed.), *Groups in context* (pp. 137–155). Stamford, CT: JAI Press.

Hayek, F. A. (1988). *The fatal conceit: The errors of socialism.* Chicago: University of Chicago Press.

Heifetz, R. A. (1994). *Leadership without easy answers.* Cambridge, MA: Harvard University Press.

Helmreich, R. L., & Foushee, H. C. (1993). Why crew resource management? Empirical and theoretical bases of human factors training in aviation. In E. L. Wiener, B. G. Kanki, & R. L. Helmreich (Eds.), *Cockpit resource management* (pp. 3–45). Orlando, FL: Academic Press.

Helmreich, R. L., & Merritt, A. C. (1998). *Culture at work in aviation and medicine.* Aldershot, England: Ashgate.

Hirokawa, R. Y. (1985). Discussion procedures and decision-making performance: A test of a functional perspective. *Human Communication Research, 12,* 203–224.

Hirschman, A. O. (1989, May). Reactionary rhetoric. *The Atlantic Monthly,* 63–70.

Hoffman, L. R. (1965). Group problem solving. In L. Berkowitz (Ed.), *Advances in experimental social psychology* (Vol. 2, pp. 99–132). New York: Academic Press.

Hogan, R., Curphy, G. J., & Hogan, J. (1994). What we know about leadership. *American Psychologist, 49,* 493–504.

Hollander, E. P. (1958). Conformity, status, and idiosyncrasy credit. *Psychological Review, 65,* 117–127.

Hollander, E. P. (1985). Leadership and power. In G. Lindzey & E. Aronson (Eds.), *Handbook of social psychology* (3rd ed., Vol. 2, pp. 485–537). New York: Random House.

Hornstein, H. A. (1986). *Managerial courage: Revitalizing your company without sacrificing your job.* New York: Wiley.

House, R. J. (1977). A 1976 theory of charismatic leadership. In J. G. Hunt & L. L. Larson (Eds.), *Leadership: The cutting edge* (pp. 189–207). Carbondale: Southern Illinois University Press.

House, R. J., Spangler, W. D., & Woycke, J. (1991). Personality and charisma in the U.S. presidency: A psychological theory of leadership effectiveness. *Administrative Science Quarterly, 36,* 364–396.

Hutchins, E. (1991). The social organization of distributed cognition. In L. B. Resnick, J. M. Levine, & S. D. Teasley (Eds.), *Perspectives on socially shared cognition* (pp. 283–307). Washington, DC: American Psychological Association.

Ilgen, D. R. (1999). Teams embedded in organizations: Some implications. *American Psychologist, 54,* 129–139.

Jackson, J. (1965). Structural characteristics of norms. In I. D. Steiner & M. Fishbein (Eds.), *Current studies in social psychology* (pp. 301–309). New York: Holt.

Jackson, P. R., Mullarkey, S., & Parker, S. (1994, January). *The implementation of high-involvement work teams: A four-phase longitudinal study.* Paper presented at the British Psychological Society Occupational Psychology Conference.

Jackson, S. E. (1996). The consequences of diversity in multidisciplinary work teams. In M. A. West (Ed.), *Handbook of work group psychology* (pp. 53–75). Chichester, England: Wiley.

Janis, I. L. (1982). *Groupthink: Psychological studies of policy decisions and fiascoes* (2nd ed.). Boston: Houghton Mifflin.

Jehn, K. A. (1995). A multimethod examination of the benefits and detriments of intragroup conflict. *Administrative Science Quarterly, 40,* 256–282.

Jehn, K. A., & Mannix, E. A. (2001). The dynamic nature of conflict: A longitudinal study of intragroup conflict and group performance. *Academy of Management Journal, 44,* 238–251.

Jehn, K. A., Northcraft, G., & Neale, M. (1999). Why differences make a difference: A field study of diversity, conflict, and performance in work groups. *Administrative Science Quarterly, 44,* 741–763.

Jensen, M. C. (1993). The modern industrial revolution, exit, and the failure of internal control systems. *Journal of Finance, 48,* 831–880.

Jensen, M. C. (2000). Value maximization, stakeholder theory, and the corporate objective function. In M. Beer & N. Nohria (Eds.), *Breaking the code of change* (pp. 37–57). Boston: Harvard Business School Press.

Jones, E. E., & Pittman, T. S. (1982). Toward a general theory of strategic self-presentation. In J. Suls (Ed.). *Psychological perspectives on the self* (Vol. 1, pp. 231–262). Hillsdale, NJ: Lawrence Erlbaum.

Juran, J. M. (1974). *The quality control handbook* (3rd ed.). New York: McGraw-Hill.

Kahn, W. A. (1990). University athletic teams. In J. R. Hackman (Ed.), *Groups that work (and those that don't)* (pp. 250–264). San Francisco: Jossey-Bass.

Kahn, W. A., & Kram, K. E. (1994). Authority at work: Internal models and their organizational consequences. *Academy of Management Review, 19,* 17–50.

Kaplan, R. E. (1979). The conspicuous absence of evidence that process consultation enhances task performance. *Journal of Applied Behavioral Science, 15,* 346–360.

Katz, D., & Kahn, R. L. (1978). *The social psychology of organizations* (2nd ed.). New York: Wiley.

Katz, N. (2001). Sports teams as a metaphor and model for workplace teams. *Academy of Management Executive, 15* (3), 56–67.

Katz, R. (1982). The effects of group longevity on project communication and performance. Administrative Science Quarterly, 27, 81–104.

Katz, R., & Allen, T. J. (1982). Investigating the Not Invented Here (NIH) syndrome: A look at the performance, tenure, and communication patterns of 50 R&D project groups. *R&D Management, 12,* 7–19.

Katzenbach, J. R., & Smith, D. K. (1993). *The wisdom of teams.* Boston: Harvard Business School Press.

Klein, J. A. (1994). The paradox of quality management. In C. Heckscher & A. Don-nellon (Eds.), *The post-bureaucratic organization* (pp. 178–194). Thousand Oaks, CA: Sage.

Klein, J. A., & Kleinhanns, A. (2001). *Maximizing the contribution of diverse voices in virtual teams* (Paper 01-3, Program on Negotiation). Cambridge, MA: Harvard University.

Knight, D., Durham, C. C., & Locke, E. A. (2001). The relationship of team goals, incentives, and efficacy to strategic risk, tactical implementation, and perfor-mance. *Academy of Management Journal, 44*, 326–338.

Komaki, J. L. (2000, April). *An operant conditioning approach to team coaching.* Paper presented at the annual meeting of the Society of Industrial and Organizational Psychology, New Orleans.

Komaki, J. L., Desselles, M. L., & Bowman, E. D. (1989). Definitely not a breeze: Extending an operant model of effective supervision to teams. *Journal of Applied Psychology, 74*, 522–529.

Kozlowski, S. W. J., & Bell, B. S. (in press). Work groups and teams in organizations. In W. C. Borman, D. R. Ilgen, & R. J. Klimoski (Eds.), *Comprehensive handbook of psychology: Industrial and organizational psychology* (Vol. 12). New York: Wiley.

Kozlowski, S. W. J., Gully, S. M., Salas, E., & Cannon-Bowers, J. A. (1996). Team lead-ership and development: Theory, principles, and guidelines for training leaders and teams. In M. Beyerlein, D. Johnson, & S. Beyerlein (Eds.), *Advances in inter-disciplinary studies of work teams: Team leadership* (Vol. 3, pp. 251–289). Greenwich, CT: JAI Press.

Langeler, G. H. (1992, March–April). The vision trap. *Harvard Business Review*, 4–11.

Langer, E. J. (1989). *Mindfulness.* Reading, MA: Addison-Wesley.

Latane, B., Williams, K., & Harkins, S. (1979). Many hands make light the work: The causes and consequences of social loafing. *Journal of Personality and Social Psy-chology, 37*, 822–832.

Lawler, E. E. (1969). Job design and employee motivation. *Personnel Psychology, 22*, 426–435.

Lawler, E. E. (1978, Winter). The new plant revolution. *Organizational Dynamics*, 31–39.

Lawler, E. E. (1999). Creating effective pay systems for teams. In E. Sundstrom (Ed.), *Supporting work team effectiveness* (pp. 188–212). San Francisco: Jossey-Bass.

Lawler, E. E. (2000). *Rewarding excellence: Pay strategies for the new economy.* San Francisco: Jossey-Bass.

Lawler, E. E. (in press). Pay systems for virtual teams. In C. Gibson & S. G. Cohen (Eds.), *Creating conditions for effective virtual teams.* San Francisco: Jossey-Bass.

Lehman, E. V., & Hackman, J. R. (2001). The Orpheus Chamber Orchestra: Case and video. Boston: Kennedy School of Government, Harvard University.

Lepper, M. R., & Greene, D. (1978). *The hidden costs of reward.* Hillsdale, NJ: Lawrence Erlbaum.

Lepper, M. R., Greene, D., & Nisbett, R. E. (1973). Undermining children's intrinsic interest with extrinsic reward: A test of the "overjustification" hypothesis. *Journal of Personality and Social Psychology, 28*, 129–137.

Levine, J. M., & Moreland, R. L. (1998). Small groups. In D. T. Gilbert, S. T. Fiske, & G. Lindzey (Eds.), *The handbook of social psychology* (4th ed., Vol. 2, pp. 415–469). New York: McGraw-Hill.

Liang, D. W., Moreland, R., & Argote, L. (1995). Group versus individual training and group performance: The mediating role of transactive memory. *Personality and Social Psychology Bulletin, 21,* 384–393.

Liebowitz, J. (1993, Winter). Self-managing work teams at PPG. *Self-Managed Work Teams Newsletter,* 1–4.

Lipton, M., & Lorsch, J. (1992). A modest proposal for improved corporate governance. *Business Lawyer, 48,* 59–77.

Locke, E. A., & Latham, G. P. (1990). *A theory of goal setting & task performance.* Englewood Cliffs, NJ: Prentice-Hall.

Locke, E. A., Soari, L. M., Shaw, K. N., & Latham, G. D. (1981). Goal setting and task performance: 1969–1980. *Psychological Bulletin, 90,* 125–152.

Louis, M. R., & Sutton, R. I. (1991). Switching cognitive gears: From habits of mind to active thinking. *Human Relations, 44,* 55–76.

Lowin, B., & Craig, J. R. (1968). The influence of level of performance on managerial style: An experimental object-lesson in the ambiguity of correlational data. *Organizational Behavior and Human Performance, 3,* 440–458.

Maitlis, S. (2001). *Variations on a theme: Forms of organizational sensemaking.* Manuscript submitted for publication.

Mankin, D., Cohen, S. G., & Bikson, T. K. (1996). *Teams and technology.* Boston: Harvard Business School Press.

Mann, J. B. (2001). *Time for a change: The role of internal and external pacing mechanisms in prompting the midpoint transition.* Unpublished honors thesis, Harvard University.

Mann, R. D. (1959). A review of the relationships between personality and performance in small groups. *Psychological Bulletin, 56,* 241–270.

Manz, C. C., & Sims, H. P., Jr. (1993). *Business without bosses: How self-managing teams are building high-performing companies.* New York: Wiley.

Margolis, J. D. (2001). *Dignity in organizations.* Manuscript submitted for publication.

Mathieu, J. E., Heffner, T. S., Goodwin, G. F., Salas, E., & Cannon-Bowers, J. A. (2000). The influence of shared mental models on team process and performance. *Journal of Applied Psychology, 85,* 273–283.

McClelland, D. C. (1973). Testing for competence rather than intelligence. *American Psychologist, 28,* 1–14.

McGrath, J. E. (1962). *Leadership behavior: Some requirements for leadership training.* Washington, DC: U.S. Civil Service Commission.

McGrath, J. E. (1984). *Groups: Interaction and performance.* Englewood Cliffs, NJ: Prentice-Hall.

McGrath, J. E., & Hollingshead, A. B. (1994). *Groups interacting with technology.* Thousand Oaks, CA: Sage.

McGrath, J. E. & Kelly, J. R. (1986). *Time and human interaction: Toward a social psychology of time*. New York: Guilford Press.

McGrath, J. E., & O'Connor, K. M. (1996). Temporal issues in work groups. In M. A. West (Ed.), *Handbook of work group psychology* (pp. 25–52). Chichester, England: Wiley.

McLeod, P. L., Lobel, S. A., & Cox, T. H. (1996). Ethnic diversity and creativity in small groups. *Small Group Research, 27,* 248–264.

Meindl, J. R. (1990). On leadership: An alternative to the conventional wisdom. *Research in Organizational Behavior, 12,* 159–203.

Meindl, J. R., Erlich, S. B., & Dukerich, J. M. (1985). The romance of leadership. *Administrative Science Quarterly, 30,* 78–102.

Melville, H. (1993). *Typee: A peep at Polynesian life*. London: J. M. Dent. (Original work published 1846.)

Meyer, A. D., Goes, J. B., & Brooks, G. R. (1993). Organizations reacting to hyperturbulence. In G. P. Huber & W. H. Glick (Eds.), *Organizational change and redesign* (pp. 66–111). New York: Oxford University Press.

Miller, D., & Friesen, P. H. (1980). Momentum and revolution in organizational adaptation. *Academy of Management Journal, 23,* 591–614.

Moreland, R. L. (2000). Transactive memory: Learning who knows what in work groups and organizations. In L. Thompson, D. Messick, & J. Levine (Eds.), *Shared cognition in organizations* (pp. 3–31). Mahwah, NJ: Lawrence Erlbaum.

Moreland, R. L., Argote, L., & Krishnan, R. (1998). Training people to work in groups. In R. S. Tindale et al., (Eds.), *Theory and research on small groups* (pp. 37–60). New York: Plenum.

Moreland, R. L., & Levine, J. M. (1988). Group dynamics over time: Development and socialization in small groups. In J. E. McGrath (Ed.), *The social psychology of time: New perspectives* (pp. 151–181). Newbury Park, CA: Sage.

Moreland, R. L., & Levine, J. M. (1992). The composition of small groups. *Advances in Group Processes, 9,* 237–280.

Morrison, R. (1991). *We build the road as we travel*. Philadelphia: New Society Publishers.

Myers, J. A., & Norris, R. E. (1968). *Summary of results: B-737 crew complement evaluation*. Elk Grove Village, IL: United Airlines.

National Center for Employee Ownership (1991). The benchmark companies: Lessons from leading employee ownership firms. *Employee Ownership Report, 11* (6), 1–5.

National Transportation Safety Board. (1982). *Aircraft accident report* (NTSB Report No. AAR-82-8). Washington, DC: Author.

National Transportation Safety Board. (1994). *A review of flightcrew-involved major accidents of U.S. air carriers, 1978 through 1990*. Washington, DC: Author.

Nemeth, C. J., & Staw, B. M. (1989). The tradeoffs of social control and innovation in groups and organizations. In L. Berkowitz (Ed.), *Advances in experimental social psychology* (Vol. 22, pp. 175–210). San Diego: Academic Press.

Neuman, G. A., & Wright, J. (1999). Team effectiveness: Beyond skills and cognitive ability. *Journal of Applied Psychology, 84*, 376–389.

Newman, K. (1980). Incipient bureaucracy: The development of hierarchies in egalitarian organizations. In G. M. Britan & R. Cohen (Eds.), *Hierarchy and society* (pp. 143–163). Philadelphia: Institute for the Study of Human Issues.

Nicholson, N. (2001, Spring). Gene politics and the natural selection of leaders. *Leader to Leader,* 46–52.

O'Reilly, C. A., III, Williams, K. W., & Barsade, S. (1998). Group demography and innovation: Does diversity help? In D. Gruenfeld (Ed.), *Research on managing groups and teams: Composition.* Stamford, CT: JAI Press.

Osburn, J. D., Moran, L., Musselwhite, E., & Zenger, J. H. (1990). *Self-directed work teams: The new American challenge.* Homewood, IL: Business One Irwin.

Osterman, P. (1994). How common is workplace transformation and who adopts it? *Industrial and Labor Relations Review, 47*, 172–188.

O'Toole, J. (1977). *Work, learning, and the American future.* San Francisco: Jossey-Bass.

Paletz, S. B. F., & Maslach, C. (2000, August). *The effect of agreeableness on group creative writing.* Poster presentation at the annual meeting of the American Psychological Association, Washington, DC.

Pascale, R. T. (1990). *Managing on the edge.* New York: Simon and Schuster.

Powell, W. W. (1990). Neither market nor hierarchy: Network forms of organization. *Research in Organizational Behavior, 12*, 295–336.

Poza, E. J., & Marcus, M. L. (1980, Winter). Success story: The team approach to work restructuring. *Organizational Dynamics,* 3–25.

Pritchard, R. D., Jones, S. D., Roth, P. L., Stuebing, K. K., & Ekeberg, S. E. (1988). Effects of group feedback, goal setting, and incentives on organizational productivity. *Journal of Applied Psychology, 73*, 237–358.

Pritchard, R. D., & Watson, M. D. (1992). Understanding and measuring group productivity. In S. Worchel, W. Wood, & J. A. Simpson (Eds.), *Group process and productivity* (pp. 251–275). Newbury Park, CA: Sage.

Rand, G. (1998, December). MD-88 crew pairing test results. *Up Front* (published by Delta Air Lines), 19–22.

Rhodes, L. (1982, August). The un-manager. *Inc.,* 2–10.

Roethlisberger, F. J., & Dickson, W. J. (1939). *Management and the worker.* Cambridge, MA: Harvard University Press.

Romanelli, E., & Tushman, M. L. (1994). Organizational transformation as punctuated equilibrium: An empirical test. *Academy of Management Journal, 37*, 1141–1166.

Saglio, J. H., & Hackman, J. R. (1982). *The design of governance systems for small worker cooperatives.* Somerville, MA: Industrial Cooperative Association.

Salas, E., Rozell, D., Mullen, B., & Driskell, J. E. (1999). The effect of team building on performance: An integration. *Small Group Research, 30*, 309–329.

Salzman, M. (1994). *The soloist.* New York: Vintage Books.

Schein, E. H. (1988). *Process consultation* (Vol. 1). Reading, MA: Addison-Wesley.

Schneider, B. (1987). The people make the place. *Personnel Psychology, 40*, 437–453.

Schneider, B., Goldstein, H. W., & Smith, D. B. (1995). The ASA framework: An update. *Personnel Psychology, 48,* 747–773.

Schultheiss, O. C., & Brunstein, J. C. (1999). Goal imagery: Bridging the gap between implicit motives and explicit goals. *Journal of Personality, 67,* 1–38.

Schumacher, E. F. (1973). *Small is beautiful.* New York: Harper & Row.

Schutz, W. C. (1958). *FIRO: A three dimensional theory of interpersonal behavior.* New York: Rinehart.

Schwarz, R. M. (1994). *The skilled facilitator.* San Francisco: Jossey-Bass.

Schweiger, D. M., & Sandberg, W. R. (1989). The utilization of individual capabilities in group approaches to strategic decision-making. *Strategic Management Journal, 10,* 31–43.

Scott, K. D., Bishop, J. W., & Casino, L. S. (1997, August). *A partial test of Hackman's normative model of group effectiveness.* Paper presented at the annual meeting of the Academy of Management, Boston.

Scott, W. R. (1991). Unpacking institutional arguments. In W. W. Powell & P. J. DiMaggio (Eds.), *The new institutionalism in organizational analysis* (pp. 164–182). Chicago: University of Chicago Press.

Seifter, H., & Economy, P. (2001). *Leadership ensemble.* New York: Henry Holt.

Shipper, F., & Manz, C. C. (1992, Winter). An alternative road to empowerment. *Organizational Dynamics,* 48–61.

Simon, H. A. (1990). Invariants of human behavior. *Annual Review of Psychology, 41,* 1–19.

Simons, T. L., & Peterson, R. S. (2000). Task conflict and relationship conflict in top management teams: The pivotal role of intragroup trust. *Journal of Applied Psychology, 85,* 102–111.

Sinclair, A. (1992). The tyranny of a team ideology. *Organization Studies, 13,* 611–626.

Smith, K., Johnson, D. W., & Johnson, R. T. (1981). Can conflict be constructive? Controversy versus concurrence seeking in learning groups. *Journal of Educational Psychology, 73,* 651–663.

Smith, K. A., Salas, E., & Brannick, M. T. (1994, April). *Leadership style as a predictor of teamwork behavior: Setting the stage by managing team climate.* Paper presented at the ninth annual conference of the Society of Industrial and Organizational Psychology, Nashville, TN.

Smith, K. K. (1983). An intergroup perspective on individual behavior. In J. R. Hackman, E. E. Lawler, & L. W. Porter (Eds.), *Perspectives on behavior in organizations* (pp. 397–408). New York: McGraw-Hill.

Smith, K. K., & Berg, D. N. (1987). *Paradoxes of group life.* San Francisco: Jossey-Bass.

Snook, S. A. (2000). *Friendly fire.* Princeton, NJ: Princeton University Press.

Spreitzer, G. M., Noble, D. S., Mishra, A. K., & Cooke, W. N. (1999). Predicting process improvement team performance in an automotive firm: Explicating the roles of trust and empowerment. In R. Wageman (Ed.), *Groups in context* (pp. 71–92). Stamford, CT: JAI Press.

Staw, B. M. (1975). Attribution of the "causes" of performance: A general alternative interpretation of cross-sectional research on organizations. *Organizational Behavior and Human Performance, 13*, 414–432.

Staw, B. M., & Boettger, R. D. (1990). Task revision: A neglected form of work performance. *Academy of Management Journal, 33*, 534–559.

Staw, B. M., Sandelands, L. E., & Dutton, J. E. (1981). Threat-rigidity effects in organizational behavior: A multilevel analysis. *Administrative Science Quarterly, 26*, 501–524.

Steiner, I. D. (1972). *Group process and productivity*. New York: Academic Press.

Steinhardt, A. (1998). *Indivisible by four: A string quartet in pursuit of harmony*. New York: Farrar Straus & Giroux.

Stevens, M. J., & Campion, M. A. (1994). The knowledge, skill, and ability requirements for teamwork: Implications for human resource management. *Journal of Management, 20*, 503–530.

Stogdill, R. M. (1948). Personal factors associated with leadership: A survey of the literature. *Journal of Personality, 25*, 35–71.

Strang, D., & Macy, M. W. (in press). "In search of excellence": Fads, success stories, and adaptive emulation. *American Journal of Sociology*.

Sundstrom, E. (Ed.). (1999). *Supporting work team effectiveness*. San Francisco: Jossey-Bass.

Sundstrom, E., McIntyre, M., Halfhill, T., & Richards, H. (2000). Work groups: From the Hawthorne studies to the work teams of the 1990s. *Group Dynamics, 4*, 44–67.

Torbert, W. R., & Hackman, J. R. (1969). Taking the fun out of outfoxing the system. In P. Runkel, R. Harrison, & M. Runkel (Eds.), *The changing college classroom* (pp. 156–181). San Francisco: Jossey-Bass.

Traub, J. (1996, Aug. 26/Sept. 2). Passing the baton: What C.E.O.s could learn from the Orpheus Chamber Orchestra. *The New Yorker*, 100–105.

Trist, E. L. (1981). The evolution of sociotechnical systems as a conceptual framework and as an action research program. In A. H. Van de Ven & W. F. Joyce (Eds.), *Perspectives on organization design and behavior* (pp. 19–75). New York: Wiley.

Tschan, F., Semmer, N. K., Naegele, C., & Gurtner, A. (2000). Task adaptive behavior and performance in groups. *Group Processes and Intergroup Relations, 3*, 367–386.

Tuckman, B. W. (1965). Developmental sequence in small groups. *Psychological Bulletin, 63*, 384–399.

Tyler, L. E. (1983). *Thinking creatively: A new approach to psychology and individual lives*. San Francisco: Jossey-Bass.

Tyre, M. J., & Orlikowski, W. J. (1993, Fall). Exploiting opportunities for technological improvement in organizations. *Sloan Management Review*, 13–26.

Tziner, A., & Eden, D. (1985). Effects of crew composition on crew performance: Does the whole equal the sum of its parts? *Journal of Applied Psychology, 70*, 85–93.

Vroom, V. H., & Jago, A. G. (1988). *The new leadership: Managing participation in organizations*. Englewood Cliffs, NJ: Prentice Hall.

Wageman, R. (1995). Interdependence and group effectiveness. *Administrative Science Quarterly, 40*, 145–180.

Wageman, R. (Ed.). (1999). *Groups in context*. Stamford, CT: JAI Press.

Wageman, R. (2000). The meaning of interdependence. In M. E. Turner (Ed.), *Groups at work: Advances in theory and research.* Hillsdale, NJ: Lawrence Erlbaum.

Wageman, R. (2001). How leaders foster self-managing team effectiveness: Design choices versus hands-on coaching. *Organization Science, 12,* 559–577.

Wall, T. D., Kemp, N. J., Jackson, P. R., & Clegg, C. W. (1986). Outcomes of autonomous work groups: A long-term field experiment. *Academy of Management Journal, 29,* 280–304.

Waller, M. J. (1996). Multiple-task performance in groups. *Academy of Management Proceedings,* 303–306.

Walton, R. E. (1980). Establishing and maintaining high commitment work systems. In J. R. Kimberly & R. H. Miles (Eds.), *The organizational life cycle: Issues in the creation, transformation, and decline of organizations* (pp. 208–290). San Francisco: Jossey-Bass.

Walton, R. E. (1985). From control to commitment: Transformation of workforce management strategies in the United States. In K. B. Clark, R. H. Hayes, & C. Lorenz (Eds.), *The uneasy alliance: Managing the productivity-technology dilemma* (pp. 237–265). Boston: Harvard Business School Press.

Walton, R. E., & Hackman, J. R. (1986). Groups under contrasting management strategies. In P. S. Goodman (Ed.), *Designing effective work groups* (pp. 168–201). San Francisco: Jossey-Bass.

Walton, R. E., & Schlesinger, L. S. (1979, Winter). Do supervisors thrive in participative work systems? *Organizational Dynamics,* 24–38.

Wasserman, N., Nohria, N., & Anand, B. (2001). *When does leadership matter?* Manuscript submitted for publication.

Watson, W., Michaelsen, L. K., & Sharp, W. (1991). Member competence, group interaction, and group decision making: A longitudinal study. *Journal of Applied Psychology, 76,* 803–809.

Watson, W. E., Kumar, K., & Michaelsen, L. K. (1993). Cultural diversity's impact on interaction process and performance: Comparing homogeneous and diverse task groups. *Academy of Management Journal, 36,* 590–602.

Wegner, D. M. (1987). Transactive memory: A contemporary analysis of group mind. In B. Mullen & G. R. Goethels (Eds.), *Theories of group behavior* (pp. 185–205). New York: Springer-Verlag.

Weick, K. E. (1993). Sensemaking in organizations: Small structures with large consequences. In J. K. Murnighan (Ed.), *Social psychology in organizations* (pp. 10–37). Englewood Cliffs, NJ: Prentice Hall.

Weick, K. E., & Roberts, K. H. (1993). Collective mind in organizations: Heedful interrelating on flight decks. *Administrative Science Quarterly, 38,* 357–381.

Weingart, L. R., & Weldon, E. (1991). Processes that mediate the relationship between a group goal and group member performance. *Human Performance, 4,* 33–54.

Weiss, H. M., & Ilgen, D. R. (1985). Routinized behavior in organizations. *Journal of Behavioral Economics, 114,* 57–67.

Weldon, E., & Weingart, L. R. (1993). Group goals and group performance. *British Journal of Social Psychology, 32*, 307–334.

Wells, W. P., and Pelz, D. C. (1976). Groups. In D. C. Pelz & F. M. Andrews (Eds.), *Scientists in organizations: Productive climates for research and development* (Rev. ed., pp. 240–260). Ann Arbor: Institute for Social Research, University of Michigan.

Wetlaufer, S. (1994, November–December). The team that wasn't. *Harvard Business Review*, 22–38.

Wheatley, M. J. (1999). *Leadership and the new science: Discovering order in a chaotic world*. San Francisco: Berett-Koehler.

Whyte, W. F., & Whyte, K. K. (1988). *Making Mondragon: The growth and dynamics of the worker cooperative complex*. Ithaca, NY: ILR Press, Cornell University.

Wicker, A. W. (1979). *An introduction to ecological psychology*. Monterey, CA: Brooks-Cole.

Wiener, E. L., Kanki, B. G., & Helmreich, R. L. (Eds.). (1993). *Cockpit resource management*. Orlando, FL: Academic Press.

Williams, R. (1986, October 27). FYs reject graded group projects. *HARBUS News*, 3, 5.

Williamson, O. E. (1975). *Markets and hierarchies*. New York: Free Press.

Wood, J. D. (1990). New Haven Nighthawks. In J. R. Hackman (Ed.), *Groups that work (and those that don't)* (pp. 265–279). San Francisco: Jossey-Bass.

Woodman, R. W., & Sherwood, J. J. (1980). The role of team development in organizational effectiveness: A critical review. *Psychological Bulletin, 88*, 166–186.

Woolley, A. W. (1998). Effects of intervention content and timing on group task performance. *Journal of Applied Behavioral Science, 34*, 30–49.

Woolley, A. W. (2001, August). *The unanticipated consequences of clear work procedures on shared goal priorities*. Paper presented at the annual meeting of the Academy of Management, Washington, DC.

Wruck, K. H. (1994). Financial policy, internal control, and performance: Sealed Air Corporation's leveraged special dividend. *Journal of Financial Economics, 36*, 157–192.

Yeatts, D. E., & Hyten, C. (1998). *High-performing self-managing work teams*. Thousand Oaks, CA: Sage.

Yorks, L., & Whitsett, D. A. (1989). *Scenarios of change: Advocacy and the diffusion of job design in organizations*. New York: Praeger.

Yukl, G. (2002). *Leadership in organizations* (5th ed.). Upper Saddle River, NJ: Prentice Hall.

Zajonc, R. B. (1965). Social facilitation. *Science, 149*, 269–274.

Zaleznik, A. (1997, November–December). Real work. *Harvard Business Review*, 5–11.

Zander, A. (1971). *Motives and goals in groups*. New York: Academic Press.

Zenger, T. R., & Marshall, C. R. (2000). Determinants of incentive intensity in group-based rewards. *Academy of Management Journal, 43*, 149–163.

Zucker, L. G. (1977). The role of institutionalization in cultural persistence. *American Sociological Review, 42*, 726–743.

Index

About the Author

J. Richard Hackman is the Cahners-Rabb Professor of Social and Organizational Psychology at Harvard University. He received his undergraduate degree in mathematics from MacMurray College in 1962 and his doctorate in social psychology from the University of Illinois in 1966. He taught at Yale until 1986, when he moved to Harvard.

Hackman conducts research on a variety of topics in social and organizational psychology, including team dynamics and performance, social influences on individual behavior, and the design and leadership of self-managing groups and organizations. He is on the editorial board of several professional journals and has consulted to a variety of organizations on issues having to do with work design, leadership, and team effectiveness.

He has published numerous articles and books on social and organizational behavior. He was awarded the Sixth Annual AIR Creative Talent Award in the field of "Measurement and Evaluation: Individual and Group Behavior," the Distinguished Scientific Contribution Award of the American Psychological Association's division on industrial and organizational psychology, and both the Distinguished Educator Award and the

Distinguished Scholar Award of the Academy of Management. He is a Fellow of the American Psychological Association and of the American Psychological Society, and in 1998 was Hewlett Fellow at the Center for Advanced Study in the Behavioral Sciences at Stanford University.

DATE DUE

AUG 0 5			